# The Taming of Democracy Assistance

Few government programs that aid democracy abroad today seek to foster regime change. Technical programs that do not confront dictators are more common than the aid to dissidents and political parties that once dominated the field. What explains this "taming" of democracy assistance? This book offers the first analysis of that puzzle. In contrast to previous research on democracy aid, it focuses on the survival instincts of the non-governmental organizations (NGOs) that design and implement democracy assistance. To survive, Sarah Sunn Bush argues that NGOs seek out tamer types of aid, especially as they become more professional. Diverse evidence – including three decades of new project-level data, case studies of democracy assistance in Jordan and Tunisia, and primary documents gathered from NGO archives – supports the argument. This book provides new understanding of foreign influence and moral actors in world politics, with policy implications for democracy in the Middle East.

SARAH SUNN BUSH is an Assistant Professor in the Department of Political Science at Temple University, Philadelphia, and a Senior Fellow at the Foreign Policy Research Institute. Her research focuses on democracy promotion, non-state actors in world politics, and gender and human rights policy, and has been published in several journals, including *International Organization* and *International Studies Quarterly*. Dr. Bush was the 2014 winner of the Deborah Gerner Grant for Professional Development.

D1596985

# The Taming of Democracy Assistance

## Why Democracy Promotion Does Not Confront Dictators

Sarah Sunn Bush

# CAMBRIDGE
## UNIVERSITY PRESS

University Printing House, Cambridge CB2 8BS, United Kingdom

Cambridge University Press is part of the University of Cambridge.

It furthers the University's mission by disseminating knowledge in the pursuit of
education, learning and research at the highest international levels of excellence.

www.cambridge.org
Information on this title: www.cambridge.org/9781107642201

© Sarah Sunn Bush 2015

First published 2015
First paperback edition 2016

*A catalogue record for this publication is available from the British Library*

ISBN 978-1-107-06964-0 Hardback
ISBN 978-1-107-64220-1 Paperback

# Contents

# Figures

# Tables

# Preface

My interest in democracy assistance began in 2007 when I had the opportunity to travel to Rwanda as part of a policy workshop sponsored by the Woodrow Wilson School of Public and International Affairs at Princeton University. The workshop was on the subject of "Managing Elections in Fragile States" and was led by brilliant elections guru Jeff Fisher of Creative Associates International, Inc. In 2007, Rwanda was preparing for a three-year electoral cycle that would determine whether the country would match its post-genocide strides in terms of good governance with strides in terms of liberal democracy. At the time, there was cautious optimism about the leadership's democratizing intentions. As of 2014, that optimism is gone.

Observing international aid to promote democratization in Rwanda was eye-opening. I remember visiting the country's shiny new National Electoral Commission, which was filled with desks and computers, but hardly any staff members. The electoral institutions were ready to hold technically sound elections, but they were not empowered to ensure that the campaigning environment was genuinely open and competitive. I also became intrigued by the buzzwords on the lips of international donors – observers, gender quotas, early warning systems – and their limits. The Rwandan government was mightily concerned with international legitimacy at the time, depending heavily on foreign aid, but the goals targeted by foreign-assistance programs did not seem to be fundamentally altering the political environment. Why was the international community not seizing the opportunity to push hard for the institutional reforms that might lead to meaningful democratic change, I wondered. More generally, what accounts for the prevalence of technical programs that do not confront dictators in fundamentally undemocratic environments? Why is democracy assistance so often tame?

This book represents the fruits of my efforts to answer those questions over the ensuing years. The argument that I develop in it focuses on the survival instincts of the non-governmental organizations (NGOs) that design and implement democracy assistance. In Chapter 1, I develop the puzzle that the book seeks to address in more detail; and then in Chapter 2 I develop my argument. In a nutshell, my key insight is that in order to survive and thrive, NGOs seek out tamer types of aid, especially as they become more professional. Diverse evidence – including three decades of new project-level data, case studies of democracy assistance in Jordan and Tunisia, and primary documents gathered from NGO archives – supports the argument in Chapters 3–8. In Chapter 9, I conclude the book by discussing its implications for how we understand foreign influence, transnational activism, and ongoing policy debates about world politics.

Many people and institutions supported me as I worked on this project. I am delighted to have the opportunity to acknowledge them and express my gratitude.

I began this project as a graduate student at Princeton University. There, I had the great fortune to be advised by a dissertation committee consisting of Robert Keohane (chair), Mark Beissinger, Amaney Jamal, and John Ikenberry. Miles Kahler generously became the dissertation's fifth reader through the Miller Center fellowship program. All of my advisors are notable for their careful, engaged scholarship and warm mentorship. I aspire to follow their examples during my career. Special thanks are due to Bob Keohane, who had the uncanny ability to send me from our meetings feeling both challenged and excited. His fundamental insights into world politics, including transnational actors' significance and the importance of incomplete information, have influenced this project in countless ways. I am proud to be one of his advisees.

While in graduate school, I began the field research in Washington, DC, Jordan, and Tunisia that is reflected in the later pages of this book. Many people that work in democracy assistance were generous with their time and expertise. I sincerely thank the more than 150 people who agreed to be interviewed for this book. Though I am sure that not all my conclusions are ones that they would share, I am indebted to them for their insights. I hope that my research does their difficult and important work justice.

I transformed my dissertation into a book manuscript first as a research fellow at the Belfer Center for Science and International Affairs at the Harvard Kennedy School and then as an assistant professor at Temple University. Colleagues at both institutions provided key advice and support. I am particularly grateful to Richard Deeg, Orfeo Fioretos, and Mark Pollack for their guidance on the last stages of publishing this book. While at Temple, I also benefited from a book conference sponsored by Marc Lynch's Project on Middle East Political Science. My readers at that conference, Sheila Carapico and Susan Hyde, each read the full manuscript and offered critiques that forced me to sharpen my thinking and writing in significant ways. Mark Buntaine, Judith Kelley, Amanda Murdie, Tsveta Petrova, and Hans Peter Schmitz also provided detailed and highly constructive comments on the penultimate draft of the book. I am fortunate to work in a field with such smart and generous colleagues.

Comments benefited this project at a number of other venues. I am especially indebted to seminar attendees at Cornell, Harvard, Princeton, and Yale Universities and to practitioners in attendance at a seminar on my research organized by the Project on Middle East Democracy in Washington, DC. In addition to those seminar presentations, I presented portions of this book at the annual meetings of the American Political Science Association, the International Studies Association, and the Midwest Political Science Association. The discussants and attendees at all of those venues provided feedback that influenced my thinking in significant ways.

In addition, many friends and colleagues provided feedback and fun along the way. From Princeton, I especially thank Lamis Abdel-Aaty, Jeff Colgan, Lauren Davenport, Andrea Everett, Jessica Green, Kristen Harkness, Marina Henke, David Hsu, Mareike Kleine, Noam Lupu, Michael McKoy, and Mike Miller. From Jordan, I especially thank Eleanor Gao and Yael Zeira. In Philadelphia, I especially thank Jennifer Dixon and Erin Graham. I would also like to acknowledge Ian Hurd, my undergraduate mentor at Northwestern, who got me excited about international relations and research in the first place. What he taught me continues to shape my research.

In addition to receiving support from many individuals, I have also received generous support from a number of institutions. Grants and fellowships during graduate school came from the American Center of Oriental Research in Jordan, the University of Virginia's Miller Center of Public Affairs, the Lynde and Harry Bradley Foundation, the Bobst Center for Peace and Justice, and Princeton University. Since Princeton, I have benefited from support from the Belfer Center for Science and International Affairs at the Harvard Kennedy School, the Project on Middle East Political Science, and Temple University.

Finally, thank you to my family. My late mother Grace inspired me with my early memory of her completing a PhD. I miss her and hope that she would be proud. My father Julian has constantly supported me. His belief in me continues to be the force that enables me to take risks and achieve my goals. He has also provided helpful feedback on my research and writing. My husband David has patiently served as a sounding board for all the major ideas in this book and many of the minor ones, too. I could not be more grateful to have such a game partner in all of life's adventures. Thank you, everyone.

# Abbreviations

| | |
|---|---|
| AFL–CIO | American Federation of Labor and Congress of Industrial Organizations |
| CIA | Central Intelligence Agency |
| CIPE | Center for International Private Enterprise |
| DG | democracy and governance |
| DRL | Bureau of Democracy, Human Rights, and Labor (US State Department) |
| EIDHR | European Instrument for Democracy and Human Rights |
| ENP | European Neighbourhood Policy |
| ERIS | Electoral Reform International Services |
| EU | European Union |
| GAO | Government Accountability Office |
| GDP | gross domestic product |
| GPRA | Government Performance and Results Act |
| IDEE | Institute for Democracy in Eastern Europe |
| IFES | International Foundation for Electoral Systems |
| INGO | international non-governmental organization |
| IO | international organization |
| IRI | International Republican Institute |
| MCC | Millennium Challenge Corporation |
| MEPI | Middle East Partnership Initiative |
| MP | member of parliament |
| NDI | National Democratic Institute |
| NED | National Endowment for Democracy |
| NGO | non-governmental organization |
| OAS | Organization of American States |
| OECD | Organisation for Economic Co-operation and Development |
| OSCE | Organization for Security and Co-operation in Europe |
| OSF | Open Society Foundations |

| OTI | Office of Transition Initiatives (USAID) |
| RONGO | royal non-governmental organization |
| UN | United Nations |
| UNDEF | United Nations Democracy Fund |
| UNDP | United Nations Development Programme |
| USAID | United States Agency for International Development |

*Part I*

# Introduction and argument

# 1    Introduction

*I do have an unyielding belief that all people yearn for certain things: the ability to speak your mind and have a say in how you are governed; confidence in the rule of law and the equal administration of justice; government that is transparent and doesn't steal from the people; the freedom to live as you choose. These are not just American ideas; they are human rights. And that is why we will support them everywhere.*[1]

The global spread of democracy was among the most remarkable transformations in world politics of the twentieth century. Democracies represented a small minority of the world's states in 1900. Owing to the spread of European fascism, the number of democracies declined further during the interwar years. Although the Allied victory in World War II bolstered democracy once again, the century's largest sustained period of global democratization began in Portugal in 1974. The "third wave" of democratization swept across states in every region of the world other than the Middle East.[2] As of 2014, over half the world's states are electoral democracies.[3]

The third wave of democratization coincided in part with the end of the Cold War and a stunning shift toward democracy promotion in the foreign policies of the world's advanced democracies. The United States led the charge. Presidents since at least Woodrow Wilson have proclaimed the United States' commitment to aiding democracy abroad. For years, however, the *realpolitik* of security and foreign economic interests overwhelmed *idealpolitik*. Cold War worries encouraged the United States to ally with autocracies and even support the overthrow of democratically elected governments in a few ignominious instances. Today, the United States continues to prize its relationships with certain dictators, especially in the "war on terror." But although the United States is far from a universal or selfless advocate of democracy, the rise of

---

[1] Obama (2009).
[2] Huntington (1991).
[3] Freedom House (2014).

3

democracy promotion has fundamentally altered how American leaders make foreign policy in many countries.[4] The rationales for that change of heart are varied and include the beliefs that democracies are linked to economic development, peaceful transfers of power, and pacific relations with other democracies.[5]

The European Union (EU) has also been a powerful democratizer. Some of the earliest roots of democracy promotion lie in Germany, where political parties aided their counterparts abroad through foundations after World War II. More recently, the tantalizing benefit of EU membership has encouraged Central and East European states to embrace liberal democracy after the fall of communism.[6] Democracy promotion is so prevalent in Europe that even newly democratized European states, such as Poland and Slovakia, now sponsor programs aiding democracy in Africa, the Middle East, and Central Asia.[7]

Democracy promotion takes many forms, including economic sanctions and rewards, diplomatic pressure, and military intervention. Although each tool has its place, democracy assistance, which I define as aid given with the explicit goal of advancing democracy overseas, is one of the most visible facets of post-Cold War democracy promotion. Indeed, it is the tool of democracy promotion used most regularly, being implemented on a daily basis in more than one hundred countries.[8] Today, Western states spend billions of dollars annually with the aim of advancing democracy, human rights, and good governance abroad, whereas they spent virtually nothing on that goal in 1980. They do so through programs that, among other things, teach civics, support civil society groups, train the media, and encourage women to run for political office.

Although democracy aid continues apace, it is under fire. Fraught wars in Iraq and Afghanistan, backlash against foreign organizations in Egypt and elsewhere, setbacks to democracy in the former Soviet states despite considerable foreign aid, the rise of Islamist parties – all those events have led policy-makers to question democracy promotion's efficacy and even desirability. The lively debate about the ethics and efficacy of international democracy promotion rages among practitioners and scholars alike. In response, democracy assistance organizations in the United States and Europe have rushed to document their positive influence and justify their existence.

[4] Cox, Ikenberry, and Inoguchi (2000).
[5] McFaul (2010, ch. 2).
[6] Kelley (2004); Vachudova (2005).
[7] Petrova (2014).
[8] Carothers (2009b).

Yet the ongoing debate often rages in a vacuum, without a strong understanding of what democracy assistance actually does. In contrast, this book dives directly into how democracy aid works on the ground. It reveals that many "democracy assistance" efforts today in fact do not confront dictators. In the 1980s, prominent donors such as the United States' National Endowment for Democracy frequently challenged autocrats by supporting dissidents, political parties, and unions overseas via the majority of their programs. Now they are more likely to support technical programs, such as efforts to improve local governance, that do not disturb the status quo in other countries. Despite the overall growth of democracy assistance, the confrontational programs of yesterday have been replaced – even in countries that have remained authoritarian – by international programs that conform more closely to their host environments. Why has democracy assistance been tamed over time? In posing that question, I do not seek to understand why democracy assistance has become "bad." Rather, following the definition of "tame" in the Oxford English Dictionary, I seek to understand how and why democracy assistance has been "reclaimed from the wild state," becoming in the process less adventurous and overtly political.[9]

Most research on foreign influence emphasizes the importance of Western states' self-interests and target states' characteristics in determining variations in types of international pressure. Rather than only examining states' preferences, this book also considers the role of the non-governmental organizations (NGOs) that design and implement democracy assistance overseas in shaping the nature of democracy promotion. Those organizations want to foster democratization, but they also want to survive and thrive as organizations. To do so, they must obtain two crucial resources: donor-government funding and physical access to non-democratic states. Relatively tame democracy-assistance programs, which I define as activities associated with measurable outcomes that refrain from directly confronting dictators, help organizations promote their survival. Problems arise because such programs can at times conflict with organizations' stated goal of effecting democratization, and may even occasionally reinforce authoritarian rule. Beyond their effects on democracy, such programs can also have far-reaching consequences. Dictators wishing to appear democratic, for example, increasingly adopt the institutions promoted by democracy promoters, such as quotas for women's representation in politics, in order to cultivate domestic and international legitimacy.[10]

---

[9] "Tame." Def. 1. *Oxford English Dictionary* (2014).
[10] Bush (2011).

If it can demonstrate that non-governmental organizations shape democracy assistance, then this book will make a significant contribution to theories about world politics as well as to the practice of democracy assistance. Synthesizing insights from literatures in economics, politics, and sociology, the book seeks to show that understanding states' attempts at foreign influence requires looking not just at the preferences of donor and target states, but also at the non-state actors that inhabit the space in between them. For that reason, this book adopts what I refer to as a *transnational* approach to understanding democracy assistance. The evidence is diverse. Statistical methods allow me to analyze a broad sample of countries and three decades of new data on democracy assistance projects. Qualitative methods – including field research in Washington, DC, Jordan, and Tunisia and the analysis of primary materials from organizational archives – allow me to analyze specific organizations and countries in depth. In the end, the project sheds new light on the debate about democracy promotion. Rewarding the programs that are most likely to advance democracy may require reform in how governments delegate democracy assistance.

### What is democracy assistance?

Many activities conducted by states, as well as private foundations, fall under the banner of "democracy assistance." In 2010, the United Nations Democracy Fund (UNDEF) – the UN's main democracy-promotion initiative – sought to strengthen the media in Albania, mobilize women for elections in Azerbaijan, increase women's representation in Jamaica, create youth councils in Lebanon, empower youth leaders in Burma, and address AIDS-related discrimination in Tanzania. The funding for those activities, which took place in almost fifty countries, ranged between $50,000 and $400,000.[11] Should those programs be considered democracy assistance?

I define democracy promotion as any attempt by a state or states to encourage another country to democratize, either via a transition from autocracy or the consolidation of a new or unstable democracy. Democracy promotion can involve rewards or punishments. Its methods are various: social pressure; economic carrots and sticks; conditionality; diplomacy; and military intervention. Democracy assistance is another method. Thomas Carothers, a foremost expert on the subject, defines democracy assistance as "aid specifically designed to foster a democratic opening in a nondemocratic country or to further a democratic transition

---

[11] United Nations Democracy Fund (2014).

in a country that has experienced a democratic opening."[12] In some cases, all the tools of democracy promotion, including democracy assistance, work together in a state's foreign policy; in other cases democracy-assistance programs can become decoupled, or separated, from the other tools of democracy promotion as well as states' broader foreign policies.

For the purposes of this book, identifying democracy-assistance projects according to what seems likely to foster democratization would be impossible. Even if it is possible to agree about what democracy is and why countries democratize – very challenging tasks, as I discuss below – critics have argued that many so-called "democracy-assistance" efforts do not lead to democratization at all.[13] Therefore, excluding projects that seem to me unlikely to cause democratization from this study could exclude a number of programs that donors intend to promote democracy. Instead, in this study, I define democracy assistance as aid that states, international organizations, and other donors explicitly give to promote democracy abroad. I thus consider UNDEF projects "democracy aid" because UNDEF claims that its projects "support democratization efforts around the world."[14]

Defined as such, it is clear that democracy assistance is a new, and growing, phenomenon. Figure 1.1 illustrates the rise of democracy assistance since 1985. What in the early 1980s consisted of the work of a few governments is now an international enterprise. The rise of democracy assistance does not simply reflect an increase in foreign aid since the end of the Cold War. In the United States, for example, democracy aid increased from 8 percent of the annual foreign-aid budget in 1990 to 16 percent in 2009.[15]

The activities sponsored as part of democracy assistance fall into several loose clusters. Civil society projects support the media and various overseas NGOs. Governance projects support more transparent and accountable government institutions. Political-processes projects aid elections, legislatures, and political parties. Rule-of-law projects strengthen constitutions, human rights, and legal institutions.[16] The projects are implemented in diverse ways – through government

---

[12] Carothers (1999, 6).
[13] Carapico (2002); Carothers (1999); Guilhot (2005); Henderson (2002); Mendelson (2001); Traub (2008).
[14] United Nations Democracy Fund (2014).
[15] Calculations from Azpuru *et al.* (2008, 152) and United States Agency for International Development (2009, 18).
[16] Finkel, Pérez-Liñán, and Seligson (2007, 406–7).

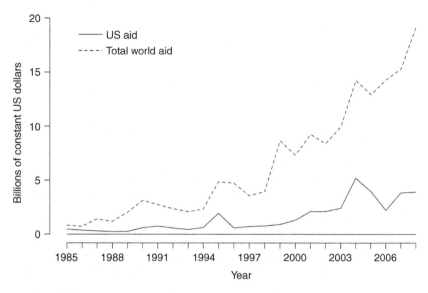

Figure 1.1 The rise of democracy assistance.
*Data source:* Tierney *et al.* (2011).

agencies, domestic and foreign non-governmental organizations, and multilateral institutions. Their defining characteristic is that recipients take the funds with the stated goal of fostering democracy.

To be sure, some of the activities such recipients engage in may seem unlikely to lead to democratization in the short or medium term. That is, however, part of the book's puzzle. Understanding, as scholars Christopher Hobson and Milja Kurki have put it, "democracy's meaning in democracy promotion" is significant for scholars working across a range of epistemologies and methodologies, yet it has been a task rarely pursued by political scientists.[17] What explains the strategies that donor states and intergovernmental organizations pursue via democracy-assistance programs? Previous research points to two possible answers: the preferences of donor governments and the characteristics of target states.

### The anatomy of foreign influence: what we know

Under what conditions can states and international institutions successfully influence a target state's domestic political institutions and

---

[17] Hobson and Kurki (2012, 2).

practices? In a well-cited article from 1978, political scientist Peter Gourevitch wrote about the "second-image reversed," or the international sources of domestic politics.[18] A growing literature has expanded on his seminal insights to show how international actors promote or otherwise encourage the spread of liberal democracy. In addition to research on democracy promotion, the literature includes studies about human rights, political conditionality, and compliance with international law.[19]

The research on foreign influence falls into two camps, which differ in terms of which factors they emphasize as being most important for the design and effects of foreign influence. The first camp emphasizes the ideologies and self-interests of donor states.[20] A large body of research shows that security and economic interests shape how donors give foreign aid. Rather than conditioning aid on the quality of governance, donors – even when acting through multilateral institutions such as the International Monetary Fund and the World Bank – frequently use it to reward and bribe target countries for pursuing donors' preferred policies. Thus, the story goes, foreign aid often fails at, for example, promoting economic growth or improving governance, since donor states did not design aid to achieve growth or governance in the first place.

The second camp emphasizes the characteristics of the target states. Target states vary in how likely they are to resist foreign influence. Attempts to liberalize target states are more likely to succeed in countries that have "good" economic policies and liberal political intentions; they may backfire and lead to corruption or repression in countries that do not.[21] The likelihood of foreign influence's success thus depends in part on how well sending states tailor their efforts to the characteristics of target states. Scholars adopting this perspective suggest some cause for cautious optimism about foreign influence because many donor states have improved at taking into account target states' needs and characteristics over time.[22]

Previous research therefore suggests that we should be able to understand variations in the allocation and effectiveness of democracy assistance by looking at just two factors: the preferences of donor countries and the characteristics of target states. The scant literature that investigates the allocation of democracy assistance confirms that those

---

[18] Gourevitch (1978).
[19] Donno (2010); Hyde (2011); Kelley (2012); Marinov and Goemans (2014); Pevehouse (2002); Simmons (2009); Stone (2002).
[20] Alesina and Dollar (2000); Bueno de Mesquita and Smith (2009); Easterly (2006); Hancock (1989); Stone (2002).
[21] Burnside and Dollar (2000, 2004); Wright (2008b).
[22] Bermeo (2008); Wright and Winters (2010, 63–5).

explanations offer important insights into the process.[23] Specifically, donor states factor in target states' regime types and their foreign-policy relationships when deciding whether and how to sponsor democracy assistance. Other research on democracy assistance also emphasizes donor states' interests by noting that countries tend to export their political ideologies and institutions overseas.[24] But state-based explanations paint an incomplete picture of how democracy assistance works on the ground. Indeed, although donor states provide funding, NGOs often design and implement programs overseas. Donor states have a hard time observing and controlling those NGOs, which work far away and seek to aid foreign citizens, who may not want or be able to communicate information about the programs back to donors. To the extent that organizations' preferences differ from donor states', they therefore have room to significantly shape the international community's efforts.

## The argument in brief

To explain the taming of democracy assistance as well as other interesting patterns in the content of democracy assistance, I develop a two-part argument that focuses on how the organizations that design and implement democracy-assistance programs interact with donor and target states. The argument seeks to explain variation across both space and time. The first part of the argument emphasizes how delegation dynamics – including what are referred to as "principal–agent problems" in political science and economics – shape the design and implementation of democracy assistance at a given point in time. The second part of the argument emphasizes how organizational changes – especially competition and professional norms – change the preferences of the actors involved and thus influence the evolution of democracy-assistance programs. In developing those ideas, I often refer to the professional field of organizations that design and implement democracy-assistance programs as the *democracy establishment*. An organization – whether non- or quasi-governmental – that obtains funding to design and implement democracy-assistance programs is a member of the democracy establishment.

In making my two-part argument, I do not argue that organizations in the democracy establishment are the only actors that matter in democracy assistance. Many of the findings in this book affirm the significance of donor governments' preferences and key events such as

---

[23] Finkel, Pérez-Liñán, and Seligson (2007); Scott and Steele (2011).
[24] Kopstein (2006); Petrova (2014).

the end of the Cold War. But I argue that organizations in the democracy establishment are an important, and often overlooked, part of the causal story. In a nutshell, organizations in the democracy establishment take part in strategic games with both donors (for funding) and target states (for access). As they compete for funding and become more professional, they pursue programs that better match their survival incentives. In addition to clarifying several puzzles about democracy assistance, the argument also suggests new ways to think about foreign influence and non-governmental actors in world politics.

### Transnational delegation in democracy promotion

As with many other international phenomena that involve delegation, governments delegate authority and funding to non-state actors to design and implement democracy assistance.[25] They do so for a variety of reasons, including to benefit from other organizations' expertise and legitimacy. Authority and aid typically pass through several institutions, not to mention moving across state boundaries. That lengthy process of delegation makes it hard for donor states to fully observe and control the projects that they fund, and gives organizations in the democracy establishment some room to design projects that satisfy their desires to survive and thrive.

Consider an American government-funded project in the Central African Republic in 2010. At the time, Freedom House ranked the war-torn country as "partly free," noting that it was "not an electoral democracy" due to unfair elections and various restrictions on freedoms.[26] In that environment, the US-sponsored program, which cost $42,953, sought to "ensure that women [in the Central African Republic] are more empowered and understand their socio-economic and political rights and legal processes for defending them."[27] Although the program's goal of promoting women's "greater involvement in local political life" was in many ways noble, it generally fits this book's definition of tame, which is to say that it was both measurable and regime-compatible. Not only could the program be plausibly evaluated using quantitative outcome measures about women's participation (e.g., the number of women in parliament), but it also did little to directly confront the government of President François Bozizé by fostering competition or mobilizing regime-challenging groups.

---

[25] Bradley and Kelley (2008); Hawkins *et al.* (2006); Nielson and Tierney (2003); Pollack (1997); Weaver (2008).

[26] Freedom House (2010).

[27] National Endowment for Democracy (2010).

Consider another American government-funded project in the same year. This $120,000 project took place in Jordan, a constitutional monarchy ranked by Freedom House as "not free" that year. Although the country's leader, King Abdullah, did permit elections, he dismissed the elected parliament at will and made use of extensive executive and legislative authority at the time.[28] As was the case in the Central African Republic, one of the democracy-assistance programs supported by the US government in Jordan that year aimed "to support women parliamentary candidates and newly-elected women parliamentarians."[29] Again, this program fits the book's definition of a tame program. Jordan has made remarkable improvements in terms of women's representation in the twenty-first century, but many experts on the country's politics suggest that these improvements have done more to enhance the regime's international reputation than they have to advance democracy.[30]

How were these American programs, which sought to engage citizens in fundamentally undemocratic political systems, designed and funded? The democracy-assistance projects in the Central African Republic and Jordan began, in a distant sense, with the American public, which elects representatives to make foreign policy on its behalf. In 2010, as in other years, the United States Congress delegated authority and funding for democracy promotion to several institutions, including the Department of State, the United States Agency for International Development (USAID), and the National Endowment for Democracy (NED). Congress delegated because it lacks the capacity to directly run democracy-assistance programs and because some separation from the government serves democracy promotion well. Some formal separation benefits democracy promotion because a heavy US-government imprint can delegitimize reform efforts[31] and also undermine diplomatic relations. For the Central African Republic project, the NED, a quasi-governmental American foundation, awarded a grant to Mercy Corps, an American non-governmental organization. Mercy Corps organized activities locally in collaboration with local civil-society organizations, including a Central African NGO, Association des Femmes Juristes de Centrafrique. For the Jordanian grant, the NED awarded a grant to the National Democratic Institute (NDI), which then made a sub-grant to Women Helping Women, the Jordanian Women's Election Network, which had been launched by the NDI in 2006 and was governed by female Jordanian leaders.

---

[28] Freedom House (2010).
[29] National Endowment for Democracy (2010).
[30] Baylouny (2005, 41–2); David and Nanes (2011).
[31] Bush and Jamal (2015).

What were the preferences and strategies of the actors involved in the Central African Republic and Jordanian projects? First, donor governments, including the United States, fund democracy aid in countries such as the Central African Republic and Jordan at least in part because they support democracy. That idea may seem obvious, but it is not: Western states, including the United States, have often supported stability rather than democracy in their autocratic allies and even supported the overthrow of democratically elected governments. Competing strategic interests can and do still trump democracy promotion, especially in cases such as Jordan, and we would expect those competing interests to affect the types of aid program donors fund. Despite all that, as Figure 1.1 suggested, since the end of the Cold War, democracy donors have made a real commitment to aiding democracy abroad. At the same time as they hope to support democracy, however, democratically elected officials also worry about satisfying their publics, who may be skeptical of foreign assistance and democracy promotion. Consequently, donor officials want to document democracy assistance's efficacy to justify spending public money.

Second, organizations in the democracy establishment – such as the NED, Mercy Corps, NDI, and local civil-society organizations in the Central African Republic and Jordan – share general preferences. Fundamentally, they want greater democracy. Promoting democracy in a partly free country such as the Central African Republic or Jordan is hard – even dangerous – work that organizations pursue because they believe it is right. But to survive and thrive, organizations must secure several resources. First, organizations need government funding. Without it, they cannot work. Second, they need access to target countries. Again, without it, they cannot work; without it, they may also face legal problems, as illustrated most famously by the 2012 crackdown on NGOs in Egypt. Yet, as is shown later in the book, there is no evidence that the tame projects that best generate funding and access are effective at democratizing countries.

Organizations pursue predictable strategies for achieving funding and access. To win funding, they prefer to pursue programs with measurable outcomes: programs that are linked to clear, quantitative outcomes. Organizations can show donors that they are making democratic progress through, for example, an improvement on a cross-national index of women's representation. Practical, ethical, and methodological limitations still make it hard to assess the causal impact of democracy programs, but at least measurable programs have concrete indicators that measure their associated outcomes, which are plausible, if minimal, barometers of success. Although more subjective dimensions of democracy also matter, they do not form clear signals to far-off funders. It is important to note that the pursuit of measurable programs represents in many cases responsiveness to donor preferences on the part of organizations in the democracy establishment. At the same time, research on democracy assistance reviewed in the next two chapters does suggest that measurable programs can conflict with effective democracy promotion. If that research is correct, then government officials are sending mixed messages to organizations in the democracy establishment: they want effective aid programs and they want measurable programs. In that case, delegation dynamics may be relevant.

To win access, organizations prefer to pursue programs that do not directly confront dictators. Incumbents want to stay in power and can and do block access to democracy-assistance organizations that threaten them. Indeed, autocrats in Egypt, Russia, the United Arab Emirates, and elsewhere have used legal and extralegal means to thwart democracy promoters.[32] Even if foreign funding is permitted, as it was in 2010 in the Central African Republic and Jordan, leaders such as Bozizé and Abdullah can set up other obstacles to democracy practitioners, such as difficult and non-transparent procedures for mandatory NGO registration. If NGOs support dissidents in such countries today, then their staff may be kicked out of the country or arrested. Organizations therefore often choose to support programs that target countries will at least tolerate, if not embrace.

Organizations' survival incentives therefore help explain why they prefer certain democracy-assistance programs, such as support for women's political participation – which are both measurable and regime compatible – over other types of programs, such as support for dissidents – which are neither measurable nor regime-compatible. Rational organizations will choose the democracy-assistance programs that help them survive. When donors cannot observe and control those NGOs, they should be more likely to reward measurable programs. Moreover, they should be less likely to punish organizations for pursuing regime-compatible programs. Thus, the more discretion that organizations in the democracy establishment have, the more we can expect them to pursue tame programs.

### The professionalization of democracy promotion

Yet even given a constant delegation structure, I expect organizations in the democracy establishment to have responded differently to the

---

[32] Gershman and Allen (2006).

same incentives over time. As democracy assistance grew, a transnational field emerged with shared ideas about the appropriate institutions and practices for developing democracies.[33] As organizational theories would predict, organizations in the democracy establishment came to promote democracy in similar ways over time due to competition and professionalization.[34] Organizations converged on approaches that treated democratization as an incremental process rather than as a political struggle. Despite the field's ideological origins and sometimes grand rhetoric, its organizations are "normal" in the sense that they care about many of the same mundane tasks that other organizations care about.

A Weberian process of competitive learning winnowed the democracy establishment's strategies. Democracy practitioners learned about effecting democratic change and also about attaining funding. The rise of democracy assistance encouraged organizations to enter the lucrative field, heightening competition. Competition in turn focused practitioners on monitoring and evaluation and reinforced the incentives for measurable programs. The organizations that survived successfully adapted. Certain characteristics of democracy assistance – such as the field's short-term projects and concentrations of practitioners in certain countries – especially fostered information-sharing and adaptive learning. Practitioners could quickly replicate models that they saw succeed elsewhere.

Professional norms locked in lessons about obtaining funding and access. Certain programs and goals became taken for granted. Supporting women's groups may have initially worked well at gaining access, for example, but it later came to be viewed as an appropriate practice. Associations, university programs, and an elite spread and reinforced the field's body of knowledge. The democracy establishment's reliance on state funding and frequent turnover especially fostered convergence. As is common among organizations that focus on vague and complex goals, the means (organizational survival) gradually became the ends in the democracy establishment. For all of those reasons, organizations in the democracy establishment will be more likely to pursue tame programs as they compete and professionalize.

Although competition and norms encouraged organizations in the democracy establishment to promote democracy in ways that helped them survive, idealism in the field endures. The point is that the balance between idealism and incentives has evolved. Optimists tend to view

[33] Guilhot (2005).
[34] Weber (1978 [1922]); DiMaggio and Powell (1983); Barnett (2009).

transnational activists as generally motivated by ideals.[35] Cynics tend to view them as just as materially-motivated as firms despite their high-minded rhetoric.[36] The truth lies somewhere in between the two perspectives for the democracy establishment, and, crucially, it varies in predictable ways. Indeed, part of what is novel about this book when compared to previous pioneering studies of NGOs in world politics is that it identifies and explains important variations in organizational behavior even when a variety of pertinent factors that we know influence NGOs – such as the extent of principal–agent problems, short-term contracts, and multiple-principals problems – are held constant.[37] The approach that I use to study democracy-assistance organizations can also be extended to study fields in a variety of issue areas in world politics relating to foreign influence, from developmental to environmental assistance.

## Organization of the book

This book has three main parts. The first part motivates the project and provides a theoretical framework for what follows. Chapter 2 develops my argument in more detail. I derive testable hypotheses from the argument that I contrast with complementary and alternative explanations, which emphasize donor countries' preferences and target countries' characteristics.

To test the argument, I develop a new typology of democracy assistance projects in Chapter 3. Measurable programs have quantitative indicators that can be used to evaluate their outcomes. Regime-compatible programs are not judged by autocrats to be likely to lead to their overthrow. In this chapter, several illustrative cases also show how measurable and regime-compatible projects can come at the expense of effective democracy assistance and thus document the principal–agent problems on which the book focuses.

Part II turns to testing my argument and represents the book's empirical core. In it, I track variations in how measurable and regime-compatible democracy-assistance programs are across time and space. The order of the chapters in Part II loosely mimics the order of the

---

[35] Keck and Sikkink (1998).

[36] Cooley and Ron (2002); Dicther (2003); Kennedy (2005); Prakash and Gugerty (2010); Sell and Prakash (2004).

[37] This study is also novel when compared to important previous studies, such as Cooley and Ron (2002), because it looks at a new sector of transnational NGOs, systematically theorizes the influence of target states (not just donor states), and contains a multi-method empirical test that explains variations in transnational NGOs' programs (rather than a qualitative-only empirical test).

transnational delegation chain in democracy assistance that I study, moving from the practices of donor governments to quasi-governmental organizations, to donor-country-based NGOs, and finally to target-country-based NGOs. The chapters in Part II also rely on a combination of empirical research methods. I draw on existing and original cross-national, over-time data sets of democracy-assistance projects, which I examine statistically, including using matching techniques for causal inference, to identify general correlations and make some counterfactual inferences. I also draw on a survey of practitioners and detailed case studies to validate my assumptions, provide context, and show the intermediate causal steps that are necessary to have more confidence in the statistical causal inferences. The data for the case studies come from more than 150 interviews, documents from organizational archives, and extensive fieldwork that I conducted in Jordan, Tunisia, and Washington, DC. In addition to testing the book's argument, by examining democracy assistance in the Middle East before and after the "Arab Spring," the chapters also contribute to ongoing policy debates.

It is worth noting that researchers face numerous barriers to entry when it comes to studying democracy-assistance organizations, as is the case with many international organizations.[38] In the wake of US interventions in Afghanistan and Iraq, many practitioners feel that their work is vulnerable to political criticism. They fear for their livelihoods and for their organizations, themes which are at the heart of this book. As such, many professionals have an understandable skepticism of academic and journalistic interviewers who could be coming to write the next exposé on democracy promotion. As a consequence, most of the interviews that I undertook for this book were conducted using "unattributable" or "off-the-record" terms so as to reassure interviewees and enable them to speak with candor. To ease the book's exposition, I occasionally use fictitious names when referring to particular interviewees. The appendix lists the organizations where my interviewees worked to give readers a sense of the sources I relied upon. Given the obvious concerns about the reliability of information gleaned from such interviews, I also relied heavily on practitioners' public statements and organizations' primary documents, including both official and unofficial documents that were leaked to me or the public by organizations' staff.

Using the aforementioned strategies, Chapter 4 tests the proposition that when democracy donors have a more difficult time observing and controlling the organizations they fund, tame programs will be more likely to occur. I test the proposition using recent data on more than

---

[38] Weaver (2008, 14).

12,000 democracy-assistance programs funded by more than twenty government donors. Using statistical methods for causal inference, I show that several indicators of the degree of difficulty observing and controlling aid-recipient organizations – such as the use of donor-state rather than target-state non-governmental organizations as implementers – are strongly related to how likely programs are to be tame.

Chapter 5 statistically tests the proposition that competition and professional norms fostered convergence within American democracy assistance on measurable and regime-compatible programs over time and across countries. To do so, it analyzes a random sample of 5,000 democracy-assistance projects from an original data set of projects funded by the NED, a US government-supported foundation that seeks to advance democracy abroad. After explaining why the NED's projects provide a useful test of the argument from a research design perspective, I show that competition and professionalism are associated with relatively tamer democracy-assistance programs, even after controlling for a number of other relevant factors. Those factors include the amount of American military aid received by the target countries, indicators for the Cold War and post-September 11 eras, indicators for changes in American domestic politics, the level of democracy and regime type of the target country, and indicators for the regions where programs take place. The over-time trend also holds among projects funded by the other main American democracy donor, USAID. Moreover, the analysis reveals that target countries that have strategic relationships with the United States receive "tamer" forms of democracy assistance.

Drawing on qualitative data, Chapter 6 focuses on the historical development of several American organizations that were significant early activist organizations promoting democracy – Freedom House, the Institute for Democracy in Eastern Europe, and the Open Society Foundations. I show how competitive learning and professional norms fostered convergence across those organizations about how to promote democracy in tamer ways. I also describe how donor governments interact with organizations in the democracy establishment, documenting the network structure of the democracy establishment using internet connections and a survey of more than 1,000 democracy-assistance practitioners.

To complement that analysis, the next two chapters (Chapters 7 and 8) turn to case studies of democracy assistance in the Middle East. Among other things, what these case studies help demonstrate is what a tame program looks like on the ground, what problems of observation and control look like in practice, and how democracy-assistance professionals make tough decisions in particular contexts about how to trade off between their ideals and incentives. To examine those dynamics, I focus on the cases of Jordan and Tunisia.

Considerations of research design as well as current policy debates guided my case selection. When country case studies are chosen to complement cross-national statistical analysis that is generally robust and confirms the argument, political scientist Evan Lieberman recommends choosing cases that are well predicted by statistical models with the goal of confirming that the hypothesized causal mechanisms are at work.[39] In Chapters 4 and 5, Jordan and Tunisia were two cases that were typically well predicted by the statistical models, which makes them appropriate countries for in-depth study. If the transnational approach to democracy assistance is correct, then Jordan and Tunisia are cases where we would expect to see some support for it.

Moreover, as a pair, Jordan and Tunisia are similar: they are both Arab countries that have relatively small populations and are relatively developed, falling into the World Bank's upper-middle-income economies group during the period of research. At the start of my period of field research, 2008, they had one particularly salient difference: Jordan was a security ally of the United States, whereas Tunisia was not. By 2012, an additional difference had emerged: Tunisia had experienced a democratizing revolution, whereas Jordan's monarchy remained relatively impervious to the Arab Spring. The case studies thus allow for across- and within-case comparisons. They afford me an opportunity to see how different relationships with donors and, later, different domestic regime types affect or do not affect the design of democracy assistance on the ground. It is worth noting that since the Middle East is thought to be a region where donor countries have major countervailing strategic interests, which may prevent them from truly pushing for democracy, evidence in favor of my argument from this region should be especially powerful.

Moreover, in terms of practical importance, the case studies make sense. The Arab world has been the focus of the greatest interest in terms of democracy promotion among policy-makers and pundits alike since September 11, 2001. Both American and European donors have dramatically increased their funding on the Middle East since 2001 and, as outlined above, Jordan, and now Tunisia, have been particular foci of new foreign-aid initiatives tied to political reform, such as the Millennium Challenge Corporation (MCC) and the European Neighbourhood Policy (ENP).[40] Yet serious doubts remain about such

[39] Lieberman (2005, 444).
[40] Youngs and Wittes (2009).

democracy-promotion efforts, including about their sincerity, practicality, and consistency.[41] Thus, it makes sense to focus on the Middle East for the analysis because doing so can help show us what factors influence the design of important democracy-assistance programs and what changes might be necessary to promote democracy more effectively in the future.

Chapter 7 examines democracy assistance on the ground in Jordan among the final "agents" in the transnational delegation chain. After discussing my selection of the Jordanian case and providing some context about liberal authoritarianism in Jordan, I show that – in contrast to conventional wisdom – donor governments' strategic interests do not offer a complete explanation of the salient variations in democracy assistance in Jordan, even after the "Arab Spring." I thus develop a more complete explanation for the design of democracy assistance in Jordan that builds on the previous chapters' transnational approach. My findings illustrate the importance of organizational survival, in terms of both funding and access, as well as professional norms with concrete examples of programs. The chapter also considers democracy-assistance efforts funded in Jordan by private foundations. The analysis draws its conclusions on the basis of more than seventy semi-structured interviews conducted in Amman, Jordan, as well as news articles from the Jordanian press and internal documents from donor organizations.

I shift focus in Chapter 8 to Tunisia, again drawing on field research. I show how little democracy promotion occurred in Tunisia prior to the 2011 Jasmine Revolution and explain what donors chose to support in the plentiful post-revolution funding environment. With less funding competition, NGOs in Tunisia pursued a relatively tame set of activities. Nevertheless, the common forces of funding competition and professionalism had already appeared and started influencing programs, even in 2012 despite the relatively free environment.

Chapter 9 summarizes the book's findings and discusses their implications for the study of world politics and the practice of democracy promotion. It argues that the book's transnational approach to democracy assistance can be fruitfully applied to the study of other types of foreign influence, such as environmental aid. It also draws out the policy implications of the book's argument, suggesting ways that the government funding structure could be reformed to reward democracy assistance that confronts dictators. Most of those reforms involve steps that can improve the observation and control of funded organizations or that can amplify the strategies used by private foundations.

---

[41] Brownlee (2012); Carapico (2002); Ottaway (2005b); Wittes (2008).

In the end, are the consequences of the democracy establishment's influence positive or negative for democracy around the world? Much remains uncertain about democracy promotion's effectiveness and hinges on one's definition of democracy. But my findings that democracy-assistance programs increasingly prioritize quantitative measurement and compatibility with the target countries' regimes are troubling for people who are interested in fighting for democracy fiercely in the short and medium term. At a minimum, important democracy-assistance programs that supported dissidents, political parties, and unions are disappearing because they fail to generate measurable outcomes. At a maximum, some democracy-assistance programs today may inadvertently reinforce strategies of authoritarian survival as a consequence of organizations' drives for funding and access. Although my conclusions are necessarily cautious, given the challenges of making causal inferences with observational data, a rigorous series of tests suggests that survival concerns have prompted organizations in the democracy establishment to increasingly pursue tame forms of democracy assistance across a variety of target states in all the world's regions.

Advancing democracy worldwide remains a noble goal. Yet one of our major tools to accomplish this goal is weaker than it might otherwise be because of how government donors fund democracy assistance. Most of our previous analysis of democracy assistance has focused on the importance of landmark political events, such as the end of the Cold War and the Iraq War, to Western countries' strategies. Such events are key to understanding the intentions of donor governments, the extent of their aid commitments, and the contexts in which overseas programs operate. Yet how democracy assistance works on the ground also depends on many small, everyday organizational decisions and battles. Institutional reforms that promote observation and control can get the incentives right in order to reward democracy-assistance programs that more directly challenge authoritarian rulers in the future.

# 2 The argument: structure, agency, and democracy promotion

*It's frustrating to work in this field because you have your DC funders as stakeholders as well as local stakeholders.*[1]

*The scattered and diffuse democracy movement of decades past has been transformed into a worldwide industry of sorts, led but not controlled by the United States. The industry has done much good. But it has also put a stamp of legitimacy on Potemkin-village democracies in Cambodia, Egypt, Armenia, and other countries. It has frustrated local democratic activists from Indonesia to Peru, and it has provided autocratic rulers with ammunition to dismiss courageous local democrats as lackeys of foreign powers.*[2]

Forty years ago, foreign aid aiming to promote democracy in other countries did not exist. Today, states and international organizations spend billions of dollars each year to promote democratic transition and consolidation abroad. This book seeks to understand how democracy assistance has evolved over that time. It is not the first book to explore the spread of democracy promotion at the end of the twentieth century.[3] Where it parts ways with previous studies, however, is in its focus on how states aid democracy, rather than why and to what effect they do so.

The analysis presented in this book suggests that today many government programs seeking to aid democracy abroad are not designed to confront dictators. Today's democracy-assistance activities emphasize activities, such as in programs supporting local governance and women's representation, that do not threaten the survival of autocrats in at least the short term. They contrast with the more confrontational aid to dissidents, political parties, and trade unions that dominated the early era of democracy assistance. *What explains the taming of democracy assistance?*

---

[1] Interview 23, with director of an INGO, in person, Amman, October 21, 2009.
[2] Bjornlund (2001, 180).
[3] Some of the most important contributions are: Burnell (2000); Carothers (1999); Cox, Ikenberry, and Inoguchi (2000); Donno (2013); Guilhot (2005); Henderson (2003); Hyde (2011); Kelley (2012); McFaul (2010); Schmitz (2004); Traub (2008); Wedel (2001); Wittes (2008); Youngs (2004).

Answering that question matters for several reasons. First, there is concrete evidence that states are likely to adopt the policies, such as gender quotas,[4] and practices, such as election observation,[5] encouraged via democracy promotion. Understanding how states promote democracy thus helps us understand some of the sources of political change in the developing world. Second, democracy assistance seems at times to have played into dictators' survival strategies.[6] Yet, at other times, democracy assistance seems to have effectively democratized countries and promoted peace after civil conflict.[7] Understanding why donors select the programs they do can therefore help inform better selection strategies in the future. Finally, the book's argument can be used to study how other forms of foreign influence and principled action take place. Developing a framework to study the taming of democracy assistance helps explain broader patterns about world politics.

To understand the taming of democracy assistance, this chapter adopts a transnational approach, which is to say that it focuses on both states and transnational organizations. The argument has two steps. The first step treats the key players in democracy assistance – donor states, target states, and aid-recipient organizations – as rational actors. The argument is that because of the constraints imposed by donor and target states, organizations in the democracy establishment prefer to implement tame programs to enhance their chances of survival. The more discretion from donors that organizations have, the more likely they will be to design and implement their preferred programs. The second step relaxes the rational-actor assumption, treating organizations in the democracy establishment as being motivated by logics of both consequences and appropriateness. It makes the case that professional norms and competition will encourage democracy-promotion organizations to pursue tamer programs.

This chapter begins by reviewing the dominant state-based approaches to the study of foreign influence. Those approaches rightly emphasize how donor states' preferences and target states' characteristics shape attempts at foreign influence. What they ignore, however, is how difficult it is for donors to observe and control the organizations that they fund

---

[4] Bush (2011).
[5] Hyde (2011); Kelley (2012).
[6] Brownlee (2012); Carapico (2002); Carothers (1999); Henderson (2003); Mendelson (2001); Roessler (2005).
[7] Finkel, Pérez-Liñán, and Seligson (2007); Savun and Tirone (2011); Scott and Steele (2011).

to design and implement democracy assistance. Those organizations, which want to survive and thrive, have some preferences that diverge from donors' preferences. All else being equal, organizations prefer to implement tame programs – programs that donor governments do not necessarily prefer across the board. When organizations focus more on their survival, I expect them to converge on the tame programs that help them accomplish that goal.

## International politics and attempts at foreign influence

As noted previously, scholars of international relations and comparative politics tend to disagree about the ability of international actors to promote democracy abroad. One potential source of the continuing debate is that many scholars have focused on the preferences of *states* – both the senders and the targets – at the expense of considering the preferences of the *transnational organizations* that design and implement many states' attempts at foreign influence. What would explain the taming of democracy assistance in a state-driven world? An international (rather than transnational) vantage point suggests that the design and impact of democracy promotion will be dictated by state power and interests. Variations in the preferences and characteristics of donor states as well as target states will impact the way that democracy is aided abroad.

### *The conventional wisdom: donor countries' preferences matter*

The first place to look when seeking to understand democracy aid is the donor state. When Western governments promote democracy, they typically attempt to do so in a way that reflects their interests. At certain times or in certain places, we would expect donors to prefer tamer democracy assistance. Those preferences should be translated into democracy-assistance programs overseas.

That donor-centric point of view jibes with the broader literature on international pressure. If there is a scholarly conventional wisdom about international efforts to promote economic development, for example, it is that donor governments' political and economic concerns drive how they give aid. A landmark study by economists Alberto Alesina and David Dollar found that indicators of states' interests – specifically, donor and target countries' similarities in UN voting and shared colonial legacies – mattered significantly more in terms of how rich countries give foreign aid than did indicators of target countries' abilities to use aid effectively.[8] Other research shows that rich countries use foreign aid to reward poorer countries for their past behavior as well as to buy future influence.[9] In that way, Western donor states shape even the programs of international institutions such as the World Bank and the International Monetary Fund.[10]

Wealthy states give economic aid under the guise of humanitarianism, but they promote democracy for explicitly political reasons. Thus, it would come as no surprise if donor countries' interests explain where and how they allocate democracy aid. Democracy aid, given as it often is to non-state actors, cannot typically be used to buy influence. Instead, to reward or bribe favored countries – whether measured by UN votes, colonial pasts, or economic or military value – donors can send them tamer programs, reserving more directly confrontational programs for non-aligned target states. Donor governments can also withhold democracy assistance as a way to enhance their alliances with friendly dictators. Whereas donor states may be willing to confront dictators through democracy aid in countries where regime opponents are pro-Western, they may be less willing to do so in countries where regime opponents are anti-Western or could otherwise endanger donors' strategic interests were they to come to power.[11] That perspective is consistent with some, but not all, previous research on American democracy assistance, which has found that US military assistance is negatively correlated with the allocation of USAID democracy assistance.[12]

Strategic incentives are not the only relevant source of donor states' preferences over democracy assistance. Domestic values could also affect their preferences over the design and implementation of democracy aid. During the 1980s and 1990s, for example, a "march of quantification" swept through governments, which sought greater efficiency, transparency, and measurable outcomes in the public sector.[13] Accordingly, donor states' changing preferences could account for a rise in measurable democracy assistance over time. At the same time, the end of the Cold War and September 11, 2001, reconfigured the international system and gave rise to new beliefs about the ascendancy of liberalism and the role of democracy in the "war on terror." Those events affected Western states'

---

[8] Alesina and Dollar (2000). See also McKinlay and Little (1977) and Schraeder, Hook, and Taylor (1998).
[9] Bueno de Mesquita and Smith (2009).
[10] Stone (2004); Winters (2010, 444–50).
[11] McKoy and Miller (2012).
[12] Scott and Steele (2011, 62).
[13] Hood (1998).

foreign policies in a number of ways and could also explain any taming of democracy assistance.[14]

Partisan political dynamics are another potential source of donor states' preferences. In the United States Congress, for example, representatives' ideologies and local economic interests have been shown to shape how they vote on foreign aid.[15] Yet domestic political competition may matter less for democracy aid than it does for foreign assistance. First, democracy promotion tends not to be a left–right ideological issue.[16] Second, democracy aid does not mobilize interest groups outside of organizations in the democracy establishment, unlike foreign aid, which sends goods from donor states overseas and thus mobilizes local manufacturers. Organizations such as the NED do rely on political connections during funding battles and can lobby elected representatives in favor of their interests.[17] But democracy aid predates the creation even of prominent organizations such as the NED. Moreover, the rise of democracy assistance is part of a broader turn toward democracy promotion in states' foreign policies,[18] suggesting that the rise of the democracy establishment as a lobbying group is not the best explanation of the rise of democracy assistance.

To sum up, the core idea about democracy assistance suggested by a perspective grounded in donor states' preferences is this: donor states promote democracy abroad with certain objectives in mind and those objectives will be reflected in democracy-assistance programs. If donors are sincere about promoting democracy, then programs will seek to effectively democratize target states. If they are strategic, then programs will avoid destabilizing the governments of allied states. If donors' preferences vary over time, then democracy-assistance programs will reflect those changes, too. In other words, governments will get the democracy assistance they pay for.

### Including target states' preferences

If donor states sincerely seek to promote democratic change abroad, then we would expect them to factor in target states' traits when designing democracy assistance. Target states vary in their levels of democracy, and even complete autocracies vary in their strategies of survival. Those

---

[14] Cox, Ikenberry, and Inoguchi (2000); Traub (2008).
[15] Milner and Tingley (2010).
[16] Bjornlund (2004, 20–7).
[17] Corn (1993).
[18] Cox, Ikenberry, and Inoguchi (2000); McFaul (2010).

variations may determine how effective democracy-assistance programs are. Focusing on donor states' preferences is therefore not enough – we should also consider the preferences of target states.

Although donors may not target foreign aid as effectively as they could, research suggests that they do attempt to target it. Humanitarian ideals at least partially explain why Western states give scarce resources to needy countries.[19] Donors' humanitarian impulses were particularly strong during the interval between the end of the Cold War and September 11, 2001.[20] Indeed, donor governments have sometimes genuinely sought to foster development in poor countries, factoring in the quality of target states' governance in aid sectors that especially require target governments' involvement to succeed. Moreover, they have responded generously when target states have experienced natural disasters or hosted many refugees – events that represent genuine human emergencies.

Similarly, donor governments may consider target countries' regime types when designing democracy-assistance programs. Although donors generally lack quality information about which democracy-assistance programs will be effective, a point that I discuss at some length in Chapter 3, the projects that will, for example, effectively foster competition in a liberal monarchy likely differ from ones that will successfully foster democratic consolidation in a fragile post-conflict environment. This framework suggests that any taming of democracy assistance may be the result of variations in target countries' regime types. Since target states may engage in various actions that prevent or thwart the types of democracy assistance they find challenging, it would make sense for donors to tailor their aid programs to at least some degree. Research that finds a positive correlation between countries' levels of democracy and amounts of democracy aid supports that point of view.[21]

### The potential limits of state-based theories

Although they offer important insights, the aforementioned approaches may not, and, I will argue later, do not, offer a fully satisfying account of the taming of democracy assistance. Recognizing when and where donor states prefer tame democracy assistance is crucial for understanding what programs get funded because donors control the purse-strings. Noting the regime type of target states is crucial, too, since target states'

---

[19] Lumsdaine (1993).
[20] Arvin (2002, 28); Bermeo (2008); Wright and Winters (2010, 63–5).
[21] Finkel, Pérez-Liñán, and Seligson (2007, 422); Scott and Steele (2011, 62).

characteristics affect what programs are possible and likely to succeed. But what state-centric vantage points ignore are the organizations that donors fund to design and implement democracy aid abroad. Like all organizations, democracy-assistance organizations have their own ideas and interests, to which this book pays careful attention. By doing so, it advances a transnational approach to democracy assistance that can be applied to the study of foreign influence more broadly.

Donor governments delegate to organizations in the democracy establishment because doing so performs several functions.[22] First, designing and implementing democracy-assistance programs requires expert knowledge that donor governments often lack. Especially since democracy-assistance programs occur year in, year out, in more than a hundred countries, it makes sense for specialists to perform the task. Second, designing and implementing democracy assistance is a political activity that is often better served by non-state implementers than state implementers. Perceptions that donor governments are engaged in foreign meddling can harm not only donors' reputations, but also democracy's legitimacy. Finally, government officials may want to cede some control to independent institutions as a way of ensuring that their strategic interests (or future officials' strategic interests) do not overwhelm democracy assistance. Independently run institutions such as the NED, for example, require government officials to have their hands tied somewhat, preventing them from directly manipulating programs and thus "locking in" a pro-democracy policy bias. Such a delegation relationship may be deliberate on the part of government officials who wish to protect democracy assistance from political opponents in the future.

Delegation therefore performs useful functions for government offi-cials. It also, however, creates *information problems* that make it difficult for donor states to observe and control their programs overseas. To give an example: one former grant-maker for the United States government told me that she had unwittingly funded a militia in Africa that was posing as an NGO – a clear violation of government policy not to aid groups that are associated with violence.[23] As her experience suggests, although donor governments set the goals for democracy assistance, the organizations they fund to design and implement programs often have some discretion. Donors' difficulties observing and controlling such organizations are significant because the organizations have preferences

---

[22] By delegation, I refer to a "conditional grant of authority from a principal to an agent that empowers the latter to act on behalf of the former." See Hawkins *et al.* (2006, 3).

[23] Interview 53, with former donor official, in person, Washington, DC, August 19, 2009.

that diverge from donor governments' preferences. As I explain in the next section, organizations worry about their survival – something about which government officials care little. Survival-seeking behavior can encourage organizations to pursue programs that donors concerned primarily with effective democracy promotion do not prefer.

Although information problems are common for government programs, they are particularly severe for democracy assistance for at least five reasons. Although all five traits are characteristic of democracy assistance, how many of them are present shapes the severity of the information problems involved in any particular democracy-assistance program. That variation will be leveraged empirically later on in the book. First, democracy-assistance programs take place overseas and typically involve multiple steps of delegation. Rather than directly funding the NGOs that design and implement projects, government funds usually pass through several organizations. As a consequence, multiple organizations have the opportunity to incrementally shift their tasks away from the original descriptions. Second, the intended beneficiaries of democracy assistance are foreign citizens, who have no formal way to communicate performance information back to donors. Third, multiple donors often fund similar projects in the same country, enabling the best local NGOs to pick donors to work with that are closer to their preferences. Fourth, democratizing countries is difficult and the state of knowledge about best practices is poor. Donors' uncertainty about the most effective democracy-promotion strategies gives organizations leeway. Finally, donor governments sometimes fund democracy assistance collectively, either when they sponsor aid programs multilaterally or when multiple parts of the same government come together to back a specific program (e.g., USAID and the US State Department jointly funding the Middle East Partnership Initiative). In such cases, multiple actors must write contracts, monitor, and punish NGOs together – all of which are harder to coordinate jointly than individually, especially when the actors have different preferences.

As this discussion suggests, although many democracy-assistance grants and contracts are lengthy and explicit, even official evaluations of democracy assistance suggest that funded organizations have some discretion. Five out of seven reports about democracy assistance by the United States' Government Accountability Office (GAO), for example, have scrutinized American democracy assistance for inadequate monitoring of programs. The highlighted problems ranged from a lack of information about what activities the US government is funding[24]

[24] United States Government Accountability Office (2009).

to inadequate financial oversight,[25] to misuse of funds and failure to comply with American law on the part of aid recipients.[26] Overcoming the problems of observation and control has no easy solution, although donors have especially sought to improve their monitoring and reporting requirements as a strategy for reducing organizations' discretion. Because the information problems in democracy assistance are severe, even the efforts most criticized by the GAO, such as those by the United States in Cuba, have still not fully solved those information problems according to repeated evaluations.[27] As such, government officials' preferences for democracy assistance (and ultimately the public's preferences) may not be fully executed by funded organizations. That is particularly so because funded organizations not only implement, but actually design, many democracy-assistance programs themselves. If organizations in the democracy establishment influence program design, then they are able to opt for programs that they prefer along a number of dimensions, including the dimensions of measurability and regime compatibility that are discussed below.

I therefore argue that an explanation of the taming of democracy assistance is difficult to develop if we focus exclusively on states, whether donors or targets. Donors fund democracy assistance, but they rarely design and implement programs themselves. For all the reasons mentioned above, it is difficult for donor states to gather quality information about programs that take place abroad. Thus, if the preferences of organizations in the democracy establishment and donor states differ, then there will be predictable effects on the content of democracy assistance.

### A transnational approach to democracy promotion

Drawing on the research of other scholars of foreign assistance contracts, such as Alexander Cooley and James Ron, this book develops a new approach to understanding democracy assistance.[28] It is grounded in the preferences of the organizations that design and implement democracy-assistance programs overseas and the way those preferences interact with the preferences of state governments. I collectively refer to organizations involved in designing and implementing democracy assistance, which are both idea-driven and incentive-driven, as the democracy establishment. I argue that as organizations have competed for funding and become

---

[25] United States Government Accountability Office (2013).
[26] United States Government Accountability Office (2006).
[27] United States Government Accountability Office (2006, 2008, 2013).
[28] Cooley and Ron (2002).

more professional, they have more often pursued democracy-assistance programs that promote their survival. The argument suggests that much (but not all) of the real politics of democracy promotion takes place outside of and between donor and target states – at the transnational level, in organizations in the democracy establishment.

The argument that I develop draws on both economic models and sociological theories. It begins with some observations about the preferences of donor states, target states, and democracy-assistance organizations. To survive and thrive, such organizations want to obtain donor funding and maintain access to target states. Generally, they pursue those goals through programs that are associated with quantitative outcomes (i.e., are measurable) and that do not directly confront dictators (i.e., are regime-compatible). Although such programs help organizations survive and thrive, they do not necessarily or clearly lead to democratization. Thus, there is a principal–agent problem since donor governments fund democracy assistance to promote democracy rather than to promote the survival of organizations in the democracy establishment. The harder it is for donors to observe and control organizations in the democracy establishment, the more I expect those organizations to pursue measurable and regime-compatible programs.

But people in the democracy establishment are not solely driven by funding and access concerns. They are also committed to their organizations' principled missions of advancing democracy. Those ideals sometimes conflict with their incentives to seek funding and access. How organizations resolve such conflicts varies. As democracy assistance has developed as a profession, organizations have become more likely to pursue programs that help them survive, even given constant information problems. Two mechanisms encourage organizations to converge on incentive-compatible democracy-assistance programs: competition and professionalization.

The discussion that follows first describes how states fund democracy assistance. It then considers the preferences and strategies of three actors: donor states, target states, and organizations in the democracy establishment. My argument is that organizations in the democracy establishment are rewarded for pursuing tame democracy-assistance programs, although the extent of those rewards varies according to donors' preferences and how closely donors observe and control them. Furthermore, I argue that the rewards for tame programs will increase – and increase in importance – to organizations over time. Competition and professionalization should have thus focused organizations in the democracy establishment more on their survival. As I demonstrate in the book's empirical chapters, organizations in the democracy establishment are, on the whole, highly dependent on democracy-assistance funding, which is why survival pressures are so acutely felt in the field.

### The delegation structure of democracy assistance

Economists' delegation models have been fruitfully applied to the study of various political relationships, including between lawmakers and government agencies and between states and international organizations. The textbook delegation, or principal–agent, relationship, is between an employer and an employee. The employer (principal) hires the employee (agent) to perform a job that the employer either cannot or does not want to do. The employer uses contracts to reward or punish the employee, but the employer cannot fully observe the employee's work. Unfortunately for the employer, her preferences may differ from the employee's preferences. Two common problems arise. First, agents act in ways that promote their goals rather than the principal's goals. Second, agents manipulate information in ways that promote outcomes that harm the principal.

The delegation structure of democracy assistance differs in several ways from the canonical models: it crosses state boundaries, sometimes involves collective principals with diverse preferences, and usually requires multiple transfers of authority. Nevertheless, the principal–agent analogy offers a useful way of understanding democracy assistance, which typically passes through a *transnational delegation chain*, beginning with government donors and ending with organizations in the democracy establishment. Figure 2.1 illustrates the delegation chain with an example of a United States government-funded democracy-assistance program in Jordan. Shorter and longer delegation chains occur in the field – a type of variation that will be relevant for testing the argument. Still, this delegation chain offers a useful example from which to build a stylized model of democracy assistance.

In Figure 2.1, the original principal is the American public. In the United States, the public elects the President and Congresspeople to govern on its behalf and make foreign-policy decisions. In that role, Congress has allocated funding to promote democracy since the 1980s. To implement programs, Congress delegates authority to other institutions, including the NED. As discussed above, Congress delegates because it lacks the capacity to run democracy-assistance programs itself, and because some separation from the government serves democracy promotion well. The NED is a foundation that awards grants to NGOs, such as the US-based Center for International Private Enterprise (CIPE). CIPE then delegates funds to overseas organizations, such as

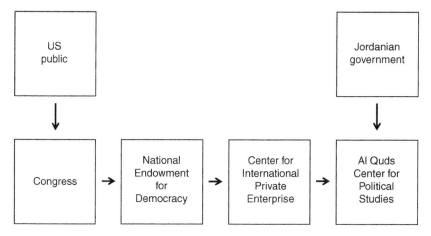

Figure 2.1 An example of the transnational delegation chain in democracy assistance.
*Note:* Bottom row depicts delegation from Congress to the final aid recipient, the Al Quds Center. Top row depicts the American public and Jordanian government as monitors.

the Al Quds Center for Political Studies in Jordan, which designs and implements projects, such as a dialogue on Jordan's national budget. The Jordanian government, a monarchy, is the final actor, although it is not an agent. Because the Jordanian government monitors aid programs, it affects actors in the delegation chain, starting with the Al Quds Center.

What are the preferences and strategies of the actors in the transnational delegation chain? I examine three types of actors: officials in donor governments, organizations in the democracy establishment, and officials in target states. My focus is on how organizations in the democracy establishment interact with states at either end of the transnational delegation chain. As the first quote in this chapter's epigraph suggests, those organizations are caught between "funders" and "local stakeholders." Strategic interactions thus occur between democracy practitioners and the leaders of the countries where they work as well as between democracy practitioners and leaders of the countries that fund them. That transnational context should significantly affect democracy assisters' strategies.

In making this argument, I draw on previous studies of transnational organizations that emphasize how such organizations, despite their grand rhetoric, behave in many ways like any other organizations.[29] In that

---

[29] Cooley and Ron (2002); Prakash and Gugerty (2010); Sell and Prakash (2004).

way, transnational organizations' changes over time are similar to the changes that many social movements and domestic NGOs have been shown to experience.[30] Where the theoretical approach developed here is particularly novel vis-à-vis previous studies of transnational actors is in its examination of a new sector (democracy assistance), systematic theorization of the importance of target states (not just donor states), and exploration of the full life-cycle of a field.

*The preferences of government officials*  Government officials want to promote democracy.[31] Yet Western governments have a long history of prioritizing other objectives over democracy promotion. After all, they want to maintain strong relationships with allies, even authoritarian ones. The US Navy's Fifth Fleet, for example, is based in dictatorial Bahrain. When tens of thousands of protesters took to Manama's streets in 2011 and the ruling Al Khalifa family cracked down with arrests, police violence, and torture, American leaders stood quietly by.[32] Indeed, when other foreign-policy preferences conflict with democracy promotion, they often win. Donor states' other foreign-policy preferences therefore ought to affect where and how they fund democracy aid.

Nevertheless, evidence suggests that donor governments fund democracy aid because they want countries to democratize, even if their other preferences can trump democracy promotion. In the United States, democracy promotion has historically enjoyed bipartisan support in the government, including among Presidents Ronald Reagan, George H. W. Bush, Bill Clinton, George W. Bush, and Barack Obama. Moreover, it has deep historical roots in American grand strategy and ideology.[33] Surveys conducted by the Chicago Council on Global Affairs between 1978 and 2004 indicate that consistently large majorities of American opinion leaders support democracy promotion.[34] Although public support for democracy promotion declined after September 11, 2001, the issue remained generally supported among political elites. Outside the United States, other Western countries and international organizations, including the European Union, the Organization of American States, the

[30] McCarthy and Zald (2011); Staggenborg (1988).
[31] "Government officials" refers to both elected officials and bureaucrats involved in funding democracy assistance. Although this category might be fruitfully disaggregated in future studies, I believe that both elected officials and bureaucrats can be theorized jointly as an initial investigation of this book's research questions.
[32] Fahim (2012).
[33] Bjornlund (2004, 20–7); Ikenberry (2000); Monten (2005).
[34] Chicago Council on Foreign Relations and the German Marshall Fund of the United States (2002, 37, 58–9).

Organization for Security and Co-operation in Europe, and the United Nations, have stated their commitments to democracy and punished countries that violate democratic norms.[35] Such actions are part of a broader acceptance of democracy as an internationally legitimate form of governance.[36] Although some politicians care little for democracy assistance, few vocally oppose it, especially since it is a relatively small budget item.

Beyond wanting to support democracy-assistance programs that effectively democratize countries and do not jeopardize other foreign policy objectives, government officials have few preferences about how to accomplish that goal. There is, however, one important preference that they have that could affect democracy assistance. Because they are often elected, government officials want to implement foreign policies successfully enough to stay in office. American and European publics tend to be supportive of democracy promotion in the abstract, but repeated polls suggest that they have little support for specific, and potentially costly, strategies of democracy promotion, such as military intervention and democracy assistance.[37] As such, elected officials do not prefer democracy assistance to be visible or highly salient to the public. And to the extent that it is visible, they hope that they will be able to demonstrate that it has been effective.

What is important to conclude from this discussion is that government officials' preferences for effective democracy assistance create the incentives to which organizations in the democracy establishment respond. At the same time, those organizations enjoy some "agency slack," which refers to their autonomy from government officials. That donor states contain diverse, often conflicting preferences concerning democracy promotion worsens the problems of observation and control discussed above. That delegation sometimes involves collaboration between multiple governments or multiple actors within the same government bureaucracy only complicates matters further. Thus, although organizations in the democracy establishment must respond to their donors' preferences, they also have an opportunity to craft programs in ways that suit their own interests. But what are those interests? Answering that question requires that we also appreciate the constraints put on democracy assisters by leaders in the countries where they work.

---

[35] Crawford (2001, 100–9); Donno (2010); Hyde (2011, ch. 3); Kelley (2008, 247); McFaul (2004–5).
[36] Franck (1992).
[37] Brancati (2014); Drezner (2008); Faust and Garcia (2013); Holsti (2000).

*The preferences of target-country leaders* Like the elected officials in donor states, incumbent politicians in target states want to stay in power. Although there are notable exceptions to that rule – politicians that willingly step down from office in order to advance a democratic transition – most incumbents in states that are the targets of democracy assistance want to stay in office. After all, when leaders in non-democratic states lose office, which they typically do in an irregular manner, they have a low probability of avoiding exile, imprisonment, or death.[38]

Because they want to stay in power, most incumbents in target states dislike, and try to prohibit or undermine, democracy-assistance programs that they think could challenge their survival. Some countries, such as Syria, have consistently prohibited democracy aid, although international actors have still managed to support some civil society groups there anyway. Other countries, such as Egypt, Russia, Venezuela, and Zimbabwe, have formally allowed democracy assistance at various times but typically imposed legal and extralegal restrictions on the NGOs that implemented it while doing so.[39]

When incumbents attempt to prohibit or limit democracy assistance, they do not necessarily succeed. Despite President Hosni Mubarak's prohibitions against NGOs in Egypt accepting foreign funding, from 2005 to 2010, for example, Congress mandated that "democracy and governance activities shall not be subject to the prior approval of the GoE [government of Egypt]."[40] Unsurprisingly, that mandate provoked considerable frustration in the Egyptian government, which, among other retaliatory restrictions, ordered the American NGO IRI to close its offices in 2005. The comments of Sherif Mansour, a senior program officer at Freedom House, illustrate the Egyptian government's extralegal attempts to derail his organization's work during President Hosni Mubarak's last year in power. Mansour said, "They [Egyptian officials] were constantly saying: 'Why are you working with those groups [Freedom House's local partners], they are nothing.'" When Freedom House refused to stop working with the criticized groups, its staff members were followed, and they found that hotels where training sessions were about to be held were closed.[41]

Of course, not all countries are like Egypt in their efforts to curb democracy assistance. In an important study of election-monitoring,

---

[38] Goemans, Gleditsch, and Chiozza (2009, 276).
[39] Carothers (2006a); Gershman and Allen (2006).
[40] Sharp (2012, 8).
[41] Nixon (2011, A1).

political scientist Susan Hyde divides the leaders of transitional democracies into two types: true democrats, who abide by democratic principles, even at some personal cost, and pseudo-democrats, who attempt to stay in office at all costs.[42] But even true democrats have reasons to prohibit democracy assistance, especially in its less tame varieties. First, programs that promote open contestation and political mobilization can endanger fragile democratic transitions. To take one example: researchers have found that electoral assistance can destabilize democratizing countries that are emerging from civil conflict.[43] Even sincere democrats may wish to avoid international assistance in such cases. Second, permitting a heavy international aid footprint, especially one that is closely linked to the United States, may be unpopular and delegitimizing for political leaders. Around the 1994 election in the Dominican Republic that ultimately led to the country's Pact for Democracy, for example, USAID and NDI elections efforts ran into problems because both elite and ordinary citizens were (perhaps understandably) suspicious of US influence.[44] Survey experiments have also confirmed that certain types of foreign intervention can also be polarizing in terms of public opinion.[45] As a consequence, target-country leaders may seek to prohibit democracy assistance, especially if it is heavy-handed.

To sum up, leaders in target countries at various levels of freedom ought to seek to limit democracy assistance. Such preferences create another important set of conditions on the work of organizations in the democracy establishment. In general, and even outside closed societies, such organizations are likely to worry about gaining and maintaining access.

*The preferences of organizations in the democracy establishment*
Outside and between donor and target states are organizations in the democracy establishment. Those organizations – such as the NED, CIPE, and the Al Quds Center in Figure 2.1 – differ in important respects, but they share fundamental goals. First, they want target states to democratize, although they may disagree about how to promote democracy. Second, they want funding from donor states so that they can survive and thrive as organizations. Third, they want access to target states for similar reasons. The extent to which winning funding

---

[42] Hyde (2011, 31–3).
[43] Brancati and Snyder (2011); Flores and Nooruddin (2012); Paris (2004).
[44] Donno (2013, 184–5).
[45] Bush and Jamal (2015); Corstange and Marinov (2012).

or gaining access matters more for an organization depends in part on its location in the delegation chain. The Al Quds Center in Figure 2.1, for example, arguably cares more about being able to legally work in Jordan than the NED because the Al Quds Center is based in Jordan, whereas the NED is not and could thus fund programs elsewhere. Still, all organizations that are available to donor governments as potential agents for democracy assistance are generally characterized by having similar preferences for funding and access, which is why I theorize them together.

Like other transnational organizations working on moral issues, organizations in the democracy establishment contain a mix of principled and pragmatic motives. Some cynics view transnational human rights and development organizations to be just as materially motivated as firms – as William Easterly puts it, a "cartel of good intentions."[46] But democracy aid is neither easy nor is it always safe. In February 2012, for example, the post-Mubarak military government in Egypt rescinded travel privileges and put more than a dozen Americans and many more Egyptians working for democracy-promotion NGOs on trial for serving foreign interests.[47] Although most of the foreigners were eventually permitted to leave Egypt on bail, the Egyptians were not, and American NDI staff member Robert Becker stayed with his employees to face the charges.[48] Meanwhile, as the Egyptian NGO crisis was escalating, Belarus President Alexander Lukashenko was overseeing raids on dozens of NGOs and sending many political activists into exile after a crackdown on protests after the fraudulent election of December 19, 2010.[49] Under such conditions, working in the field often requires a firm moral commitment to promoting democracy.

Given the dangers highlighted by the cases of Belarus and Egypt, organizations in the democracy establishment must worry about their survival, for both principled and pragmatic reasons. After all, advancing democracy in target states requires that organizations survive. Yet organizational survival can also become its own end – even at the expense of promoting democracy effectively. Fostering organizational survival typically entails two goals: securing donor funding and gaining or maintaining access to target countries.

---

[46] Easterly (2002). See also Kennedy (2005).
[47] Kirkpatrick (2012).
[48] Fahmy (2012).
[49] Schwirtz (2010).

Organizations need donor funding to enact programs and to maintain their staffs, offices, health insurance, and so on. Democracy-assistance organizations are, in that way, like all organizations. As one longtime practitioner who runs an American NGO put it: "One of my friends runs a $50 million organization and so he has to generate $50 million to keep everyone employed. It means that you have to go where the money is."[50] That organizations in the democracy establishment want to obtain more donor funding should matter for what types of democracy-assistance projects they pursue. They must identify and pursue programs that will win them favor with donors that have a hard time observing and controlling them.

Organizations also need access to target countries to survive and thrive. To keep working and winning grants, organizations must secure access to as many countries as possible. Doing so helps organizations survive not only by increasing the number of available grants, but also by establishing a successful reputation and global brand. If organizations in the democracy establishment lose access to Egypt, for example, they lose a valuable revenue source and a prominent country in terms of their image. Losing access is also a visceral worry, since it can jeopardize the safety of organizations' employees. As was the case with seeking to secure donor funding, that organizations in the democracy establishment want to maintain access to target states matters for what types of democracy-assistance projects they pursue. They must not anger target countries' leaders so much that their offices will meet major local resistance or be closed. Yet, as I discuss below, in some cases, and perhaps especially in countries that would find it diplomatically problematic to kick out foreign NGOs, programs that challenge dictators may be what are needed for democratization.

Donor-government officials do not generally care about organizations in the democracy establishment surviving. When donors fund democracy assistance, they do so to promote democracy, not to help organizations thrive or expand overseas. They may be happy, for example, to fund democracy-assistance programs in fewer countries due to access problems if it means that that doing so is likely to lead to democratization. Thus, to the extent that democracy practitioners shift programs toward their preferences for funding and access, there is a principal–agent problem. But what types of programs generate funding and access for organizations in the democracy establishment? And do they actually contradict donor states' preferences?

[50] Interview 70, with director of democracy assistance NGO, in person, Washington, DC, April 30, 2010.

*Rewards for tame democracy assistance*

In a nutshell, organizations in the democracy establishment pursue their goals of donor funding and overseas access through the pursuit of measurable and regime-compatible programs. Distinct mechanisms can lead to each type of program, although in both cases, the fact that donor states' information about democracy-assistance projects is often scarce plays an important role. On the one hand, donor states will be more likely to reward programs associated with measurable outcomes when the observation and control of organizations are relatively difficult. On the other hand, they will also be more likely to unwittingly tolerate programs that generate target-state access under the same circumstances. I consider each process in turn.

*Measurable programs* I hypothesize that, under conditions of difficult observation and control, organizations are more likely to pursue democracy-assistance programs that are *measurable* because such programs help them please donors and win funding. I define measurable programs as democracy-assistance efforts that are associated with country-level quantitative outcomes. There are practical, ethical, and methodological challenges that obscure the causal impact of democracy-assistance programs.[51] Measurable programs still face such limitations and do not necessarily involve clear impact measures. But at least they have concrete indicators that measure their associated outcomes, which are plausible, if minimal, barometers of success for far-off donors.

Aid-recipient organizations use the strategy of pursuing measurable programs to help them survive because they want to signal success to donors. Indeed, organizations can and do use measurable programs to demonstrate their results in terms of tangible outcome indicators. Increasing the number of women in parliament in a country, for example, sends a clearer signal to donors of an efficacious program than does reporting that an organization has aided dissident groups, an action that does not have an obvious outcome measure to which it could be attached. Such a signaling strategy is not inevitable. In many cases, organizations use inputs, outputs, or non-quantitative outcomes as their measurement strategies – or use no measurement strategy at all.[52] Although measurable programs send a particularly appealing signal to donors, organizations also use other signaling strategies to convince them

---

[51] National Research Council (2008, ch. 5).
[52] Bollen, Paxton, and Morishima (2005); Epstein, Serafino, and Miko (2007, 11–17); Green and Kohl (2007); National Research Council (2008, ch. 5).

of programs' efficacy, such as pursuing photo opportunities or programs with short time horizons. I discuss some of those strategies in the case studies, although my primary focus in this book is on the strategy of pursuing tame programs.

An analogy to the pressure for measurement in democracy assistance comes from the field of education, where psychologist Donald Campbell's "law" is often invoked: "The more any quantitative social indicator is used for social decision-making, the more subject it will be to corruption pressures and the more apt it will be to distort and corrupt the social processes it is intended to monitor."[53] Governments want state-funded schools to educate students. Schools can demonstrate educational success to governments in various ways, including through measures of students' attendance. Although attendance fails to capture important aspects of school performance, such as instructional quality or student learning, it is a ready, quantitative, and plausibly objective outcome indicator. In other words, attendance is a noisy but loud signal of school performance. Since it is hard for outsiders to monitor schools, schools win by reporting rosy attendance figures, even if focusing on attendance comes at the expense of pursuing other valuable goals.

As with public schools, the principals in democracy assistance are usually donor governments. Elected officials seek reelection, hoping that no scandals about democracy assistance will alarm voters. As discussed above, although democracy promotion is popular among elites, it has historically garnered little support from the general public. Public skepticism encourages elected officials to use positive results to justify spending public money on democracy promotion. As US Secretary of State Hillary Rodham Clinton warned USAID staff in 2009: "You've got to be able to make the case that what you do for America is important, even in these tough times."[54]

In the fight for organizational survival, strategic organizations in the democracy establishment will seek to please donors by pursuing measurable programs. That strategy is not unique to democracy aid; organizations involved in development assistance also use it.[55] I posit that the harder it is for donor states to observe and control organizations in the democracy establishment, the more likely they are to reward measurable programs. Thus, strategic organizations will pursue more measurable programs when observation and control are difficult.

---

[53] Campbell (1976, 49).
[54] Clinton (2009).
[55] Ferguson (1990); Jackson (2005).

But if measurable programs please democracy donors, what is the principal–agent problem? As noted above, measurable programs seem to satisfy government officials' preferences. Thus, it may not be appropriate to conceive of measurable programs as the consequence of a principal–agent problem. Research on democracy assistance does, however, suggest that measurable programs can conflict with effective democracy promotion. If that research is correct, then government officials are sending mixed messages to organizations in the democracy establishment: They want effective aid programs and they want measurable programs. In that case, delegation dynamics are relevant. I take up this issue more fully in Chapter 3, but I briefly touch on the issue here.

In a landmark study of democracy assistance, Thomas Carothers of the Carnegie Endowment for International Peace sharply criticized measurable programs, concluding that the field's emphasis on quantitative results harmed democracy promotion by encouraging myopia and wasting time and other resources.[56] A USAID program in Cambodia in 1997, for example, was evaluated as achieving progress that "exceeded expectations" on preexisting indicators even though a democracy-thwarting coup had occurred. A number of other studies of democracy assistance have also faulted programs for unduly emphasizing quantitative outputs and outcomes.[57]

Consistent with their findings, many practitioners believe that crucial outcomes of democracy-assistance programs are not measurable. Some practitioners are "true believers" when it comes to measurement, perhaps due to professionalism, which is studied later in the book. Others view it as a necessary evil. Some donors and practitioners have even publicly fought against pressure from elected officials to measure. According to the National Endowment for Democracy, for example, "measurement of the effect of democracy promotion projects on democratization is … an overwhelming, if not impossible, task."[58] But using measurable programs helps organizations in the democracy establishment to win funding, so even many skeptical practitioners will do it. As of 2013, six years after making the above statement, it is important to note that the NED's approach to monitoring and evaluation has changed dramatically. The NED's approach to evaluation came to involve a multilayered strategy of external evaluations, in-house evaluations, and grantee self-assessments.[59]

---

[56] Carothers (1999, 291–3).
[57] Brown (2006); Burnell (2000); Henderson (2003); Ishkanian (2008); Mendelson and Glenn (2002).
[58] Epstein, Serafino, and Miko (2007, 17).
[59] Usatin (2013).

*Regime-compatible programs* I hypothesize that, under conditions of difficult observation and control, organizations are more likely to pursue democracy-assistance programs that are *regime-compatible* in order to gain access to target states. I define regime-compatible programs as democracy-assistance efforts that are unlikely to threaten the survival of an incumbent regime in the near future due to regime collapse or overthrow. Regime-compatible programs may promote normatively desirable ends, such as women's representation, that could be associated with long-term democratization. Crucially, however, regime-compatible programs do not directly confront dictators. For that reason, target states' leaders will be less likely to prohibit them than other types of democracy assistance.

Why would organizations in the democracy establishment prefer to design and implement regime-compatible programs, all else being equal? The answer again relates to organizational survival. If a dictator blocks access to NGOs in the democracy establishment, organizations cannot promote democracy there. Thus, they will choose regime-compatible programs for both principled and pragmatic reasons. Such strategic calculations are consistent with existing studies of organizations involved with democracy assistance. Indeed, previous research shows that democracy practitioners are often willing to compromise with pseudo-democrats. In one important study, for example, political scientist Judith Kelley found that international election monitors hesitate to criticize countries that are improving after an authoritarian past in their reports.[60]

The rewards for compromising with pseudo-democrats in terms of access are real. Countries frequently block access to democracy practitioners. As diplomatic cables released by Wikileaks from Bahrain and Egypt show, high-level officials have complained to donor governments about NGOs in the democracy establishment operating in their countries specifically because of the help that those organizations give to regime opponents.[61] Outside the Middle East, in 2006, Russia passed a law to monitor the activities of local and foreign NGOs, significantly constraining democracy-assistance organizations.[62] Later, in 2012, Russia expelled USAID, halting its democracy-assistance activities. Although those actions seem to have been at least partially rooted in the Kremlin's concerns about specific American foreign-assistance programs, they also represent a broader type of domestically rooted backlash to foreign

[60] Kelley (2009, 782–3).
[61] Embassy Cairo (2007); Embassy Manama (2010).
[62] Carothers (2006a, 55–7).

interference.[63] Democracy practitioners therefore will prefer to support practices and institutions that target countries will tolerate, if not embrace. Doing so allows them to obtain access and, arguably, make some progress.

In that way, regime-compatible democracy assistance is connected to the phenomenon of competitive authoritarian regimes. Although researchers define countries that are lacking in some but not all democratic credentials in various ways, the key is that many countries today have some democratic institutions but lack important political and civil liberties, peaceful transfers of power, or both.[64] In such countries, democratic institutions such as elections can be used as "instruments of authoritarian rule."[65] Pseudo-democrats' policy choices thus influence the democracy establishment, such as when pseudo-democrats began inviting election observers and fostered an international norm that is now endorsed and enforced by the democracy establishment.[66] At the same time, the democracy establishment's preferences, such as its support of women's representation, influence the practices of pseudo-democrats. Countries seeking to signal their liberal credentials often attempt to do so according to what organizations in the democracy establishment promote.

Of course, donors themselves may want to send certain countries, such as their security partners, regime-compatible democracy aid. Yet organizations in the democracy establishment prefer to pursue regime-compatible programs to gain and maintain access regardless of donor states' preferences. Consequently, if organizations influence the design of democracy assistance, programs can get decoupled, or separated, from donor states' broader foreign policies. Consider a case study of democracy assistance during Georgia's Rose Revolution in 2003 by Lincoln Mitchell, a scholar–practitioner who led NDI's Georgia office at that time.[67] On the eve of the revolution, the US government was disillusioned with President Eduard Shevardnadze, but the White House was not interested in supporting his ouster, viewing Shevardnadze as a reformer and a friend in the Iraq War. Despite that perspective in Washington, DC, American democracy aid played an important role in mobilizing the Georgian dissidents that overthrew him after fraudulent elections. As I show in the later chapters, such decoupling

---

[63] Christensen and Weinstein (2013).
[64] Collier and Levitsky (1997); Levitsky and Way (2010).
[65] Gandhi and Lust-Okar (2009); Schedler (2006).
[66] Hyde (2011).
[67] Mitchell (2009, 4).

can also happen in the opposition direction: when donor states want regime transition, organizations in the democracy establishment may compromise with the target states' regimes.

### Change in the democracy establishment

The preceding section discussed democracy assistance as if the actors' preferences are constant over time. That is not, however, the case. First, and as noted previously, American government officials' preferences may have changed such that measurable or regime-compatible programs have become more valued. Second, and as discussed in this section, organizations in the democracy establishment have come to value the tame programs that help them survive more. I hypothesize that those changing preferences affect the design and implementation of democracy assistance. Specifically, I hypothesize that competition and professionalization will encourage organizations in the democracy establishment to pursue tamer programs.

The hypotheses developed below entail both a logic of consequences, which involves actors motivated by costs and benefits, and a logic of appropriateness, which involves actors motivated by right and wrong.[68] Both logics could explain convergence on measurable and regime-compatible democracy assistance. Organizations adapt both to further their interests and to do what they think is right. Canonical sociological research on organizations suggests that they can become more homogeneous because of competition as well as desires for legitimacy.[69] I expect that the democracy establishment will have experienced both processes. Competition for funding encourages learning, while professional norms spread standards and ideas.

*Competition* As democracy assistance has grown, organizations that did not originally promote democracy (for example, development consultants such as ARD, later known as Tetra Tech, or Chemonics) entered the field of democracy assistance to take advantage of new opportunities. New organizations, both non-profit and for-profit, and departments within existing organizations were formed. Although NGO competition can involve fights over resources, attention, or policy influence,[70] competition for funding to execute democracy-assistance programs was especially salient in light of such developments.

---

[68] March and Olsen (1998).
[69] Weber (1978 [1922]); DiMaggio and Powell (1983).
[70] Bloodgood (2011, 116–18).

Under such circumstances, I argue that competitive learning will have winnowed the strategies of organizations in the democracy establishment. Democracy practitioners have learned about effecting political change and attaining funding. Because new organizations entered the lucrative field, competition grew. I expect the organizations that survived successfully, such as Freedom House, to have won projects and gained access to target countries relatively often through tame programs. In contrast, I expect the organizations that remained less professional and adhered to older models, such as the Institute for Democracy in Eastern Europe, to have receded in importance over time. Organizations in the democracy establishment failed to follow the well-known evolutionary axiom at their peril: "Adapt or die."

Certain characteristics of democracy assistance should have fostered information-sharing and competitive adaptation in the democracy establishment. First, programs usually last for one or two years. That short time horizon gives organizations the opportunity to frequently update their strategies and replicate models that they have seen succeed elsewhere in terms of funding and access.[71] In that way, change in democracy assistance should be similar to opportunistic adaptation in other competitive fields with short-term contracts, such as international humanitarian relief.[72] The concentration of democracy assisters in post-conflict countries should have also fostered adaptive learning and information-sharing among organizations in the democracy establishment. Large expatriate communities create informal communication and coordination channels through which relevant information can pass.

Competition should have also reinforced organizations' preferences for measurable programs. Creating neutral standards has helped democracy-assistance organizations justify the continued need for aid after the end of the Cold War.[73] Since donors want to justify the money they spend on democracy assistance but have a hard time observing and controlling programs, organizations need to signal that their efforts are successful, which prompts them to pursue measurable programs. The harder they have to compete for funding, the more measurable programs benefit them. In Armenia, competition for democracy assistance was so fierce that it drove NGO leaders to call each other "grant chasers," "grantrepreneurs," and even "prostitutes."[74] In such situations, I expect

[71] Henderson (2002, 153–4).
[72] Cooley and Ron (2002).
[73] Guilhot (2005, 72).
[74] Ishkanian (2008, 146).

NGOs to shift toward measurable programs in a particularly rapid fashion.

*Professional norms* I hypothesize that professionalization should have also encouraged organizations in the democracy establishment to pursue tamer democracy-assistance programs. By professional, I draw on a long-standing definition from sociology and refer to people holding "systematic knowledge or doctrine acquired only through long prescribed training ... [and] a set of professional norms."[75] Building on that definition, professionalization refers to the process by which a field is increasingly inhabited by professionals.

Professional norms should have helped spread and institutionalize what organizations in the democracy establishment learned through competition and experience. Professionals share a cognitive base about the appropriate practices and structures of work in their field.[76] Many early leaders in democracy assistance started out as idealistic volunteers. In the twenty-first century, entrants to the field have studied development and democracy in college or graduate school. Multinational groups of experts on managing elections, supporting political parties, fostering independent media, and so on travel the world on contract aiding democracy in diverse settings.[77]

As in other fields, professional associations, links with universities, conferences, and the creation of an elite all could have spread and reinforced the democracy establishment's body of knowledge.[78] In 1999, for example, the NED created the World Movement for Democracy, which holds periodic international conferences for "a global network of democrats."[79] Other organizations in the democracy establishment launched the ACE Network in 1998 to unite resources on elections for practitioners.[80] Universities, such as American University in 2002 and Georgetown University in 2004, reinforced the field's growing body of knowledge by creating graduate programs for would-be democracy professionals. Not only did they encourage people in the field to think of themselves as professionals, but they also emphasized the technical and less politicized aspects of democracy promotion – thus encouraging measurable and regime-compatible programs. Courses at American

---

[75] Wilensky (1964, 138).
[76] Finnemore and Sikkink (1998, 905).
[77] Wedel (2001).
[78] DiMaggio (1991).
[79] See http://wmd.org/about.
[80] See http://www.aceproject.org.

University covered technical topics – such as election administration, electoral process, and governance, democracy, and development – beyond the general issues of democratization or democracy promotion that once characterized the field of study. When practitioners are taught to focus on the technical side of democracy promotion, they will value untame programs less than tame ones.

Although aiding democracy remained in many ways more of an art than a science, the emerging field became more epistemic as knowledge about promoting democracy accumulated. Research by Carothers, Diamond, McFaul, and others gradually built common techniques as well as shared normative and cause–effect beliefs.[81] In the Dominican Republic's 1990 presidential election, for example, international election observers lacked the technical ability to reject or accept the opposition's allegation that widespread fraud had caused President Joaquín Balaguer to steal the close election. By the 1994 election, quick count techniques – by then a fairly routine component of election observations – allowed the international community to take a much stronger stand against Balaguer's misconduct.[82]

Professional norms should have also led organizations in the democracy establishment to take certain programs and goals for granted. Professionals often have faith in measurement systems for domains such as human rights.[83] As such, norms should have reinforced professionals' growing desire to implement measurable programs. A program that an organization initially pursued instrumentally could later become viewed as appropriate. Authoritarian rulers, for example, tend to tolerate programs supporting women's representation. But professionals can value women's representation in and of itself, even if it may not lead to immediate democratization. More generally, professionals should place a stronger priority on organizational survival and job security and the more technical (as opposed to political) work that comes with it. Their means become their ends, a pattern familiar from studies of goal displacement in sociology.

Changes in higher education and public sector management should have encouraged professionalization in democracy assistance.[84] In that way, changes in the democracy establishment have been caused exogenously by a broader "evidence-based" transformation of public policy. Yet certain unique characteristics of democracy assistance should have

[81] Goldstein and Keohane (1993).
[82] Donno (2013, 177).
[83] Merry (2011).
[84] Hopgood (2008).

fostered professionalization endogenously, too. First, research shows that organizations are more likely to converge in fields that rely on few funding sources and interact often with the state, which prefers to work with professional organizations.[85] The democracy establishment is precisely that type of field, and competition for donor funding only heightens the pressures. Second, short-term contracts foster professionalization. As people transfer across organizations and countries according to new contract opportunities, ideas and practices get cross-fertilized across organizations.[86] For all those reasons, I expect professional norms to play an important role encouraging organizations in the democracy establishment to converge on tamer programs.

If I can show that professional norms have caused convergence, my findings will in many ways be surprising. That organizations in the democracy establishment could share common ideas about promoting democracy is striking. In many policy areas, experts disagree about how to achieve a goal. Even in cases of politically influential expert consensus, such as the one that occurred among Keynesian economists after World War II, the consensus is often momentary and masks many divisions.[87] Moreover, donor states vary in their democratic institutions and traditions. We might therefore expect their programs to "export" their unique models of democracy, and previous studies have emphasized such logics.[88] Indeed, considerable differences in foreign-aid strategies exist across bilateral donors as well as between bilateral and multilateral donors.[89]

## Empirical expectations

Testing the two-pronged argument developed above requires developing many concrete observable implications and scrutinizing them with diverse types of evidence. This section summarizes the main empirical implications of the argument, which were laid out above. In the chapters that follow, I seek to test these observable implications.

First, *the rewards that organizations gain from pursuing measurable and regime-compatible democracy assistance will come at some cost in terms of effective democratization* (Hypothesis 1). Donors fund democracy-assistance programs to democratize target states. Organizations in the democracy establishment seek democratization, too, but they also want

---

[85] DiMaggio and Powell (1983, 155).
[86] On turnover in democracy assistance, see Coles (2007, 24, 42).
[87] Ikenberry (1993).
[88] Kopstein (2006); Petrova (2014).
[89] Alesina and Dollar (2000); Milner (2006).

to obtain funding and access to target countries to survive and thrive. The programs that best further those goals are measurable and regime-compatible. Thus, when organizations have more discretion over the design and implementation of democracy assistance, they will be more likely to pursue those preferred programs. Although my goal in this book is *not* to study the effects of tame democracy assistance, a testable assumption of the argument is that the programs that promote organizational survival will not always effectively democratize countries.

Building on that logic, *the more difficult it is for donors to observe and control organizations in the democracy establishment, the more those organizations will pursue programs that are measurable, regime-compatible, or both* (Hypothesis 2). Again, organizations want to win funding and maintain access to survive. Their strategies for achieving those ends involve pursuing measurable and regime-compatible programs. When donor governments can more easily observe and control organizations, they will reward measurable programs less and punish regime-compatible programs more. Organizations will respond accordingly to enhance their chances of survival. As I discuss in Chapter 4, there are a number of ways to test this hypothesis that depend on variations in the nature of delegation relationships, as well as variations in the characteristics of government donors and organizations in the democracy establishment.

Turning now to the taming of democracy assistance, *competition and professional norms in organizations in the democracy establishment should exist and should have increased over time* (Hypothesis 3). I expect organizations in the democracy establishment to worry about their survival, especially under conditions of high competition and strong professional norms. Competition and professionalization will both increase over time and thus exert an increasing influence on program decisions. Organizations will feel some tension between their ideals and incentives as a consequence. Such dynamics are not unique to democracy assistance, although, as discussed above, certain characteristics of the field should exacerbate the trends.

Growing competition and professionalism should impact the design and implementation of democracy assistance in tangible ways. *The more organizations compete for funding, the more programs that are measurable, regime-compatible, or both will be pursued* (Hypothesis 4). Increasing competition in the democracy establishment focuses organizations on their survival. When competition is higher, organizations will work harder to please donors with measurable programs and to gain target-state access with regime-compatible programs. *The more organizations in the democracy establishment are professional, the more programs that are measurable, regime-compatible, or both will be pursued* (Hypothesis 5). Organizations change as they professionalize. Professionals will focus more on maintaining their organizations through tame programs than novices. Furthermore, they care more about monitoring and evaluation and thus value measurable programs more.

Donor governments' preferences will influence the design of democracy assistance, too, even though organizations in the democracy establishment ultimately implement most efforts. *The more donor governments prefer measurable or regime-compatible programs, the more organizations in the democracy establishment will pursue those programs* (Hypothesis 6). Because they want to survive, organizations in the democracy establishment will respond to donors' preferences. If donor states prefer measurable or regime-compatible programs in a particular target state or at a particular time, organizations in the democracy establishment will design and implement those programs.

Variations in donor type also will lead to variations in donor preferences. Specifically, *government-funded democracy-assistance programs will be more measurable than privately funded ones* (Hypothesis 7). Donor states are preoccupied with measurable programs in part because policy-makers are elected officials. In other words, policy-makers are the agents of the public. Donor governments typically also channel democracy assistance through multiple mechanisms, which makes it harder for them to observe and control grantees. Thus, private donors will be less likely to reward measurable democracy assistance than government donors. As discussed in the later chapters, private donors may also be bolder than public donors because they have fewer competing interests.

## Conclusions

What explains the taming of democracy assistance? Under what conditions do states promote democracy in measurable and regime-compatible ways? This chapter suggested that to answer those questions, in addition to focusing on the preferences of donor and target states, we should examine the ideas and incentives of the organizations that implement democracy assistance. Although the existing state-centric approaches offer valuable insights, they overlook important factors. Donor states cannot perfectly observe and control the democracy-assistance programs they fund. Language barriers, multiple stages of delegation, uncertainty about democratization, and multiple and collective principals – all those factors and more create problems of observation and control. Since the organizations that implement democracy-assistance programs overseas have their own preferences that diverge from government officials' preferences, focusing just on the states is not likely to tell the whole story about democracy assistance.

I suggested that we should shift some of the theoretical focus in the study of foreign influence from states to transnational organizations. Organizations in the democracy establishment want to survive and thrive and thus prefer to implement tamer programs – even when the constraints put on them by target countries do not force them to implement such programs. When donors cannot closely monitor organizations, they will be more likely to implement tame programs. Furthermore, competition and professional norms will cause organizations to focus more on incentives than ideals, and thus pursue tamer programs. As we shall see, hard evidence from democracy-assistance programs taking place in more than one hundred target states over the past thirty years, as well as from cases of specific organizations and countries, support the argument.

# 3    Tame democracy assistance: what it is and why it matters

> *US democracy assistance has "high" and "low policy" elements. High policy is reflected in the actions senior US officials take vis-à-vis other governments ... "Low policy" is much quieter and less visible, and resides mostly in the democracy-assistance programmes that operate day-in, day-out, in close to 100 countries.*[1]

In the twenty-first century, the United States government has supported many activities in Jordan under the umbrella of advancing democracy. One USAID-sponsored program purchased an electronic voting system for the national parliament in the hopes of fostering transparency and accountability there. Another program, run by NDI, sought to increase women's representation by training over fifty female candidates for an upcoming parliamentary election. Meanwhile, the International Republic Institute (IRI) trained opposition political parties, such as the Al Wasat Islamic Party, on effective platforms and messages. Finally, the Solidarity Center supported union activists that were organizing migrant workers to fight for better working conditions and wages in Jordan's qualified industrial zones, where goods produced in collaboration with Israel benefited from a free trade agreement with the United States.

Although those programs all explicitly claimed to promote democracy in Jordan, only some were designed to challenge Jordan's King Abdullah. The Jordanian legislature, for example, is a favorite institution of the monarchy, which uses the parliament as a means to distribute patronage to supporters; it is not an engine of democratization but instead a tool of autocratic survival.[2] NDI's effort to increase women's representation thus took place within a regime-sanctioned institution and played into the regime's strategy of impressing foreign donors with a progressive record (for the region) on gender.[3] Meanwhile, and as I will discuss

---

[1] Carothers (2009b).
[2] Lust-Okar (2009).
[3] Baylouny (2005, 41–2); David and Nanes (2011).

in more detail in Chapter 7, there is little evidence that the female participants in such programs used their new positions to press for change. Elsewhere, USAID's electronic voting system collected dust – especially during the lengthy periods when the king dismissed parliament at will.[4] As such, it did little to destabilize liberal authoritarianism in Jordan.

Other programs took a more confrontational approach toward the incumbent regime. IRI's program attempted to empower the weak political parties that challenge the political status quo in which the king rules without any party affiliation. The Solidarity Center's program mobilized labor activists even as the government was courting foreign investment. Such confrontational programs were not necessarily more effective or better for democracy than the less challenging ones, although they could have been. What is clear, however, is that the programs were designed and implemented in ways that differed greatly in terms of their relationships with the regime.

Building on those examples, this chapter peels back the curtain on the general concept of "democracy assistance" to reveal important variations. It focuses on two characteristics of democracy-assistance programs that are particularly salient in terms of my argument: how much the programs emphasize quantitative outcomes and how much they confront dictators in target states. In the previous chapter, I argued that practitioners prefer programs that are measurable and regime-compatible, sometimes at the expense of effective democracy promotion. Before testing that argument, it is necessary to explain what tame democracy-assistance programs look like in greater detail. What categories do democracy-assistance programs fall into? Which types of programs are generally measurable, regime-compatible, or both?

This chapter answers each question in turn. The first section offers a fine-grained typology of democracy assistance. The second section first examines measurable democracy assistance, which refers to programs with quantitative indicators that measure their desired outcomes at a national level. Donor governments can use such indicators to assess the efficacy of democracy assistance. It then examines regime-compatible democracy assistance, which refers to programs that do not threaten the imminent survival of target-country incumbents. Such programs are defined as ones that attempt neither to foster political competition nor to mobilize civil society groups that are likely to challenge dictators. The third section illustrates how measurable and regime-compatible

---

[4] United States Agency for International Development, Office of the Inspector General (2008, 4).

democracy assistance can, at least under certain conditions, harm the cause of democracy, whereas untame programs can sometimes promote it. My goal is to show that the observable patterns are consistent with my argument, even if making causal inferences about the effects of programs is outside my scope. The chapter concludes by discussing the limitations of its approach and how to overcome them.

I acknowledge at the outset that classifying democracy assistance is ultimately a subjective exercise. Although I devote considerable effort to justifying my approach, some decisions are simply more clear-cut than others. That observation is not, however, necessarily problematic since I can compare trends in the more or less clear-cut cases empirically. This chapter's goal is to determine how measurable and regime-compatible certain types of programs *generally* are, *relative to* other types. Although its approach obscures some fascinating details about programs that emerge when we look at them on a case-by-case basis, that approach also allows me to understand important broader trends in democracy assistance. As I argue in this book, democracy-assistance programs vary considerably in how measurable and regime-compatible they are and those variations may matter for how effective democracy promotion ultimately is.

## A typology of democracy assistance

To examine variations in democracy-assistance programs, we need a typology. An obvious place to start are the classification schemes already used by practitioners. Doing so helps promote the study's external validity by linking the book's concepts to their ordinary language use.[5]

The United States government divides democracy assistance into four sectors: civil society; elections and political processes; governance; and rule of law. It defines civil society projects, which aid diverse NGOs, as projects that pursue "increased development of a politically active civil society." Elections and political processes projects support elections and political parties and encourage "more genuine and competitive political processes." Governance projects foster "more transparent and accountable government institutions." Rule of law projects, which include human rights projects as well as legal aid, "strengthe[n] rule of law and respect for human rights."[6]

---

[5] Fearon and Laitin (2000).
[6] United States Agency for International Development, Office of Democracy and Governance (2010).

Table 3.1 *Categories of democracy assistance.*

| Business | Dissidents | Legislatures | Rule of law |
|---|---|---|---|
| Civic education | Elections | Local governance | Unions |
| Civil society (general) | Governance | Media | Women's groups |
| Conflict resolution | Humanitarian aid | Political parties | Women's participation |
| Constitutions | Human rights | Research on democracy | Youth groups |

*Note:* See Appendix A for definitions.

The European Instrument for Democracy and Human Rights (EIDHR), a major European initiative, sorts its democracy-assistance programs into broadly similar, if less well-defined, groups. Although a European Union report admits that the institution "has continuously changed the categories it uses in EIDHR reports," it has nevertheless identified some general categories.[7] Those categories include aid to human rights; conflict resolution; international justice; civil society and civic participation, and in particular NGOs; rule of law; media, freedom of expression, and journalists; elections; parliaments; transparency and anti-corruption; and civil–military relations.

Building from those classifications as well as interviews with practitioners, Table 3.1 divides democracy assistance into twenty categories. Using the disaggregated typology presented in the table has two key advantages. First, doing so allows me to code and compare democracy assistance across donors based on project descriptions. When they self-report aid by category, donor governments often use different, and often non-transparent, criteria. Second, doing so allows me to study not just an "elections and political processes" project, but a project that supports elections, legislative assistance, political parties, or women's representation. Such precision is necessary to test the argument, since projects in the same sector may not all be measurable, regime-compatible, or both.

It is worth noting that the typology presented in Table 3.1 classifies each project or disbursement as falling into a single category, which obscures some interesting variation, since the same project may pursue multiple goals. In the absence of detailed budgets, however, it is difficult to determine how much of a project was devoted to secondary and tertiary goals. Thus, using a categorical typology provides both simplicity and practical clarity without sacrificing too much information.[8] Another benefit of a categorical typology is that it corresponds to the way that

[7] European Parliament, Office for Promotion of Parliamentary Democracy (2010, 40).
[8] Collier, LaPorte, and Seawright (2012).

Table 3.2 *Classification of categories of democracy assistance.*

|  | Measurable | Not measurable |
| --- | --- | --- |
| **Regime-compatible** | Business and enterprise | Civic education |
|  | Constitutions | Civil society (residual) |
|  | Good governance | Conflict resolution |
|  | Local governance | Humanitarian aid |
|  | Women's groups | Legislative assistance |
|  | Women's representation | Rule of law |
| **Not regime-compatible** | Elections | Dissidents |
|  | Human rights | Political parties |
|  | Media | Research |
|  |  | Trade unions |
|  |  | Youth |

*Note:* Full details explaining the categories and the classification decisions are provided in Appendix A.

most practitioners and donor officials conceive of democracy-assistance projects, which are typically seen as falling into discrete groupings.

### Identifying tame democracy-assistance programs

Breaking down "democracy assistance" into those twenty categories reveals important variations in the extent to which programs are linked to quantitative outcomes and confront dictators. I now discuss measurable and regime-compatible democracy assistance in turn. Table 3.2 summarizes the categories.

*Measurable democracy assistance*

I define measurable democracy-assistance programs as ones that are linked to quantitative or otherwise clear and objective indicators of progress at the level of the country. That definition is deliberately narrow. It does not encompass any notions of measurable causal impact. Measurable outcomes are not causal impacts. Inferences about the causal impact of democracy assistance are difficult to make for multiple reasons, including disagreement about the appropriate evaluation criteria and methodological issues such as selection bias.[9] A program's classification as measurable does not ameliorate those difficulties. Yet measurable democracy assistance is linked to quantitative, country-level indicators,

---

[9] National Research Council (2008, 6).

which can document a country's progress (or failure) on a specific dimension and thus at least hold out the possibility of demonstrating short-term effectiveness. Since donor governments struggle to collect quality information about democracy-assistance programs, such indicators are often satisfactory for the purposes of demonstrating effectiveness to their own principals, who are the country's citizens. Although measurable outcomes would not satisfy social scientists' concerns about causal impacts, they are still one step ahead of the measures used by many development organizations. Indeed, such organizations often struggle to demonstrate results and assess their effectiveness, even going so far as to measure their impacts in terms of *inputs*.[10]

Government officials can use quantitative, country-level indicators to signal progress to distracted donor publics and politicians. Government officials might, for example, use an improvement in a target country's Freedom of the Press score to reward the success of a media-strengthening program led by NGOs such as IREX and Internews. In contrast, when the NED quietly funded dissidents in Syria through an overseas NGO, monitoring and reporting the project's outcomes to Congress were difficult, if not impossible. Such a program's outcome or impact is hard to identify short of a democratizing revolution; even then, donors may not observe a link between the aid program and revolution. Of course, the output of such a project could be measured with a tally of the number of dissidents trained through foreign funding. Still, such an output does not offer as clear and credible a signal of effectiveness as the third-party Freedom of the Press rating, which can be treated as an outcome in the context of a Congressional hearing or federal report. Thus, dissidents programs are relatively less measurable and media programs relatively more measurable within the universe of democracy assistance. It is important to note, however, that the measurable outcomes that help enhance organizations' credibility in the eyes of donors could also harm their credibility with other audiences, such as local partners – a phenomenon that is typical for NGOs that are attempting to demonstrate credibility to multiple audiences.[11]

A reasonable way to identify measurable democracy assistance is to look for related country-level indices that donor officials could use to assess progress. Independent professional organizations' indices are most credible. When the Bush administration, for example, announced the creation of the Millennium Challenge Corporation (MCC) in 2002 – a new aid program meant to encourage and reward democratic governance – officials sought out "clear and concrete" criteria that

[10] Fowler (1996); Easterly (2006, 181).
[11] Gourevitch and Lake (2012).

would identify countries that "govern justly, invest in their people, and encourage economic freedom."[12] Indicators from the World Bank and Freedom House were chosen as appropriate benchmarks.

Seven categories of democracy assistance are associated with a cross-national index that can be used to assess outcomes: (1) business (the Political Risk Services' International Country Risk Guide and the Economic Freedom Network's Business Environment rankings); (2–3) governance and local governance (Transparency International's Corruption Perceptions Index and Global Corruption Barometer, the World Bank's Worldwide Governance Indicators and Business Environment and Enterprise Performance Surveys, and the Quality of Government Institute's Index); (4) human rights (Freedom House's *Freedom in the World* reports, Gibney's Political Terror Scale, and the Cingranelli and Richards (CIRI) Human Rights Data Project); (5) media (Freedom House's Freedom of the Press database, IREX's Media Sustainability Index, and Reporters Without Borders' country reports); and (6–7) women's groups and women's representation (the UNDP's World Development Indicators, the Inter-Parliamentary Union's Women in Parliaments database, and the CIRI database). No comparable quantitative cross-national indices exist for the remaining thirteen categories to the best of my knowledge.

Of course, the existence of quantitative indices could be a consequence of rising professionalism in the democracy establishment or the overall trend toward quantification in NGOs.[13] Yet most of the aforementioned indices – and, crucially, at least one index for each measurable category – predated the explosion of democracy assistance in 1985. If those measures predate the start of democracy assistance, then my findings should not be endogenous to the rise of the democracy establishment.

Donors have identified quantitative indicators of progress for similar categories, suggesting that the relevant officials actually use such indicators to measure progress. Consulting the United States government's "Master List of Standard Indicators" for foreign aid reveals that the seven categories listed above are rightly regarded as measurable.[14] To assess countries' progress in terms of governing justly and democratically, the Department of State and USAID use indices from Freedom House and the World Bank and the number of women holding seats in national parliaments. To assess human rights, the US government uses indices from the World Bank and CIRI; to assess governance, it uses

---

[12] Girod, Krasner, and Stoner-Weiss (2009, 71).
[13] Hopgood (2008); Merry (2011).
[14] United States Department of State and United States Agency for International Development (2008). See also United States Agency for International Development, Center for Democracy and Governance (1998).

its own index; to assess media, it uses the Freedom of the Press score. Officials also use lower-level indicators to assess particular program elements; however, such indicators are so narrow and numerous that far-off principals such as Congress cannot reasonably digest them.

Donor officials also consider two additional types of democracy aid to be measurable due to strong international norms about appropriate practice: aid to support elections and constitutions. The presence of credible election monitors gauges the success of electoral assistance, while the protection of religious freedoms gauges the success of constitutional assistance. Proportional systems of representation and quotas for women and minorities in parliaments represent other constitutional norms, which are disseminated by institutions such as the US Institute of Peace and the International Institute for Democracy and Electoral Assistance (IDEA).[15] Given those clear expectations in terms of outcomes on the part of donors, I consider aid in those categories as measurable.

### Regime-compatible democracy assistance

I define regime-compatible democracy-assistance programs as those programs that target-country leaders view as unlikely to threaten their imminent survival by causing regime collapse or overthrow. I do so because, as discussed in Chapter 2, incumbents in states that are the targets of democracy assistance want to avoid being replaced and can therefore prohibit the actions of organizations in the democracy establishment. In conceptualizing regime-compatible programs, I focus on programs that support competition and mobilization. Such programs are relatively likely to lead to regime overthrow or collapse[16] and thus they are also the most likely ones to create problems of access for organizations in the democracy establishment. Recall that access problems occur even in countries that are sincerely democratizing, as they may generate controversy and political instability and thus a backlash from the incumbent regime.

It is important to note that although promoting regime replacement is not the same thing as promoting democracy, it is related: even minimalist definitions of democracy emphasize changes in power as an important condition.[17] As such, if democracy promotion does not contribute to elections that are capable of bringing multiple candidates or parties to power, then it is failing to advance the fundamental element

[15] Elkins (2009, 59); Rubin (2004).
[16] Huntington (1991, 142–51).
[17] Przeworski *et al.* (2000, 14–18); Schumpeter (1942, chapter XXI).

of democracy. Yet I emphasize regime replacement in conceptualizing regime-compatible democracy assistance mainly because testing my theory involves identifying the democracy-assistance programs that are likely to advance (or impede) the interests of the organizations that enact them. Regime replacement is therefore essential because it is what incumbents fear most about such programs. Since state leaders that do not lose office through regular elections or natural death are overwhelmingly likely (about 80 percent) to end up in exile, in prison, or dead, avoiding such a violent fate is crucial to their interests.[18]

Democracy-assistance programs can plausibly endanger the survival of incumbents in two ways. First, they can threaten incumbents by fostering open and fair political competition. Second, they can threaten incumbents by mobilizing independent groups that are likely to challenge the regime. I consider each process in turn.

Democracy-assistance programs can attempt to foster open competition and encourage the free exchange of political information by supporting a number of things associated with democracy: elections; human rights; free media; political parties; and research about democracy, which often has an activist or dissident component. Of course, programs in all those categories could be designed to be compatible with dictators. After all, many seemingly democratic institutions can be used as tools of authoritarian survival.[19] But if programs in those categories are implemented successfully – admittedly sometimes a big "if" – they will foster competition. As we would expect, research shows that elections, human rights, media, and political parties are all important causes of democratization.[20] Of the five categories, the most ambiguously classified one is research, which supports studies about democracy at think-tanks and universities and could foster competition by, for example, polling citizens about their political attitudes and making that information public so as to discourage compliance with the regime.

Democracy-assistance programs can also attempt to mobilize independent groups that are likely to challenge the regime, such as dissidents, unions, and youth. Although any civil society organization could conceivably be co-opted by a regime, those specific civil society groups have historically promoted political participation and challenged authoritarian regimes by creating alternative power bases.[21] Programs

---

[18] Goemans, Gleditsch, and Chiozza (2009, 276).

[19] Brownlee (2007); Gandhi and Przeworski (2007); Schedler (2006).

[20] For connections with democratization, see for example, Lindberg (2006) on elections, Davenport (2007) on human rights, Norris (2008, ch. 8) on media, and Hadenius and Teorell (2007) on political parties.

[21] Carothers (2005, 203–4).

aiding them have arguably helped topple dictators in Eastern Europe and the post-Soviet states by linking local activists with transnational networks.[22] Youth groups are, however, an ambiguously classified category. Although Samuel Huntington aptly calls youth the "universal opposition," democracy-assistance programs with youth groups, such as sports clubs, can also be apolitical.[23]

Other types of democracy assistance tend to be regime-compatible. Many civil society actors entrench authoritarian rule, despite their famous links with democracy.[24] Amy Hawthorne, a former senior program officer at the International Foundation for Electoral Systems (IFES), for example, has said that apolitical civil society programs "seem [to donors] like a good way to support a gradual, citizen-generated transformation of politics ... thus avoiding the risk of calling for the immediate democratization of the political sphere."[25] Programs supporting women's groups have been especially criticized on that score. Women's groups often address apolitical issues, such as domestic violence, in contrast to dissident groups, who of course can and do include women. Marina Ottaway writes that supporting women's groups, even in the Middle East, "can be translated in practice into many concrete, small projects that are not seen as threatening by most Arab regimes and are even welcomed by them as a means to demonstrate their willingness to democratize and modernize."[26] Aiding women's groups may be a worthy activity both as its own end and as a means to advance development goals. Yet neither practitioners nor dictators regard doing so as likely to challenge them.

Other democracy-assistance programs work cooperatively with incumbents in target countries to improve existing institutions, such as aid for constitutions, good governance, legislative assistance, local governance, rule of law, and women's representation. It is true that in some countries, and especially in fragile states, issues related to corruption can be politically explosive. But because capacity-building projects require government collaboration, target countries must actively permit them in a way that they must not for civil society activities. Thus, it is fair to say that most incumbents do not regard them as threatening. In fact, according to Thomas Carothers, other governments welcome such programs for more selfish purposes, "hop[ing] that the governance

---

[22] Beissinger (2007); Bunce and Wolchik (2011).
[23] Huntington (1991, 144–5).
[24] Jamal (2007).
[25] Hawthorne (2005, 85).
[26] Ottaway (2005a, 116).

programs will render the state more capable of solving citizens' problems and burnish their own legitimacy as reformist regimes."[27]

## Concluding thoughts on the typology

The preceding pages have laid out a rationale for coding democracy-assistance programs in "measurable" and "regime-compatible" groups. The empirical approach sought to establish general patterns in aid programs, fully recognizing that there are some exceptions to the general tendencies. Such an approach is typical among related studies of foreign-aid projects.[28] I am investigating why and under what conditions democracy assistance that is generally associated with quantitative outcomes and that is not generally associated with the promotion of competition and mobilization is more common. Although I will demonstrate below that such aid is not clearly effective – and is at least sometimes correlated with failure – I am not equating "tame" with "bad" or "untame" with "good." Regime compatibility is about access, not success or the lack of it.

An important critique of empirical endeavors such as this exercise in descriptive inference is that they do not sufficiently account for projects' implementation and performance.[29] To that I offer the following rejoinders.[30] First, as discussed in the next two chapters in some detail, the project descriptions that I rely on for coding have been verified as accurate sources of information about implementation. Projects do not differ radically from their reported descriptions (e.g., rather than aiding dissidents, they actually support good governance). Second, the performance of the projects remains largely outside my scope of study. It would be interesting, for example, to see how delegation and professionalization affect other dependent variables, such as how closely good-governance programs cooperate with the regime or to what extent political-party programs support opposition groups. My variables of theoretical interest could certainly affect those outcomes – although other variables, such as target-country regime type, are likely quite important, too. Yet studying such outcomes would require the collection of much additional data, the bulk of which is not available, since such information is not required in official reports. Thus, I believe that my current approach and combination of methods

---

[27] Carothers (2005, 202).
[28] See, for example, Nielson and Tierney (2003).
[29] Gutner (2005b).
[30] Here I draw on Nielson and Tierney (2005).

represent important advances in knowledge, even if more work remains to be done.

### The consequences of tame democracy assistance

This book is about what caused the taming of democracy assistance. It focuses on that issue because understanding how successful states are likely to be at promoting democracy abroad requires understanding what the democracy programs they fund actually do and what drives those selections. It also does so because understanding the taming of democracy assistance reveals important broader insights about foreign influence and the behavior of non-state actors in world politics.

Rigorously assessing the consequences for democracy of the taming of democracy assistance thus falls outside the book's scope and, unfortunately, is very difficult. The consequences of tame democracy assistance for other important outcomes of interest, such as violence or political stability, are also outside of the scope of this project. One reason why that is so relates to the availability of data. The Organisation for Economic Co-operation and Development (OECD), the official clearing-house for foreign-aid statistics, has only gathered detailed information on democracy assistance since 2002. The lack of adequate data commonly inhibits studies of aid effectiveness, although new efforts such as AidData are helping researchers overcome that problem.[31]

Inferential problems also exist beyond data limitations. An ideal research design for making causal inferences is the experiment, in which a treatment is assigned randomly to the objects of study so that the researcher can calculate the average effect of the treatment on some outcome, holding all other factors constant. Alas, studying democracy assistance usually requires researchers to work far outside the experimental ideal.[32] After all, measurable and regime-compatible democracy-assistance programs are not assigned randomly to countries. One way to cope with the lack of random assignment is to statistically control for other relevant variables, such as target states' previous democratic trajectories or their relationships with foreign governments. But many of those factors are likely both to affect target states' future democracy levels and to be affected by democracy assistance. That problem, technically called post-treatment bias, prevents us from accurately estimating the effects

---

[31] See http://www.aiddata.org.
[32] Particular interventions can, however, be fruitfully studied experimentally. See Hyde (2007, 2010); Moehler (2010).

of measurable and regime-compatible democracy assistance on target countries' democracy levels.[33]

Both data availability and research design issues thus make it difficult to establish the causal effects of measurable and regime-compatible democracy assistance on target countries' democracy levels. That observation has important implications for the book's argument. Any convergence on tame approaches within the democracy establishment has thus taken place in the absence of clear causal knowledge that such programs effectively democratize countries. The severe impediments to creating such causal knowledge jibe with several scholarly studies of democracy-assistance evaluations, which have uniformly found those evaluations lacking, and even the statements of some democracy-assistance practitioners, who have expressed doubts about their ability to make causal inferences about democracy-assistance programs' impacts.[34] A study of aid "apologetics" in Kenya, Malawi, and Rwanda noted, for example, that donor officials often feel it is impossible to judge the effectiveness of their efforts at aiding democracy until decades, or even centuries, have passed. As one official stated, "Progress will come over the long term. It is not always visible."[35]

In addition, the limited evidence that we do have about the effects of democracy assistance includes at least some signs that measurable and regime-compatible democracy aid can buttress dictators. Such evidence validates my principal–agent approach to democracy assistance: the programs that generate funding and access for democracy-assistance organizations do not necessarily democratize countries and, furthermore, they come at some cost in terms of democratization. As I discuss below, countries that experience changes in power tend to receive less tame forms of democracy aid than countries that do not. Examples, often drawn from scholar–practitioners' accounts, abound with tame democracy-assistance programs that have played directly into strategies of authoritarian survival and untame programs that did not. To be clear, the evidence does not, and cannot, show that measurable and regime-compatible democracy assistance impedes countries' democratization in all cases or even on average. What it does show, however, is that such programs reinforce authoritarian survival in at least some instances, which is a necessary implication of my theory and a significant finding for our understanding of democracy promotion that merits further exploration.

---

[33] King and Zeng (2006, 147–8).
[34] Bollen, Paxton, and Morishima (2005); Epstein, Serafino, and Miko (2007, 11–17); Green and Kohl (2007); National Research Council (2008, ch. 5).
[35] Brown (2011, 522).

*General trends*

One way to explore the effects of tame democracy aid is by comparing how often leaders lose power in countries that receive tamer (i.e., more regime-compatible and more measurable) and less tame (i.e., less regime-compatible and less measurable) programs. Leaders' loss of power is a relevant outcome for several reasons. First, and as discussed above, procedural minimum definitions of democracy emphasize changes in power.[36] If a country's leaders never change, then it is not a full democracy according to most definitions. Second, focusing on changes in power zeroes in on the question of authoritarian survival. Since many seemingly democratic institutions can help autocrats survive, incremental improvements on democracy scales may mask fundamental continuities in political systems.

Of course, countries could be nudged toward democracy via democracy assistance, and the best strategy for democracy practitioners may be to bide their time and wait for an opportunity to push hard for democratization. With that perspective, it is possible to evaluate some democracy-assistance programs in a sympathetic way. Consider, for example, a "twinning" program set up by the European Union in Morocco that fostered cooperation between state administrators in Morocco and Europe. That project succeeded in influencing the attitudes of Moroccan civil servants, but not in bringing about an "effective change of administrative governance, let alone regime change."[37] I remain skeptical that such an effort can therefore be termed democratizing, unless the meaning of democracy is stretched beyond recognition or usefulness in terms of testing social science theories. Nevertheless, the question would still remain: why should practitioners choose to enact such programs and not others in the absence of evidence about their relative efficacy? What is puzzling is why practitioners hold the view that such programs are appropriate today but were not twenty or thirty years ago, especially in the absence of epistemic learning.

It is possible to make some relevant comparisons about tame and untamed democracy assistance using several well-respected scholarly data sets that tracked political changes in all countries until 2006. One data set looks at changes in countries' executive leaders.[38] Another looks at whether incumbents or incumbent parties win national elections.[39] Since the OECD started collecting project-level data on democracy

[36] Przeworski *et al.* (2000, 14–18); Schumpeter (1942, ch. XXI).
[37] Freyburg (2011, 1002).
[38] Goemans, Gleditsch, and Chiozza (2009). See Appendix D for details.
[39] Hyde and Marinov (2012).

assistance in 2002, 139 countries have received some form of democracy assistance.

Regime-compatible programs play a prominent role in many bilateral and multilateral donors' democracy-assistance strategies and tend not to be associated with changes in executive and legislative power. Between 2002 and 2006 about 13 percent of countries *only* received regime-compatible democracy assistance, and 28 percent of them received democracy assistance that was at least 90 percent regime-compatible. None of those countries experienced changes in power between 2002 and 2006 unless they were already ranked by Freedom House as "free." In other words, in the unfree and partially free countries that arguably most need democracy aid, power does not change hands when the international community's approach to democracy promotion is overwhelmingly regime-compatible. Of course, there is potential for reverse causality, but the correlation is notable.

Meanwhile, more confrontational democracy assistance is correlated with regime change. The three unfree countries that experienced defeats of incumbents in elections (Kenya in 2002, Iran in 2005 and 2006, and Haiti in 2006) and the three unfree countries that experienced executive turnovers (Kenya in 2002, Macedonia in 2002, and Georgia in 2003) all received many millions of dollars of untame democracy assistance. On average, those countries received about one million dollars more confrontational (i.e., non-regime-compatible) democracy aid than did other states. Scholars often cite several of those cases as examples of effective democracy assistance. Foreign donors, for example, success-fully encouraged the formerly divided Kenyan opposition parties to join forces in the National Rainbow Coalition in advance of the 2002 election and to put forward a common candidate, Mwai Kibaki, who ended up winning the presidential election in a landslide.[40] One year later, in Georgia, NDI and other foreign NGOs trained and funded influential local NGOs, such as the youth dissident group Kmara (Enough!), which in turn mobilized people in the protests that led to the Rose Revolution.[41]

Of course, we cannot conclude from such correlations that regime-compatible democracy assistance caused authoritarian regimes to sur-vive, nor that more confrontational democracy assistance caused them to collapse. As previously discussed, properly studying the causal impact of democracy assistance requires researchers to "square the circle" of omitted variable and post-treatment bias. Nevertheless, the

---

[40] Brown (2004, 331).
[41] Beissinger (2007, 262); Bunce and Wolchik (2011, 160).

evidence gives no support for the idea that tame democracy assistance is associated with democratization. Moreover, regime-compatible democracy assistance tends not to be correlated with changes in power. Such patterns encourage the further study of what accounts for such programs' selection, which is what this book provides.

### A few examples

Specific examples of democracy assistance further illustrate the consequences of tame and untame programs for democracy. This section provides several tangible cases of when untame democracy assistance seems to have worked and tame democracy assistance seems to have failed from the perspective of democratization in the short and medium term. Whenever possible, I rely on the first-hand descriptions of people who worked on the democracy-assistance programs. My goal is not to offer an overall inference about the effects of democracy assistance in the countries examined. Instead, I seek to show some of the effects of particular types of democracy assistance.

*Political-party aid* Political-party aid has outcomes that are hard to measure and can directly threaten dictators' survival. In other words, it is a type of untame democracy assistance. Political-party aid is often deeply political, even partisan, in contrast to the technical programs that are more common in the twenty-first century. To take one extreme example, consider the departure of a USAID-funded IRI project from Romania in March 1996. IRI was asked to leave, not by local officials but by the US ambassador to Romania, Alfred Moses, who was a friend of the country's pseudo-democratic president Ion Iliescu. The reason for his request was that IRI was funding opposition parties there.[42] IRI has also run afoul of American diplomats in Haiti, where former US ambassador Brian Dean Curran accused it of actively undermining US relations with Jean-Bertrand Aristide during his second presidency from 2001 to 2004.[43]

It was reasonable for Iliescu to worry about the IRI project supporting opposition parties, which ended up defeating his Party of Social Democracy in the November 3, 1996 parliamentary elections. In fact, political-party assistance around that time played an important role – likely a necessary, if not sufficient one – in a number of countries' electoral

---

[42] Jordan (1996).
[43] Bogdanich and Nordberg (2006).

revolutions. It was particularly important in the democratic transition of Slovakia, a competitive authoritarian regime that was ruled by Prime Minister Vladimír Mečiar and his Movement for a Democratic Slovakia (HZDS) from the country's independence in 1993 until his electoral defeat in 1998.

Although Mečiar allowed certain freedoms, including largely free elections, he tightly controlled the media and undermined the rule of law, most famously by abducting the son of his primary political rival, Michal Kováč, in 1995. Despite those ignominious traits, autocratic Slovakia was what political scientists Steven Levitsky and Lucan Way refer to as a high linkage and high leverage environment: a country with many connections to the West and notable vulnerability to external pressure to democratize, especially from the EU.[44] After the breakup of Czechoslovakia, democracy assistance quickly started to flow into Slovakia, with the United States playing a leading role: NDI and IRI were the main foreign NGOs in Slovakia, with NED funding representing about 40 percent of all democracy assistance in Slovakia after the fall of communism.[45]

Organizations from the democracy establishment supported the Slovakian transition by encouraging opposition parties to collaborate after they had failed to do so in the 1994 elections. Scholars Valerie Bunce and Sharon Wolchik call the parties' decision to unify "a critical element in ending Mečiar's rule."[46] One way that political-party assistance promoted opposition unity was via information. For example, an IRI public opinion survey in 1997 revealed to opposition parties that youth voters were sympathetic to them but had voted in low numbers in the 1994 election. That revelation encouraged the opposition groups to form a coalition and target youth voters through civic campaigns, such as OK '98 and Rock the Vote (Rock volieb).[47] Second, NDI, IRI, and other foreign organizations put high-level pressure on opposition parties to form and stay in a coalition. In fact, a number of opposition groups in Slovakia met with diplomats and NGOs from the democracy establishment to that end at Vienna airport.[48] Finally, outside actors taught political parties useful skills, such as door-to-door campaigning, and connected them with successful leaders from other countries in order to encourage their united actions to be more successful.[49] All of

---

[44] Levitsky and Way (2010); Pridham (1999).
[45] Bjornlund (2000, 167).
[46] Bunce and Wolchik (2011, 64).
[47] Bunce and Wolchik (2011, 64–5).
[48] Bunce and Wolchik (2006a, 290).
[49] Bunce and Wolchik (2011, 76).

those tactics helped the opposition coalition stay together and win the 1998 election.

The Slovakian case built on earlier moments of successful and highly partisan political-party aid that represent the favorite examples of many democracy practitioners: support to opposition parties prior to the defeat of apartheid in South Africa and of Pinochet in Chile.[50] A more infamous, but nevertheless influential, early case of political-party aid came in the form of ideologically-motivated American support to opponents of the Sandanista National Liberation Front in Nicaragua before the 1990 election that defeated President Daniel Ortega and launched Nicaragua on a tentative transition to democracy.[51] Political-party aid was just one aspect of broad international efforts in all those cases, making it inappropriate to assign it a firm causal role in the transitions. Nevertheless, it is clear that support for political parties can be, and in some cases has been, associated with changes in power, as its untame classification would imply.

*Legislative assistance* Legislative assistance tends not to challenge dictators. As such, I consider it a regime-compatible, but not measurable, category of democracy assistance. International efforts in Kenya in the mid-1990s highlight the perils of aiding legislatures in semi-authoritarian regimes. After the end of the Cold War, President Daniel arap Moi and his Kenya African National Union (KANU) party faced considerable pressures from foreign-aid donors to reform Kenya's economy and political system. In response, Moi agreed to hold multi-party elections for Kenya's presidency and legislature.[52]

Yet multi-party elections could not guarantee an effective or democratic parliament. Moi and KANU won elections first in 1992 and again in 1997 thanks to a biased media, gerrymandering, and various forms of fraud. After elections, President Moi's regime harassed opposition leaders and excluded them from decision-making, while buying compliance from KANU MPs by doling out patronage and appointing them to cabinet positions. In that context, international donors sought to increase the capacity of MPs to make them more effective representatives of the Kenyan people. But when donors such as USAID paid for KANU MPs to visit Europe and North America on "study tours" to learn about democratic legislatures, they played into the hands of KANU's patronage scheme: the Moi-appointed Speaker of the parliament happily gave trips

[50] Carothers (2006b, 164).
[51] Levitsky and Way (2010, 141–4).
[52] Brown (2001, 726); Roessler (2005, 213).

as gifts to his favored MPs to encourage their compliance. Meanwhile, the Speaker avoided making any of the reforms encouraged by donors, ensuring that the parliament did not develop meaningful legislation or challenge Moi's power, instead arguably enhancing it.[53] Of course, we cannot know what might have happened in the counterfactual case – if USAID had not provided KANU with a new resource for patronage. The example of foreign aid to Kenya in the 1990s plausibly shows, however, how incumbents can manipulate legislative aid to subtly strengthen their hold on power.

More than a decade later, American legislative-assistance efforts continued to run into similar problems thousands of miles away. USAID delegated the American company Development Alternatives, Inc. (DAI) to implement a $5.6 million project between 2007 and 2011 to strengthen oil-rich Azerbaijan's parliament. According to an outside evaluator, DAI's goals for this project, which included strengthening the parliament's capacity, transparency, and efficacy, were "similar to the goals of USAID-supported legislative strengthening programs all over the world."[54]

Achieving such goals was challenging, to say the least. Azerbaijan had taken an initial step toward democracy after the Soviet Union's collapse. But in 1993, the former leader of Soviet Azerbaijan, Heydar Aliyev, seized power during a military revolt. His son Ilham succeeded him in 2003. At that point, Azerbaijan's democratic transition had not only stalled but had been reversed; Azerbaijan was holding elections for the presidency and parliament (Milli Majlis), but they were rigged and the parliament had little law-making authority.[55] The DAI effort did not alter that political context. The project had a number of successful outputs (not outcomes), including an improved parliamentary website, guidebooks for MPs and parliamentary staff, and new district offices, and parliamentary staff were reportedly "pleased with the support they have received and [wanted] additional assistance."[56] But an independent evaluator found the program's "political impact was less clear" and that DAI's efforts reinforced MPs' view of their role as "entirely constituent service" rather than "representation."[57] Although the evaluator recommended strategies for enhancing representation in the Milli Majlis, it is not clear that any legislative assistance could have led to a democratic transition in Azerbaijan at that time, where every MP was a member of

[53] Barkan and Matiangi (2009, 41).
[54] Democracy International, Inc. (2011, 4).
[55] Bunce and Wolchik (2011, 178–90).
[56] Democracy International, Inc. (2011, vi, 7).
[57] Democracy International, Inc. (2011, vii).

Aliyev's party.[58] Given that the Aliyev government uses elections as a way of "shamming the appearance of democratic struggle" to audiences such as the Council of Europe, a program that enhances its parliament's professionalism and reputation seems to play into the regime's survival strategy.[59]

*Women's groups* Aid to women's groups, a measurable and regime-compatible strategy, can also reinforce authoritarianism. Although such groups are often service-delivery organizations, funding them has been an important dimension of democracy assistance for many democracy donors. The trend of supporting women's groups has played a particularly important role in American efforts in the Middle East after September 11, 2001.[60] The US–Middle East Partnership for Breast Cancer Awareness, launched in 2006, for example, supported women's civic engagement as part of the Middle East Partnership Initiative (MEPI), a State Department democracy-promotion instrument. I consider such a program measurable because donors can use indicators such as the Human Development Indicators' gender inequality measures to assess progress. MEPI also used some specific, low-level indicators, such as the number of training sessions (101 in 2006), to report on its first "year of action" for interested readers.[61] That MEPI program was pursued, among other places, in Saudi Arabia, one of the world's most repressive regimes. In addition to the quantitative outputs and outcomes, the project offered other appealing signals back to Washington, DC, such as a photo opportunity for First Lady Laura Bush during her visit.

Unfortunately, according to Tamara Cofman Wittes, a Middle East expert and later a State Department official, the project ultimately strengthened the US–Saudi relationship and bolstered the regime's legitimacy. Wittes criticized MEPI for missing an opportunity to champion women's rights and democracy in Saudi Arabia, such as through support to "women columnists ... arguing for liberal reforms and criticizing clerics and others who promoted outdated views of the relationship between husband and wife."[62] In other words, even in a country like Saudi Arabia, MEPI could have aided civil society actors in a way that was not regime-compatible. Instead, it supported an anodyne program that enhanced the Saudi regime's image.

---

[58] Haring (2013).
[59] Valiyev (2006, 19).
[60] Abu-Lughod (2002, 783–4); Ottaway (2005a, 115).
[61] United States Department of State, Middle East Partnership Initiative (2007).
[62] Wittes (2008, 93).

The potentially negative consequences for democracy of aiding women's groups are not confined to the Middle East. Research on international democracy assistance supporting women's organizations in Russia suggests that foreign funds helped foster professional, bureaucratic NGOs there that were detached from Russian society.[63] According to a former consultant for the Ford Foundation in Russia, foreign-funded women's NGOs became "nonpoliticized": despite (or perhaps because of) their resources and infrastructure, they were no more likely to push for political reform than non-funded NGOs; moreover, to obtain funding, they chose to focus more narrowly on women's issues than non-funded women's groups, which addressed many issues of community concern.[64] Thanks in part to the activity of the internationally funded women's groups, the Russian Duma, Federation Council, and executive branch dedicated some attention to women's issues.[65] It is not clear, however, that such institutional changes played any democratizing role, especially given the overall trajectory of Russian politics in the 2000s. Thus, since women's groups became less connected to the public due to foreign funding, scholars have concluded that foreign aid to women's groups harmed democracy's chances in Russia.[66]

Do those observations minimize the importance of women's groups to democracy? Whether as militant revolutionaries in El Salvador during the country's civil war and its subsequent democratic transition or as anti-apartheid and later political-party activists in South Africa, female activists can and do play an important role in countries' democratic transitions.[67] Moreover, issues of gender equality are central to democratization. Finally, aiding women's groups may be worthy for reasons beyond democratization. What is crucial to recognize, however, is that neither practitioners nor pseudo-democrats view aiding women's groups as effective from the perspective of defeating dictators. Most women's groups, which generally focus on non-political issues, simply are not likely to prompt a regime change in a pseudo-democracy, at least in the short or medium term.

*Electoral assistance* Perhaps it comes as little surprise that regime-compatible democracy assistance can reinforce authoritarianism. But even measurable democracy assistance can, at times, impede democratization. Measurable programs exhaust scarce time and resources on

---

[63] Richter (2002).
[64] Henderson (2000, 73).
[65] Mendelson and Glenn (2002, 14).
[66] Richter (2002); Henderson (2000).
[67] Britton (2005); Shayne (2004).

measurement systems. Furthermore, they can encourage democracy promoters to myopically focus on quantitative outcomes to the detriment of better impact assessments.[68] According to former Freedom House executive director Jennifer Windsor, "The overarching flaw behind the current approach [to democracy assistance] is that the US government is trying to construct an aggregate measure for a wide range of programs that operate in very different contexts."[69] Likewise, one of the main conclusions of a study of democracy assistance in the former Yugoslavia is that its emphasis on quantitative results harmed democracy there.[70]

Consider, for example, electoral assistance, which often supports the efforts of international observers. Inviting international election monitors can deter election day fraud and promote long-term democratization.[71] Negative reports from election monitors have been shown to have a number of important consequences, including changes in prominent indices of democracy, reductions in what Susan Hyde calls "democracy-contingent benefits," and protests from domestic opponents.[72] Such consequences are costly for states. Much of the success of international election monitors stems from their development of increasingly sophisticated and technical strategies for detecting fraud, such as parallel vote tabulations or quick counts and voter registration audits.[73] Such developments represent the creation of a technique[74] and help establish NGOs' credibility as election monitors.[75]

But international election assistance's emphasis on measurable outcomes has also had some negative, or at least ambivalent, consequences for democracy, especially in the short term.[76] First, international support for monitors can cause dictators to use alternative, and arguably more pernicious, survival tactics. Monitors may have inadvertently encouraged dictators, such as Robert Kocharian of Armenia in 2007, to crack down on media freedom and the rule of law to maintain their rule without committing visible election day fraud.[77] Indeed, experimental studies over multiple elections in Azerbaijan, Georgia, Ghana, and

---

[68] Carothers (1999, 291–3).
[69] United States Congress, House of Representatives Committee on Foreign Affairs (2010).
[70] Brown (2006).
[71] Hyde (2007, 2010); Kelley (2012).
[72] Hyde (2011, ch. 3).
[73] Bjornlund (2004, ch. 13).
[74] Coles (2004).
[75] Hyde (2012).
[76] When international donors aid elections, they can also unintentionally cause states to expand and privatize their use of violence to stay in power, as was the case in Kenya's deadly 1992 elections. See Roessler (2005).
[77] Simpser and Donno (2012, 502).

Kyrgyzstan show that incumbents are adept at transferring fraud to unobserved polling stations and using other methods of cheating that monitors will not pick up.[78]

Second, international election monitors can legitimize unfair elections. Inviting monitors generally sends a signal about a country's democratizing intentions.[79] But technically proficient elections can take place even in non-democracies, which can lead monitors to inadvertently bolster autocrats' legitimacy by endorsing their Potemkin elections. Many people in countries with flawed elections seem to take that critical view; some research suggests that opposition parties boycott elections more often when international monitors are present because they wish to protest flawed procedures that may otherwise be enjoying legitimacy, although that finding is debated in the literature.[80] Indeed, internationally funded monitors regularly observe problematic elections despite the principles that they have publicly endorsed at the United Nations, which suggest that monitors should only observe genuine elections.[81] Yet although 36 percent of national elections since 1990 seemed unlikely beforehand to be free and fair, monitors refused to observe just around 4 percent of elections.[82]

Electoral assistance's focus on measurable outcomes is thus a double-edged sword: it is a strategy that enhances NGOs' professional reputations but it also encourages a myopic focus on technical standards with some deleterious consequences. Measurable democracy assistance thus can negatively affect democratization. Perhaps, then, it is no surprise that researchers find that democracy assistance does not clearly improve electoral quality and that electoral misconduct is not in decline, despite international assistance's role in several democratizing revolutions.[83]

## Conclusions

Democracy-assistance programs vary considerably by design, and those variations matter for how likely they are to create democratic change in target states. Those are two of the key insights of this chapter. Most previous research on democracy assistance has lumped international programs together as a single type of foreign aid or has disaggregated

---

[78] Ichino and Schuendein (2012); Sjoberg (2012).
[79] Hyde (2011); Kelley (2012).
[80] Beaulieu and Hyde (2009); Kelley (2012).
[81] United Nations (2005, 4–5).
[82] Hyde and Marinov (2012). See Appendix D for details on the data in this and other chapters.
[83] Birch (2012, 77); Donno (2013, 62).

them into just the categories of civil society, elections, governance, and rule of law. Those approaches make sense given the way that foreign-aid donors report their efforts to the OECD. But as I have argued in this chapter, from the perspective of democracy assistance's likelihood of fostering democratic change, comparing aid to dissidents with aid to women's groups or comparing aid to legislatures with aid to political parties is like comparing apples and oranges.

To overcome those limitations, I have developed a new typology of democracy assistance and identified the "tamer" types. Some categories are measurable, others are regime-compatible; some are both, others are neither. Measurable programs have quantitative, country-level indicators that donors can use to measure the program's desired outcome. Regime-compatible programs do not threaten the imminent survival of incumbent regimes in target countries. Although the categories coincide somewhat empirically, they are distinct conceptually.

Some limitations inevitably remain. In the subsequent statistical analysis, I take several steps to address those limitations. First, I recode each type of program (for example, switching it from measurable to not measurable) to address concerns that my findings are artifacts of miscoding. Unless otherwise noted, the results do not change. As a consequence, the findings that I present in the coming chapters do not depend on the coding of any particular category of democracy assistance. Second, I analyze democracy aid in the individual categories, rather than in tame and not-tame groups. That enables me to tell if measurable programs drive my findings about regime-compatible programs, or vice versa. It also allows me to perform a sort of sensitivity analysis, comparing the clearly-coded programs with the ambiguously coded ones (for example, aid to dissidents is clearly not regime-compatible, whereas aid to youth is probably not). I find, for example, that the effects of professionalization are stronger for the clear-cut programs, a reassuring finding for my argument.

It is impossible within the scope of this book to rigorously establish whether tame democracy assistance is ultimately bad for democracy. But this chapter has shown that, at least in certain contexts, tame programs do conflict with donors' fundamental goal: to promote democracy abroad. That conflict supports Hypothesis 1 and confirms that there is a principal–agent problem in democracy assistance. Since tame democracy-assistance programs can exert a considerable influence on target countries' policies and institutions, it is vital to understand why democracy-assistance programs became tame in the first place. It is to that endeavor that I now turn.

*Part II*

# Testing the argument

# 4    Delegation and the allocation of democracy assistance

*Compare the cleanliness of your dining room and your attic. The dining room is observable to your dinner guest. The attic is not. Your dining room is a lot cleaner than your attic . . . If someone comes up with a utopian plan to transform your attic, nobody will ever know if it succeeded or not.*[1]

Western governments that seek to support democracy abroad have multiple instruments of foreign policy at their disposal. They can put diplomatic pressure on political elites in target countries, using the threats of economic sanctions or the rewards of foreign aid or international-organization membership to push for political reform. They can also directly intervene in other countries by funding democracy-assistance programs, attempting to amplify the voices of certain civil society groups, increase the capacity of democratic institutions, and improve the quality of elections. But the choice of instrument is not their only decision to make. When donor governments fund democracy assistance, they must also make choices about the *channels* through which to deliver the aid – choices about whether to pass aid through government agencies, non-governmental organizations of various nationalities, or multilateral organizations. This chapter focuses on those delegation decisions and their consequences for the design of the democracy-assistance programs that have been funded by twenty-three Western governments.

One of Chapter 2's central arguments was about how the preferences of organizations in the democracy establishment interact with the preferences of donor and target states. Those organizations sincerely care about advancing democracy in unfree countries. They also prefer to pursue tame democracy assistance, if possible, because doing so helps them survive and thrive as organizations. The more difficult it is for donors to observe and control organizations in the democracy establishment, the more those organizations will pursue tame programs, which help organizations signal effectiveness to distant donor officials

[1] Easterly (2006, 170).

79

and secure access to target states but which also involve tradeoffs in terms of democratization. In addition, the more donors prefer tame programs at a particular time or place, the more organizations will pursue those programs. Ultimately, organizations in the democracy establishment are responsible to their principals.

This chapter's task is to test that argument about principals and principles. Its challenge is that donors may deliberately choose to channel programs in particular ways for reasons unrelated to my argument. Government donors do not, for example, usually want to directly support foreign dissidents. Doing so creates diplomatic problems and could endanger dissidents, who may not want to publicly take funds from foreign governments. An example of the domestic political backlash that dissidents can experience comes from Russia, where the Podkontrol website hosted an online petition in favor of restricting the foreign financing of NGOs. The petition gathered more than 10,000 signatures during its first few days in March 2012.[2] To avoid that kind of scrutiny, donors may prefer to fund dissidents in ways that are not obviously governmental. Thus, a finding that aid to dissidents is more likely to be channeled through non-governmental organizations than through government agencies could reveal little about the impact of delegation relationships on the design of programs. Comparing democracy-assistance programs funded through different channels of delivery – specifically, through non-governmental organizations, multilateral organizations, and government agencies – would be like comparing apples and oranges.

To address the inferential challenge, this chapter examines the effects of variations in donors' abilities to observe and control aid programs *within* the same channel of delivery. Using data on channels of delivery for democracy assistance from the twenty-three main government donors, I show that when donor governments have a harder time observing and controlling organizations in the democracy establishment, those organizations are more likely to pursue tame programs. I arrive at that conclusion using several indicators of donors' ability to observe and control democracy aid. First, I argue that donors have a harder time observing and controlling programs channeled through non-governmental organizations when those NGOs are foreign. Second, I argue that multilateral organizations with relatively diverse member states have a harder time observing and controlling programs than multilateral organizations with more similar members do. Third, I argue that donor governments that lack a domestic political consensus on foreign assistance observe and control their agencies' programs more closely

---

[2] Rodin (2012).

than do other governments. (They also have different preferences.) All three factors influence how tame democracy-assistance programs are, although they do so to greater or lesser degrees. The findings thus support my argument that the transnational delegation structure shapes democracy assistance in important ways.

The findings are quite robust. To be sure, the variables identified by my theory are not the only factors that influence the design of democracy-assistance programs. But the statistical correlations between tame programs and problems of observation and control are strong even when I control for a number of other relevant variables, including the level of democracy in, and regime type of, the target countries, the region of target countries, and the foreign-policy preferences of donors. I also use matching techniques as a way to boost my findings' accuracy and reduce their dependence on my choice of statistical models. Across a variety of models, delegation relationships remain the strongest predictors of tame democracy assistance – findings which bolster my transnational approach to studying democracy promotion.

The rest of the chapter proceeds as follows. The first section explains how to conceptualize and measure variations in delegation relationships in democracy assistance. The second section describes the new data on democracy-assistance projects that I analyze in this chapter and presents the main results. The third section concludes by summarizing the chapter's contribution and considering the need for the additional qualitative analysis presented in later chapters.

## Observation and control in democracy assistance

Students of foreign aid have for some time noted the principal–agent problems that ensue when economic aid is delegated across state boundaries and through multiple institutions.[3] Economist William Easterly compares utopian dreams of alleviating poverty in the developing world to plans for cleaning up a house's attic – an effort that few people will ever clearly see the results of and thus an undertaking that is unlikely to be performed well. In other words, we should not be surprised when efforts to clean up attics do not go as well as other, more observable tasks, like cleaning up dining rooms for party guests. Easterly shows convincingly how such monitoring problems affect foreign aid. This book turns its attention to another, related area where Western governments seek

[3] Easterly (2006); Martens *et al.* (2002); Milner (2006); Milner and Tingley (2013); Schneider and Tobin (2013).

to influence political outcomes in other countries through delegation: democracy assistance.

### Examples of principal–agent problems

As with foreign economic aid, a principal–agent framework can help illuminate the dynamics of democracy assistance. As discussed in Chapter 2, collecting information about the performance of democracy-assistance programs is costly and difficult for donor governments. Such information must be gathered far from home, often in other languages, and even in the best of circumstances, it is difficult to evaluate the impact of democracy-assistance programs. Moreover, the beneficiaries of democracy-assistance programs – foreign citizens – typically play no formal role in monitoring the programs. Finally, donor governments sometimes delegate collectively, and like all collective bodies, groups of governments have a difficult time working together.

A report by the United States' Government Accountability Office in 2006, *U.S. Democracy Assistance for Cuba Needs Better Management and Oversight*, illustrates some of the problems in terms of observation and control that donor governments face when aiding democracy abroad. The United States government had spent more than $75 million during the preceding decade aiding democracy in Cuba through various channels with uncertain success. Its efforts included aid to dissidents, civil society groups, independent journalists, and trade unions. The bilateral context in which those programs were funded was one of tense relations between the United States and Cuba, with the United States historically being supportive of regime change there.

The domestic context in Cuba was one in which Cuban NGOs were rightly worried about securing donor funding and avoiding confrontation with the Cuban government. On the one hand, the process for obtaining foreign-donor funding was competitive. To give one example: twenty-seven NGOs submitted applications in response to USAID's requests for applications in 2004 and 2005; out of those, twelve NGOs were deemed potentially fundable; and of those, only six NGOs were funded.[4] On the other hand, the political environment in Cuba was hostile to international democracy assistance and created genuine access concerns. According to local law, Cubans who accepted American democracy assistance could be punished with prison sentences of up to twenty years.[5]

---

[4] United States Government Accountability Office (2006, 16).
[5] United States Government Accountability Office (2006, 6).

Even though much of the United States' democracy aid in Cuba was given via cooperative agreements, a type of agreement in which the federal government expects "substantial involvement," the government still had a difficult time controlling the aid programs it financed.[6] One problem came from award agreements that "lacked the detail necessary to provide adequate guidance to grantees," allowing grantees, at least in the eyes of the GAO evaluators, to "use program funding, either unintentionally or intentionally, for purposes that are not intended by the program."[7] Another problem came from United States government officials' difficulty visiting grantees due to a "restrictive environment where the Cuban government precludes Cuba program officers from directly observing the use and outcomes of the assistance."[8] A final problem came from communications breakdowns between the State Department, USAID, and the US Interests Section, which all had private information about civil society in Cuba that they did not regularly share.[9]

According to my argument, those types of information problems will affect the design and implementation of democracy assistance in significant ways. Tame programs serve organizations' interests in survival but not necessarily donors' interests in democratization. For example, regime-compatible programs help organizations obtain access to target countries by avoiding confrontation with dictators, such as Cuba's Fidel Castro, who donor officials hoped would be replaced. The more difficult it is for donors to observe and control organizations, the more likely they are to reward measurable programs. Moreover, the more difficult it is for donors to observe and control democracy assistance, the more likely they are to permit regime-compatible programs. In sum, if organizations in the democracy establishment are rational, when the problems of observation and control faced by their funders are more severe, they will pursue tamer democracy assistance. But when are those problems most severe?

*Identifying variations in delegation relationships*

To identify variations in delegation relationships, an obvious place to look would be at the length of the delegation chain. In general,

---

[6] Grants involve less government involvement and contracts involve more. Several American NGOs, such as IRI and NDI, have lobbied Congress to force USAID to provide more aid through grants and cooperative agreements rather than through contracts, which give them less discretion and are more competitive (Melia, 2005, 8).

[7] United States Government Accountability Office (2006, 29).

[8] United States Government Accountability Office (2006, 30).

[9] United States Government Accountability Office (2006, 11). Since the United States and Cuba do not have formal diplomatic relations, the US Interests Section of the Swiss Embassy in Havana acts as the de facto American embassy.

principals have a harder time motivating and monitoring their agents when those agents are farther away.[10] Although few donors provide reliable information about their delegation processes, we can still discern some sources of variation. To take one example, multilateral democracy assistance – which typically requires delegation from governments to international organizations (IOs) and then to one or more implementing organizations – tends to involve worse problems of observation and control than bilateral democracy assistance since it involves an additional step of delegation and a collective principal. Consistent with that observation, multilateral democracy-assistance programs in 2010 were 20 percent more likely to be measurable and 13 percent more likely to be regime-compatible than bilateral democracy-assistance programs using the data described below ($p < 0.01$).

But evidence that multilateral programs are tamer than bilateral ones does not necessarily show that delegation dynamics affect the design and implementation of democracy assistance. As political scientist Simone Dietrich shows, donors make decisions about how to channel foreign aid according to the characteristics of target countries, choosing, for example, to opt for multilateral mechanisms more often when target countries are poorly governed.[11] Thus, a better way to show that certain types of delegation relationships make measurable and regime-compatible democracy assistance more likely would be through evidence that even *within* non-governmental, multilateral, or bilateral aid channels of delivery, delegation dynamics matter. My strategy is to identify variations in delegation relationships within each major channel of delivery – in other words, the first implementing partner (NGO, multilateral organization, or government agency) – used by donor governments.[12]

*Non-governmental organizations* Non-governmental organizations are the most common channel of delivery for bilateral democracy assistance, receiving 58 percent of the projects in 2010 according to data from the main clearinghouse on foreign assistance, the OECD. Within that channel, however, there exists considerable variation in the NGOs that are funded. Donor governments give democracy assistance to NGOs with headquarters in three general locations: donor states, target states, and other states. In other words, for its democracy-assistance efforts in Serbia, the United States government can fund American

[10] Nielson and Tierney (2003, 249–51).
[11] Dietrich (2013).
[12] That is the definition of "channel of delivery" developed by the OECD. See Organisation for Economic Co-operation and Development (2010).

NGOs, Serbian NGOs, or NGOs from other countries (for example, Czech NGOs or French NGOs) that want to work in Serbia. The ability of a donor government to observe and control an NGO in the democracy establishment depends, in part, on that NGO's national origins.

In general, it is easier for a donor government to observe and control NGOs headquartered in the donor country than NGOs headquartered in other countries.[13] First, donor-country NGOs are more likely to be organizationally familiar to donor governments. In a study of American, British, and French NGOs working in humanitarian assistance, Sarah Stroup shows that national origin affects organizations' internal structures, funding strategies, and advocacy goals.[14] Her analysis suggests that national environments shape organizations through multiple mechanisms, including legal rules, social networks, and political opportunity structures. It is easier for donor governments to observe and control organizations about which they already have expectations for appropriate behavior. Second, staff members at donor-country NGOs share linguistic, cultural, and social ties with donor officials. As former practitioner Paul Nuti noted, speaking the language and idioms of democracy donors is a crucial step for NGOs performing the "democracy dance."[15] Shared sociocultural and linguistic ties promote information transmission. Donor governments are better able to evaluate NGOs that conduct work in their native language, both literally and figuratively.

Examples abound of the communications failures and information breakdowns that can occur when democracy assistance crosses national borders. Consider the political-party training sessions funded by the United States government in Poland in 1990 that the anthropologist Janine Wedel attended. Despite the American trainers' often tone-deaf advice – for example, about how to use direct mail marketing in political campaigns despite Poland's abysmal postal system – Polish political clubs eagerly participated in the programs.[16] Why? They thought that they could get money and access by associating with Westerners. An exchange Wedel recorded at one session illustrates the dynamic.

A CONSULTANT (RESPECTFULLY): You were in prison, too? I admire your courage.
A POLITICIAN (SMILING MODESTLY): Yes, I was. [It didn't take any special courage. I was picked up just like all my friends.]

---

[13] On this point, see also Bush (2013).
[14] Stroup (2012). See also Clark, Friedman, and Hochstetler (1998).
[15] Nuti (2006, 87).
[16] Wedel (2001, 90).

A CONSULTANT: You suffered. If there's anything we can help you with now, just let us know.

A POLITICIAN: The workshop has been so enlightening. One thing just occurred to me. There's a shortage of paper and, you know, we don't have enough money to buy fax or photocopy machines. [Of course, we think you can help. Travel abroad? Funds? Other contacts? Anything that might give us visibility in the West and the prestige we need here that is associated with Western exposure. That's why we bothered to come to your workshop.]

A CONSULTANT: Perhaps my organization could help.

A POLITICIAN (HUMBLY): Oh, we would be most grateful![17]

We can expect such exchanges, in which grantees pursue their own agendas and interests when interacting with donor officials, to occur more often when the agents come from a different culture and political context than the principals. Even when the grant-givers are based abroad, as was the case in Wedel's example, quality information is hard to collect. When quality information is hard to collect, NGOs are more likely to pursue tame programs.

In addition to the dynamics of observation and control, organizations' preferences may also vary with their nationalities in ways that are consistent with my argument about how an organization's position in the delegation chain relates to its preferences in Chapter 2. Donor-country NGOs should be less concerned about target-country access than target-country NGOs because they can work elsewhere, if necessary. As a consequence, donor-country NGOs should feel less interested in pursuing regime-compatible programs than target-country NGOs, all else being equal.

Thus, because of organizational and cultural similarities, I expect the German government, for example, to find it easier to observe and control German NGOs working abroad, such as the Stiftungen, than NGOs headquartered in target states or in some other country, such as the United States or Canada. When it is easier for a donor government to observe and control the NGOs it funds, those NGOs have less to gain from pursuing measurable programs and more to lose by pursuing regime-compatible programs in terms of their relationships with donors. Moreover, German NGOs should value continued access less than target-state NGOs. Therefore, donor-country NGOs should pursue less tame democracy assistance than other NGOs, all else being equal.

It is important to acknowledge that donor-country NGOs could simply be better at executing untame programs than other NGOs and are selected for that reason. Several observations suggest that is not the

[17] Wedel (2001, 92).

case, although that concern is one that I address explicitly in my case studies of aid in the Arab world later in the book. First, and as discussed in Chapter 3, the findings about the efficacy of one main set of donor-country NGOs, American NGOs, are mixed, giving little credence to the notion that American NGOs are more effective at untame democracy assistance than other NGOs. Second, refined channeling tactics are at odds with the relatively poor state of knowledge about democracy-assistance effectiveness that has also been discussed above. Finally, based on my interviews with practitioners, to the extent that folk wisdom in the field suggests that donor-country NGOs are better at certain tasks than other NGOs, such tasks tend to be ones that are fairly technical and thus measurable (e.g., electoral aid), regime-compatible (e.g., rule of law aid), or both (governance aid) – rather than falling into untame categories (e.g., dissident aid). In other words, donors' concerns about aid effectiveness should, if anything, bias me against finding a positive relationship between donor-country NGOs and untame programs.

*Multilateral institutions* Donor governments can also deliver democracy assistance through multilateral organizations, an option that they chose 6 percent of the time in 2010 according to the OECD.[18] Multilateral democracy donors include the United Nations and its associated bodies, the European Union, and a host of other intergovernmental institutions, such as development banks and democracy-focused international organizations such as International IDEA. Multilateral organizations usually delegate to a non-governmental organization working in the target country to help them implement projects. Among multilateral organizations, one relevant characteristic from the perspective of observation and control is membership diversity.

When multilateral organizations delegate to NGOs, they confront collective-principal problems. That is a typical problem for international organizations.[19] In a nuanced study of the International Monetary Fund (IMF), political scientist Mark Copelovitch explained the nature of that problem: "Agency slack is ... severe in cases of common agency ... because the multiple members comprising the agent's principal may have heterogeneous preferences about the agent's behavior, which the agent can exploit to pursue its own interests."[20] Indeed, when the largest shareholder states at the IMF diverge more from each other, then the IMF's loans are often markedly different than they are when the states

---

[18] In addition to bilateral aid that is channeled through multilateral organizations, there is also purely multilateral aid, which this chapter does not focus on.
[19] Pollack (1997).
[20] Copelovitch (2010, 55).

diverge less. The principal–agent problems confronted by collective principals typically involve control more than observation, since it is difficult for such principals, with their diverse preferences, to coordinate activities such as sanctioning agents and writing complete contracts.

Some of the challenges that the United Nations faces as a democracy promoter illustrate the difficulties of formulating democracy-promotion policy in a diverse-membership organization. The UN – the epitome of a heterogeneous organization since it has every sovereign state as a member – has often been hesitant to interfere in countries' national affairs, whether by refraining from condemning Bosnia's fraudulent election in 1996[21] or avoiding calling Cambodia's 1997 coup a "coup."[22] Indeed, research shows that the UN's election monitors are notably less critical than those of other, more homogeneous (and specifically, more democratic) IOs.[23] Although the United Nations' relatively non-confrontational approach to democracy assistance undoubtedly has multiple sources, one is certainly its diverse membership, which impedes political consensus. It has long been difficult for an organization that includes such notorious dictatorships as Syria and North Korea as members to take a strong pro-democracy stance.[24] As a consequence, we would expect UNDEF, the UN's primary democracy-assistance agency, to have a relatively difficult time observing and controlling its NGO grantees when compared to more homogeneous IOs. As a consequence, the UNDEF's grantees should pursue tamer programs.

To sum up, relatively homogeneous multilateral organizations, such as the European Union, should be better able to coordinate and forge consensus about democracy assistance than politically diverse multilateral organizations, such as the United Nations. Better coordination and political consensus should help states collect better information about democracy-assistance programs and, as necessary, punish NGOs that are pursuing their own interests rather than democratization. As a result, rational organizations in the democracy establishment should pursue less tame projects when they are funded by more politically homogeneous organizations.

*Government agencies* Donor governments also channel democracy assistance through the overseas offices of their own government agencies, such as USAID in the United States or the Department for International Development (DFID) in the United Kingdom. OECD

21 Kelley (2009, 766).
22 Newman (2004, 196).
23 Kelley (2009, 778).
24 Ludwig (2004, 170).

data show that around 24 percent of democracy-assistance programs in 2010 were channeled through government agencies. As is the case for aid initially channeled through multilateral organizations, aid delegated to government agencies is usually then delegated to a non-governmental organization working in the target country that assists the donor government with the project's design and implementation.

Within democracy assistance that is channeled through government agencies, some donor officials are better than others at observing and controlling their overseas projects. I hypothesize that the sources of those variations are at least partially rooted in the domestic politics of donor states. Specifically, donor agencies vary considerably in the degree to which their work is subject to political debate at home, which should cause variations in their commitments to gathering costly information about democracy assistance. In addition, donor governments may vary in their preferences over relatively tame democracy assistance.

Previous research on foreign economic aid demonstrates that domestic political dynamics – including ideological cleavages and the activities of local interest groups – significantly affect the allocation of foreign assistance.[25] The extent to which foreign assistance activates those ideological and economic cleavages, however, varies across countries. In some countries, foreign assistance is subject to frequent political debate, and changes in domestic politics lead to changes in foreign-aid policy relatively often. In other countries, foreign-assistance policies enjoy political consensus and change little from year to year. To understand that phenomenon, consider that although most OECD donors have pledged to give 0.7 percent of their gross national products as foreign assistance, few states have come close to achieving that goal.[26] Yet a handful of countries, such as the United Kingdom in 2010, have attempted to make firm pledges to meet the 0.7 percent target, even in the midst of economic austerity.[27] Foreign aid is a relatively routine and non-controversial part of foreign policy in such countries and so we would expect their government agencies, such as DFID, to expend less effort trying to observe and control aid projects.

Debates about democracy assistance in the United States illustrate the potential consequences of domestic political debates on observation and control. After controversial American attempts to democratize Afghanistan and Iraq during the presidency of George W. Bush, the number of Americans that prioritized democracy promotion as a

---

[25] Milner and Tingley (2011); Tingley (2010).
[26] UN Millennium Project (2009).
[27] House of Commons, International Development Committee (2010).

foreign-policy goal dropped by more than 50 percent.[28] Even after President Bush's administration left office, growing public isolationism and heightened worries about the government's debt eroded support for foreign assistance; a (failed) bill in January 2011, for example, sought to eliminate USAID and all American democracy assistance and received support from 165 Republican Congresspeople.[29] Unsurprisingly, foreign-aid agencies have worked vigorously to justify their existence and to better monitor their aid programs in the midst of the post-Iraq skepticism of democracy assistance. Under the Strategic and Operational Research Agenda, USAID commissioned, for example, the first major scholarly study of the impact of democracy assistance on countries' democracy levels and a National Academy of Sciences report on monitoring methods.[30] USAID continued to expend more energy supporting independent evaluators via its Center of Excellence on Democracy, Human Rights and Governance, often turning to more rigorous experimental designs.

If governments' aid agencies vary in the amount of scrutiny they are subject to at home, they are also likely to vary in their delegation relationships with grantees. Specifically, scrutinized government agencies should be more willing to spend scarce time and resources observing and controlling their agents since they have a greater need to show their success to the public. As a consequence of their better information, they should be more likely to punish regime-compatible democracy assistance. Thus, politically vulnerable government agencies should be less likely to fund regime-compatible programs than politically secure agencies.

According to my argument, politically vulnerable agencies should also be less likely to reward programs associated with measurable outcomes because they are expending more effort observing and controlling their agents. At the same time, I expect such agencies to prefer programs associated with measurable outcomes more than government agencies with a relatively consistent budget. The reason is that government agencies ultimately seek to please their principals, the public, and measurable programs may help them accomplish that goal. As such, I have no clear prediction about the relationship between politically vulnerable government agencies and measurable programs since there are factors that could lead to either a positive or a negative correlation.

---

[28] Drezner (2008, 58).
[29] Mitchell (2011, 314).
[30] Finkel, Pérez-Liñán, and Seligson (2007); National Research Council (2008).

## Variations across twenty-three democracy donors

The above discussion describes how donor governments vary in their willingness and ability to observe and control the aid projects they fund. It also emphasizes how variations in the preferences of the different actors involved in democracy aid may be significant. If my transnational argument about democracy assistance is correct, those variations will systematically affect how tame democracy-assistance programs are. The harder it is for donors to observe and control organizations in the democracy establishment, the more those organizations will pursue programs that are measurable, regime-compatible, or both.

The previous section identified three sources of variation in preferences and donors' information about organizations in the democracy establishment. First, donors should observe and control donor-country NGOs more easily than other NGOs. Donor-country NGOs should also be less concerned about maintaining access than target-country NGOs. Second, relatively homogeneous multilateral organizations should observe and control their agents more easily than relatively heterogeneous organizations. Third, more politically vulnerable donor agencies should collect better information than more politically secure donor agencies. They should also value measurable programs more. This section tests all of these observable implications of the argument using data on the democracy-assistance programs of twenty-three Western donors.

### Data and methods

The OECD is the official data source on foreign aid.[31] When donors report to the OECD about foreign aid, they provide several valuable pieces of information which can be used to test my argument. Most importantly, donors assign to each foreign-aid project a single category number that denotes its purpose. Democracy-assistance projects fall into what the OECD refers to as the "government and civil society" sector.

As Table 4.1 shows, the United States is by far the largest democracy donor.[32] The United States spent more than $2 billion in 2010 in bilateral democracy assistance – more than six times the commitment of the next largest bilateral donor, Germany. Of course, many countries also give aid directly to multilateral institutions, especially the European

[31] Organisation for Economic Co-operation and Development (2010).
[32] After the top ten, the other countries that gave democracy assistance in 2010 were, in descending order of dollar amount spent: Belgium, Ireland, Japan, Switzerland, Finland, France, Italy, Austria, New Zealand, Luxembourg, Portugal, South Korea, and Greece.

Table 4.1 *The largest bilateral democracy donors, 2010.*

| Donor | Millions of dollars |
| --- | --- |
| United States | 2,397 |
| Germany | 372 |
| Sweden | 307 |
| United Kingdom | 254 |
| Spain | 222 |
| Denmark | 217 |
| Norway | 211 |
| Australia | 173 |
| Canada | 155 |
| Netherlands | 124 |

*Note:* Totals are in constant 2010 US dollars.
*Source:* Organisation for Economic Co-operation and Development (2010).

Union, which Table 4.1 excludes. Although countries in the Middle East and North Africa have garnered democracy-assistance headlines in recent years, countries in Asia and Africa were the main global targets of democracy assistance by donors in the sample. Notably, the sample of democracy-assistance projects in this chapter includes relatively fewer projects in Latin America than does the time-series NED sample in Chapter 5, which likely reflects both global trends in democratization as well as the United States' particular strategic interests in Latin America. As Figure 4.1 shows, OECD donors also fund democracy-assistance projects in target countries at a variety of levels of democracy. When compared to this sample of democracy-assistance projects, however, it is clear that the NED deserves its reputation for spending relatively more money in the least democratic countries in the world than many other donors.

*Identifying tame democracy assistance* In this chapter I am interested in predicting the likelihood that a democracy-assistance project is measurable, regime-compatible, or both. Thus, I create dichotomous variables that indicate whether a project is measurable, regime-compatible, both, or neither. The "government and civil society" sector in the OECD includes projects in the following categories that may be classified as democracy assistance: decentralization and support to sub-national governments; legal and judicial development; democratic participation and civil society; elections; legislatures and political

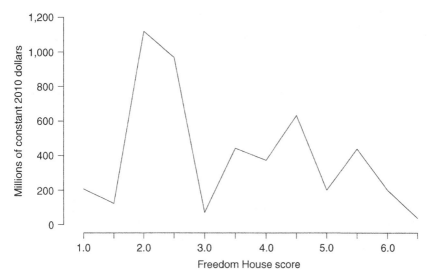

Figure 4.1 Bilateral democracy assistance, by freedom level.
*Note:* I averaged countries' political liberty and civil rights scores, which
were rescaled so that 1 represents the least democracy and 7 the most.
*Data sources:* Organisation for Economic Co-operation and Development (2010) and Freedom House (2011).

parties; media; human rights; and women's equality organizations and
institutions. I used the donor-assigned categories as a starting point
for the analysis and supplemented them with my own coding in order
to ensure that the data fit the book's purpose. For donor-assigned
categories that were broader than the categories that I described in
Chapter 3 (for example, legislatures and political parties), I hand-coded
projects so that they fell into finer-grained groups that would permit
appropriate analysis. Then I sorted the projects into measurable and
regime-compatible groups.[33] The total number of projects in the sample
was 14,150; out of those projects, 47 percent were coded as measurable
and 38 percent as regime-compatible.

*Indicators of delegation relationships* To test my argument about
how delegation relationships affect democracy assistance, I created three
variables that measure how difficult it is for democracy donors to observe

---

[33] A key nuance was that because project descriptions lacked sufficient information to
distinguish dissident groups from other types of civil society groups, I classified general
civil society projects as not regime-compatible.

and control the projects they fund. In a nutshell, the harder it is for donors to observe and control democracy assistance, the tamer the programs should be. The measures of delegation relationships that I use draw on information about donors' channels of delivery that the OECD started to require in 2011, when donors were reporting on 2010 flows. Because those data were new, the analysis in this chapter is limited in its temporal scope. The 2010 data do, however, permit analysis of more than 14,000 projects funded by twenty-three donors in 142 target states – a large and varied sample. As discussed above, I separately analyze democracy assistance channeled through NGOs, multilateral organizations, and government agencies.

First, I created a dichotomous indicator for donor-country NGOs that takes 1 if the NGO is from the donor country and 0 if the NGO is not from the donor country.[34] I expect donor-country NGOs to pursue less tame democracy assistance than other NGOs because they are easier for donors to observe and control. Donor-country NGOs are more likely to have organizational norms and structures that are familiar to donor officials. That familiarity enables officials to evaluate what NGOs are doing. In addition, donor-country NGOs are less concerned about maintaining access than target-country NGOs.

Second, I created a dichotomous indicator for EU democracy assistance that takes 1 if the multilateral institution is the European Union and 0 otherwise. I expect multilateral organizations with relatively heterogeneous members to pursue tamer democracy assistance than multilateral organizations with relatively homogeneous members. Diverse multilateral organizations have a harder time coordinating and reaching agreements, which makes it more difficult for them to effectively collect information and punish slacking agents. As a consequence, the organizations they fund will have more discretion to pursue their preferred tame programs.

When donors report information about channeling aid through multilateral institutions, they note if they give aid to the UN, the EU, the International Monetary Fund, the World Bank, the World Trade Organization, a regional development bank, or another multilateral institution. Among those organizations, the European Union is the best example of a relatively homogeneous institution, making it most likely to gather good information about its democracy-assistance programs. Moreover, it is the only international organization with a significant

---

[34] Unfortunately, the data do not generally report information about the specific organization that designs and implements a democracy-assistance program, which prevents me from organizing the data as donor–NGO dyads.

diplomatic corps, which should especially help it gather information. Thus, I expect the EU to fund relatively less-tame programs. Empirical support for that expectation would in many ways be striking given the conventional wisdom about the "relative timidity" of EU democracy assistance.[35]

Finally, I created an indicator of volatility in foreign aid. I expect government agencies that are more vulnerable politically to prefer measurable democracy aid more than government agencies that are more secure politically. Politically vulnerable agencies are more likely than politically-secure agencies to want to present results-oriented information about their foreign assistance; doing so helps them justify their existence in the face of political scrutiny. Organizations in the democracy establishment should respond to those preferences since they want to earn donor funding. At the same time, politically vulnerable agencies are also more likely than politically secure agencies to attempt to observe and control democracy-assistance projects. Given that, organizations in the democracy establishment may avoid tame programs. A good indicator of political vulnerability is the amount of year-to-year variation in a donor's foreign-assistance commitments. The most volatile donor was Portugal ($\sigma = 0.13$); the least volatile was the Netherlands ($\sigma = 0.02$).

As Figure 4.2 shows, tame democracy assistance is generally correlated with my indicators about different types of delegation relationships. First, donor-country NGOs receive less measurable and regime-compatible democracy assistance than other NGOs. Second, the EU receives less measurable and regime-compatible democracy assistance than other multilateral organizations. Finally, in countries where foreign aid is volatile, democracy assistance is more measurable and less regime-compatible. All of those descriptive relationships are consistent with my transnational approach to democracy aid and provide specific support for Hypothesis 2 about delegation relationships as well as Hypothesis 6 about donor preferences. But can we reject the null hypothesis that there is no relationship between delegation relationships and tame democracy aid from those patterns? Multivariate statistical analysis allows us to answer that question.

*Control variables* Figure 4.2 suggests a systematic relationship between information problems and how measurable and regime-compatible democracy assistance is. But what about the other factors that could affect the design of democracy assistance? To answer that question, I construct a statistical model that can account for a host of

[35] Carothers (2009a); Youngs (2003, 135).

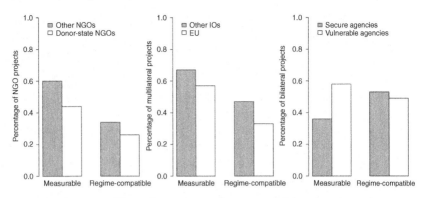

Figure 4.2 Tame democracy assistance and delegation dynamics.
*Data sources:* Organisation for Economic Co-operation and Development (2010) and author's coding.

other factors that are likely to affect the likelihood of donors funding measurable and regime-compatible programs.

First, I control for donor governments' preferences. Target countries that are strategically important to donor countries may receive relatively more regime-compatible democracy assistance than other countries, all else being equal. After all, donors often use foreign aid to reward or bribe countries for strategic purposes. The measure that I use for political alignment between donor and target countries is the affinity score in terms of UN voting. Although votes in the UN General Assembly are often symbolic, they provide an accurate indicator of countries' foreign-policy preferences and are widely used by scholars of international relations.[36]

Of course, strategic relationships with target countries are not the only potentially relevant characteristics of donor governments. To account for other donor-specific factors that may be relevant for the design of democracy assistance, I include what are known as "donor fixed effects" when I examine NGO and multilateral projects, although I do not report their coefficient estimates to enhance the presentation's simplicity.[37] Doing so means that I include separate indicator variables for each donor, which controls for the fixed characteristics of countries, from geography to domestic political institutions, to previous colonial relationships with target countries.

---

[36] Copelovitch (2010); Stone (2004, 580).
[37] Since I am interested in cross-country variation in my analysis of aid volatility, including donor fixed effects in those regressions does not make sense.

Next, I control for target countries' characteristics. Donor governments may use foreign aid as a political tool, but most donors also want aid to be effective and so they tailor aid to target countries' needs and characteristics. For democracy assistance, a country's political development needs are captured primarily by democracy levels. We might expect that the proportion of regime-compatible democracy assistance that countries receive would be curvilinear with their democracy levels, with foreign donors sending confrontational programs to highly authoritarian states, a mix of confrontational and regime-compatible programs to semi-democratic states, and programs that freely promote competition and free information in sincerely democratizing states. Since donors may also adapt democracy-assistance programs to take into consideration unique regional dynamics, I include indicator variables for target countries' regions, as well.

### Main findings

Table 4.2 presents the results of the multivariate analysis. Because my dependent variables are dichotomous (measurable programs or not, regime-compatible programs or not), I use logistic (logit) regressions to estimate the effects of delegation relationships and donor preferences while holding other factors constant. When using fixed effects, I use conditional logit models, which help me control for unmeasured heterogeneity across countries and are less biased than unconditional logit models.[38] All models use robust standard errors clustered on the donor.

To begin, recall that donor governments should find it easier to observe and control donor-country NGOs, which speak a language (literally and figuratively) familiar to donors. As a consequence, they should be less likely to reward donor-country NGOs that pursue measurable programs and more likely to punish donor-country NGOs that pursue regime-compatible programs. Table 4.2 shows that donor-country NGOs are indeed less likely to pursue tame projects than other types of NGOs. The coefficient estimates for the donor-country NGO indicators are in both cases negative and, because they are more than twice the size of their standard errors, statistically significant at conventional levels. On average, donor-country NGOs are 16 percent less likely to pursue measurable projects and 8 percent less likely to pursue regime-compatible projects than other types of NGOs, holding the other variables in the regressions at their means.

---

[38] Green, Kim, and Yoon (2001); Katz (2001).

Table 4.2 How delegation relationships affect democracy assistance.

| | DV = % measurable | | | DV = % regime-compatible | | |
|---|---|---|---|---|---|---|
| | Model 1 | Model 2 | Model 3 | Model 4 | Model 5 | Model 6 |
| **Variable** | | | | | | |
| Sample | NGOs | IOs | Government Agencies | NGOs | IOs | Government Agencies |
| Donor-country NGOs | −0.77** | | | −0.63*** | | |
| | (0.34) | | | (0.20) | | |
| EU projects | | −0.74 | | | −1.45 | |
| | | (0.93) | | | (1.16) | |
| Aid volatility | | | 1.58 | | | −3.37*** |
| | | | (1.30) | | | (1.29) |
| Affinity | −0.09 | 0.43 | 1.41*** | 0.41 | 0.53 | −0.29*** |
| | (0.42) | (1.25) | (0.08) | (0.32) | (0.84) | (0.07) |
| Democracy | −0.01 | 0.64** | −0.11 | 0.44*** | −0.26 | 0.06 |
| | (0.12) | (0.28) | (0.10) | (0.16) | (0.32) | (0.10) |
| Democracy$^2$ | −0.04 | −0.10*** | 0.01 | −0.05** | 0.04 | 0.02 |
| | (0.02) | (0.03) | (0.01) | (0.02) | (0.04) | (0.01) |
| Donor fixed effects | Yes | Yes | No | Yes | Yes | No |
| Region fixed effects | Yes | Yes | Yes | Yes | Yes | Yes |
| N | 7,225 | 712 | 4,857 | 7,225 | 712 | 4,857 |
| Donor countries | 22 | 21 | 21 | 22 | 21 | 21 |
| Target countries | 132 | 119 | 119 | 132 | 119 | 119 |

Notes: Models 1, 2, 4, and 5 are conditional logit models; Models 3 and 6 are unconditional logit models. Control variables are lagged by one year. Robust standard errors, clustered on donor, are in parentheses. *** denotes $p < 0.01$, ** denotes $p < 0.05$.

Does it matter if we are comparing donor-country NGOs to NGOs from other developed countries versus NGOs in target states? When I introduce an indicator variable for target-country NGOs to the models, I find that target-state NGOs pursue notably tamer democracy assistance than other (i.e., non-donor-country and non-target-country) NGOs on average. That finding makes sense according to the theory laid out in Chapter 2. First, NGOs in target states are likely to be the most unfamiliar to donor governments, and thus the most difficult to observe and control. In contrast, NGOs that are headquartered in other developed countries are likely to bear at least some organizational and cultural similarities to donor-country NGOs, which helps donor governments monitor them. Second, target-country NGOs are most likely to care about maintaining access, and thus have a particular preference for regime-compatible programs.

Recall also that I expected IOs with diverse member states to find it more difficult to observe and control their overseas projects than IOs with homogeneous members. I suggested that the EU is an IO with a relatively homogeneous membership when compared to other democracy donors such as the UN. As such, it should be able to better observe and control the aid projects it funds than other donors. In addition, because of its institutional design and diplomatic corps, which are unusual for an IO, it should also be able to gather high-quality information about its aid projects.

Table 4.2 suggests that European Union democracy-assistance projects may indeed be less measurable and regime-compatible than other multilateral projects since in both cases the coefficient estimates for the EU indicator are negative. On average, EU projects are 10 percent more likely to be measurable and 14 percent more likely to be regime-compatible than other multilateral projects, holding the other variables at their means. Fairly large standard errors, however, prevent me from confidently concluding that EU projects are less tame than other multilateral projects. The relatively large standard errors are related, at least in part, to the small sample of bilateral projects that were channeled first through multilateral organizations in 2010 – just 712 in comparison to 7,225 that were channeled first through NGOs. If I restrict the sample just to projects funded by European states – in other words, the countries that *could* channel multilateral projects through the European Union – and compare EU projects to other multilateral projects, the results are similar.

Another way of understanding the lack of statistical significance comes from the recognition that there is considerable diversity within European countries in terms of strategies of democracy assistance, even if it appears at first glance to be relatively homogeneous. Specifically, the East and Central European countries that transitioned to democracy after the collapse of the Soviet Union have approaches to democracy assistance that are different from each other as well as from the Western European countries.[39] As such, I may have overestimated the relative homogeneity of the EU member states in developing my hypothesis.

Finally, recall that I expected domestic political controversy about foreign aid to influence government agencies' preferences about measurable programs and their efforts to observe and control projects. I hypothesized that aid volatility, which occurs when governments change foreign-aid policy with some frequency, would be negatively associated with regime-compatible projects when channeled through government agencies because of donors' efforts at observation and control. After all, government officials, though they act as principals when it comes to democracy aid, are themselves agents of their voting publics. At the same time, I offered no clear hypothesis about the relationship between aid volatility and measurable programs. The lack of a clear prediction stemmed from my observation that, on the one hand, volatile donors should more greatly value measurable programs, but on the other hand, donors should have better information about grantees and thus less need to reward measurable programs.

Table 4.2 shows support for my expectations. On average, aid volatility is positively correlated with measurable projects, although large standard errors prevent me from saying that the effect is conclusively different from the null hypothesis of zero relationship. Given that I made no clear prediction about this relationship, the null finding is not surprising. Aid agencies are also clearly less likely to pursue regime-compatible projects when there is political volatility, as the negative coefficient for aid volatility, which is more than 2.5 times the standard error, shows. A shift from fairly low aid volatility (25th percentile) to fairly high aid volatility (75th percentile), while holding other variables at their means, is associated with a 9 percent greater likelihood of an agency pursuing a measurable program and a 18 percent lesser likelihood of pursuing a regime-compatible program.

The control variables yield some explanatory power, but not always in the predicted directions. We might expect donors to send target countries with which they have affinity more regime-compatible aid, but they do not. In fact, when it comes to aid channeled through government agencies, affinity has a clear *negative* relationship with regime-compatible democracy aid.

---

[39] Petrova (2014).

What should we make of the lack of significance of preference alignments for the design of democracy assistance? A plausible answer comes from previous research that has found that foreign-aid donors vary in the extent to which economic and military factors affect their allocation decisions, with the United States being a country that is especially likely to consider such factors.[40] Chapter 5 will show that American geostrategic interests were consistently associated with more regime-compatible democracy assistance, in keeping with previous findings about the insincerity of US democracy promotion. In contrast, this chapter's wider sample of donors includes a number of donor governments that do not seem to worry as much as the world's hegemon about geostrategic interests when giving democracy assistance.

Table 4.2 shows that target countries' democracy levels are correlated with regime-compatible programs only for aid channeled through NGOs. Since target governments can more easily prohibit aid via NGOs than aid via IOs or donor agencies, that relationship is not surprising. Meanwhile, Eurasia stands out as the region least likely to receive regime-compatible democracy assistance, whether through NGOs, multilateral organizations, or government agencies. Since some of democracy assistance's biggest triumphs in the twenty-first century occurred in Eurasia, from the electoral defeat of Slobodan Milošević in Serbia in 2000 to Georgia's Rose Revolution in 2003, it makes sense that relatively confrontational aid might continue to be targeted there. Again, in contrast to the American projects that I will examine in Chapter 5, I find little evidence that Middle Eastern countries received unusually regime-compatible projects among this large sample of donors – perhaps as an indicator of the United States' special strategic relationships with a number of Arab autocracies.

*Alternative explanations for the findings*

One advantage of the preceding analysis is that it focused on the impact of variations in information problems *within* the same channel of aid delivery. Doing so allowed me to partially sidestep the confounding issue of why donor governments choose certain channels of delivery in the first place. Not all problems related to the selection of aid channels were, however, eliminated.

Thus, I use the statistical technique of matching to help address the concern that the inferences I am drawing about the relationships between delegation relationships and tame democracy assistance may, in fact,

---

[40] Schraeder, Hook, and Taylor (1998).

be driven by other factors. I specifically use the technique to further explore allocation patterns for aid channeled via NGOs and multilateral organizations. Such aid is of particular concern in terms of alternative explanations, as I discuss below. Moreover, since the key explanatory variables in those cases are dichotomous, they are particularly well suited to matching.

To begin, programs that donors channel through donor-country NGOs may systematically differ from programs that are channeled through other NGOs in ways for which the analysis did not account. In particular, poorer donors likely have fewer donor-country NGOs than wealthier donors. Poorer donors may also be less likely to confront dictators overseas than wealthier donors since they tend to be less powerful and thus may be less willing to have aggressive foreign policies. Thus, donor-country NGOs could be associated with less-tame programs because they are more often used by wealthy, powerful countries that are not afraid to fund untame programs.

Matching is a statistical method that prunes and then pairs observations from a data set such that the resulting observations are more comparable. Preprocessing the data using matching before conducting more conventional regression analysis can successfully reduce model dependence and statistical bias.[41] A particularly appealing matching method is coarsened exact matching (CEM), which "coarsens" variables into theoretically informed groups, matches observations on the coarsened values, and saves the original uncoarsened values to use later in regression analysis. In addition to its intuitive approach, CEM has a number of statistical advantages over other matching methods.[42] I matched donor-country NGO projects and other NGO projects on three variables that could influence the donor's choice to use a donor-country NGO: donor-government region (exact match); donor-government wealth (with a cutoff point of a gross domestic product per capita of $45,000, which is around the Netherlands' GDP); and target country (exact match). In other words, I compared the effect of donor-country NGOs on the types of projects that are funded by donors from the same region and a similar level of wealth and in the same target countries. When I calculated the $L_1$ statistic, I found that the procedure effectively reduced imbalance in the data.

After using matching to improve the balance of the data, I re-estimated the effect of using donor-country NGOs on the likelihood of a democracy-assistance program being tame. Donor-country

---

[41] Ho *et al.* (2007).
[42] Iacus, King, and Porro (2012); Blackwell, Iacus, and King (2009).

NGOs, which are easier for donors to observe and control, are again associated with less-tame democracy assistance. In fact, the effects of donor-country NGOs are substantively larger: on average, donor-country NGOs are 55 percent less likely to pursue measurable projects and 44 percent less likely to pursue regime-compatible projects than other NGOs, holding the other variables in the regressions at their means.

Similarly, European Union member states may choose to target particular types of programs through the EU instead of through other multilateral organizations. Recall that I expected EU projects to be less tame than other multilateral projects because it is easier for the EU (a relatively homogeneous IO with a diplomatic corps) to collect better information than other multilateral organizations. But if European countries do not randomly select to channel programs through the EU, then my causal inference may be incorrect.

Why might European countries channel aid through the EU rather than through other multilateral organizations? First, I expect EU countries to be more likely to channel aid through the EU rather than through other multilateral organizations when the target countries are part of the European Neighbourhood Policy (ENP), a framework that includes support for political reform in sixteen nearby countries in Eurasia, the Middle East and North Africa. When target countries are outside of the ENP, European donors have less reason to send aid through the EU. Second, I expect European countries that have more control over EU policy to be more likely to channel aid through the EU. For such countries, EU democracy assistance is more likely to match their preferences about where and how to promote democracy. One way to measure a country's control over EU foreign-aid policy is through formal bargaining leverage, which tends to correlate with types of informal influence, as well.[43] Countries in the EU vote at the Council of the European Union using a system that gives more weight to larger, wealthier, and more powerful countries. I expect countries that command a larger share of the bargaining power to be more likely to give to projects through the EU since they can better influence the design of those projects.[44]

I therefore matched EU projects and other multilateral project observations on three variables that could influence the donor's choice to channel multilateral aid through the EU: target-state ENP membership (exact match); donor-government EU vote share (with a cutoff point of

[43] Schneider and Tobin (2013, 106–7).
[44] European Union (2007).

8 percent vote share); and target country (exact match). That procedure improved the balance of the data significantly; the $L_1$ statistic indicates a 53 percent reduction in imbalance in my data after matching.

I then reestimated the effect of channeling aid through the EU on the likelihood of a democracy-assistance program being measurable and regime-compatible using logistic regressions. Channeling democracy assistance through the EU, rather than some other multilateral organization, has a much stronger relationship with the outcome variables in these models. On average, EU projects are 129 percent less likely to be measurable and 150 percent less likely to be regime-compatible than other multilateral projects, holding the other variables in the regressions at their means. In sum, there is strong evidence that suggests that the donor governments' ease in observing and controlling the democracy-assistance projects they fund affects the likelihood of organizations in the democracy establishment pursuing tame projects.

## Conclusions

Bilateral governments spent more than $5 billion in 2010 on aid projects to promote democracy in the developing world. The amount countries spend on democracy assistance continues to grow each year, despite ongoing criticisms that aid projects are not well designed and general skepticism about democracy promotion's place in foreign policy. This book argues that one of the most important elements for predicting how likely democracy-assistance projects are to advance donors' wishes has to do with donors' abilities to observe and control how the projects they fund are implemented.

Do delegation relationships affect how organizations in the democracy establishment promote democracy? This chapter's answer is yes. Both the descriptive and multivariate analyses presented in this chapter showed that indicators of variations in delegation relationships – such as channeling aid through non-donor-country NGOs – are associated with tamer democracy assistance. Those findings are striking when considered in the context of much research about democracy assistance, which depicts donor governments sitting alone in the driver's seat, steering foreign aid toward their strategic allies. Donor governments' strategic interests clearly do affect democracy assistance, too, especially for some donor countries. Indeed, the findings of the next chapter illustrate how the United States takes a different and more geostrategically driven approach to democracy promotion than do some other donor countries. Despite that, the findings in this chapter suggest that the intermediaries between donor and target states – organizations in the democracy establishment – also matter in significant ways for the design of democracy assistance. Aid-recipient organizations can play an important role steering the car.

The findings are quite robust. A careful research design – which allowed me to compare information problems within rather than across channels of delivery – supplemented by statistical matching helped isolate the independent effect of information problems on the likelihood of democracy assistance being measurable and regime-compatible. The analyses controlled for other important factors, including the unique preferences and characteristics of donor governments and target states. Although the size of the impacts of information problems is difficult to estimate with precision, it is clear that they are substantively large across several channels of delivery.

Of course, the analysis has limitations. It only investigates one step in the transnational delegation chain – the delegation from bilateral democracy donors to the first organizations they fund to implement democracy assistance. There are additional levels of delegation beyond what is contained in the OECD's data. To understand some of those additional steps in the delegation chain, in the next chapter I focus on delegation relationships – and professionalization – in American democracy assistance.

# 5    Changes in American grant-making

*Speaking out . . . for democratic values and principles is good and right. But it's not just good enough. We must work hard for democracy and freedom.*[1]

*Building democracy is like building a bridge: It's something that today we think there aren't too many ways to do well.*[2]

In 1982, President Ronald Reagan elaborated his vision for democracy promotion in an address to the British parliament: "to foster the infrastructure of democracy – the system of a free press, unions, political parties, universities – which allows a people to choose their own way, to develop their own culture, to reconcile their own differences through peaceful means."[3] Reagan followed through by proposing two new democracy promotion vehicles to Congress: Project Democracy, a public diplomacy program that the US Information Agency would coordinate, and the National Endowment for Democracy, a bipartisan grants program.[4] Project Democracy failed to win Congressional support, but the NED succeeded. The NED sought to make democracy assistance public after controversial, covert actions conducted by the CIA during the Cold War. The NED was modeled on the Stiftungen, the German political-party foundations that aided Spain and Portugal's democratic transitions.

If the transnational theory of democracy assistance advanced in this book is correct, then increasing competition and professionalism in the democracy establishment should have "tamed" American aid over time. Yet demonstrating such a trend is challenging. The past three decades have witnessed major changes in global politics as a consequence of the end of the Cold War, as well as widespread democratization. Those changes are likely to affect states' democracy promotion strategies in

---

[1] Reagan (1983).
[2] Interview 30, with democracy-assistance practitioner, in person, Washington, DC, September 16, 2009.
[3] Reagan (1982).
[4] Carothers (1999, 30–2, 357).

multiple ways. Consequently, it is difficult to show that competition and professionalization in the democracy establishment *independently* tamed democracy assistance.

To cope with that challenge, this chapter uses multivariate statistical analysis to examine how competition and professionalization affect programs that have been funded in a largely constant manner over time. To do so, it focuses mainly on variations in programs funded by the National Endowment for Democracy. Studying variations in a single donor's programs – especially the NED's – holds constant a number of potentially confounding factors related to organizational structure and donor preferences. Although the NED has steadily expanded, its grant-making mission has not wavered and no major organizational changes have occurred that pertain to its assistance efforts.[5] Moreover, the organization's leaders have persisted over time; founding president Carl Gershman, for example, continues in that office as of 2014.

But according to the new data analyzed in this chapter, not everything at the NED has stayed the same. In 1986, measurable and regime-compatible programs represented around 20 percent of the NED's grants. By 2009, they represented around 60 percent. Over the same period of time, aid spent on dissidents, political parties, and unions dropped in real terms – despite the large growth in democracy assistance. What explains the transformation of democracy assistance? Consistent with the theory I developed in Chapter 2 and specifically Hypotheses 3 and 4, I find that organizations in the democracy establishment have changed how they promote democracy over time to help them survive and thrive. Organizations in the early era of democracy assistance were less professional – prompting less focus on tame programs. They also had to worry about survival less then, since there was less competition for donor funding.

Competition and professionalism are not, however, equally likely to be associated with tamer programs at all times and places. One of the other significant findings of this chapter is that democracy-assistance programs reflect growing Congressional pressures for measurable programs. That finding is consistent with my expectation that organizations in the democracy establishment want to survive and therefore respond to donors' preferences (Hypothesis 6).

---

[5] Note, however, that Nicolas Guilhot has documented other changes at the NED, such as an increasing emphasis outside of grant-making on academic programs. See Guilhot (2005, 91–100).

Can we be sure that the taming of democracy assistance would have occurred in the absence of rising competition and professionalization and changing government preferences? It is clear that there are multiple sources of change in democracy assistance. The quantitative evidence in this chapter can ultimately only show correlations between competition and professionalism and certain types of democracy assistance, not causation. The evidence presented in this chapter controls, however, for a number of other factors that could explain variations in democracy assistance, thus taking plausible alternative explanations for the findings into account. Those factors include the end of the Cold War and the associated changes in donor preferences and the nature of regimes in the developing world. Even controlling for such factors, the evidence remains consistent with my argument that competition and professionalization have caused organizations in the democracy establishment to more often pursue the democracy-assistance programs that promote their survival. Furthermore, competition and professionalization do a better job of explaining variations in democracy assistance than do other factors. The empirical record thus offers strong support for the theory. Chapter 5 further explores the causal mechanism to establish further confidence in my inferences. At the same time, it is important to acknowledge the multidimensionality of the changes that I document in democracy assistance since 1980. In particular, the end of the Cold War and the associated third wave of democratization are important variables.

To evaluate changes in American democracy assistance, the first section of this chapter explains the empirical strategy, which begins with an examination of grants given by the National Endowment for Democracy. The second section introduces a new data set of democracy-assistance projects and presents tests of the argument that competition and professionalism in the democracy establishment lead to more measurable and regime-compatible democracy assistance. The third section considers the generalizability of those findings. The fourth section concludes.

## American democracy assistance

The US government funds democracy-assistance programs via multiple institutions, including USAID and the State Department. The oldest institution – and the only one devoted exclusively to democracy aid – is the National Endowment for Democracy. I begin my analysis of American democracy assistance with a focus on the NED. Below, I explain the logic behind that decision and provide an overview of the NED's efforts at aiding democracy abroad.

### Promoting democracy at the NED: an overview

According to its website, the National Endowment for Democracy "is guided by the belief that freedom is a universal human aspiration that can be realized through the development of democratic institutions, procedures, and values."[6] To achieve its mission, the NED distributes funds to non-governmental organizations. Those funds come primarily from Congress, although the State Department also provides some money. Although the NED relies on government resources, it decides where and how to spend most of its funds. The NED accepts applications – which contain information about the NGO, a project proposal, and a budget – four times a year. NGOs design and propose projects themselves. All NGOs that are not associated with violence may submit proposals on any subject in an open call for applications that makes no demands on organizations in terms of the content of their programs.[7] Congress holds the NED accountable through audits and annual reports. The NED monitors its grantees through visits and periodic reports on at least an annual basis. Though the monitoring process is undoubtedly imperfect, it reflects the NED's desire to evaluate programs on a frequent basis, regardless of how incremental and long-term democratic progress may be. Although funded NGOs must measure a project's progress, there are no required measurements.[8]

Although the NED runs a number of programs at its Washington, DC, headquarters, around 90 percent of its budget goes to overseas grants: 135 countries – the significant majority of countries that are not consolidated democracies – have received NED grants. The average country has received seventy-two NED grants over twelve years. As Figure 5.1 shows, the NED has grown considerably as a grant-maker. Congress first authorized the NED in the FY84/85 State Department Authorization Act (HR 2915) for $31.3 million, although the appropriation was only $18 million since the organization took longer to set up than expected. In 2011 the NED's revenue from government agencies was $135.7 million.[9] The NED's resources increased significantly when the Soviet Union collapsed and during the "freedom agenda" of President George W. Bush.

[6] National Endowment for Democracy (2012a).
[7] Melia (2005, 3).
[8] National Endowment for Democracy (2012b, 5).
[9] National Endowment for Democracy (1985–2012).

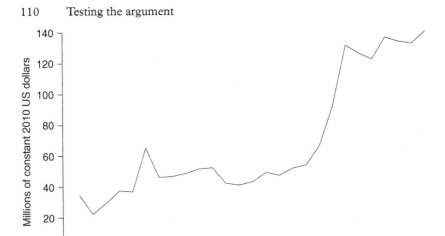

Figure 5.1 The growth of the National Endowment for Democracy.
*Note:* Funds are in constant 2010 US dollars.
*Data sources:* National Endowment for Democracy (1985–2012).

Although the NED gives out grants directly to overseas groups, four American organizations that were key to its founding political arrangement – the Solidarity Center (an affiliate of the AFL-CIO that replaced the similarly affiliated Free Trade Union Institute), the Center for International Private Enterprise (an offshoot of the Chamber of Commerce), the International Republican Institute (loosely linked with the Republican Party), and the National Democratic Institute (loosely linked with the Democratic Party) – are its largest grantees. Those organizations, referred to as the NED's core grantees, receive just over half of the NED's grants. The core grantees as well as some other recipient organizations re-grant NED funds to NGOs overseas that directly implement democracy-assistance projects.

As Figure 5.2 shows, the NED gives grants to countries at various levels of democracy. The average target country falls between 2 and 3 on Freedom House's seven-point index, on which 1 is the least democratic and 7 the most democratic. Compared with other democracy donors, the NED works in somewhat more authoritarian countries on average. The NED's grants have not been heavily concentrated in particular regions. Over the course of its history, the NED has given around 22 percent of its grants to organizations working in Asia (the largest beneficiary region)

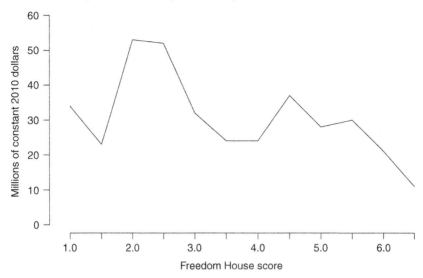

Figure 5.2 NED grants, by freedom level.
*Note:* Between 1985 and 2009, I averaged countries' political liberty and civil rights scores, which were rescaled so that 1 represents the least democracy and 7 the most.
*Data sources:* National Endowment for Democracy (1985–2010) and Freedom House (1985–2010).

and around 14 percent to organizations working in Africa (the smallest beneficiary region).

Findings about the impact of NED grants are mixed. Supporters of the NED credit it with helping successful democratic transitions in Czechoslovakia, South Africa, and Chile.[10] As a consequence, former NDI and Freedom House executive (and subsequent Obama administration official) Thomas Melia described the NED as "The best money available in the democracy promotion business," and called for a quintupling of its budget and slashing of USAID and the State Department's democracy budgets.[11] But systematic, cross-national evidence of the NED's positive impact is less forthcoming. Research shows that NED grants are not associated with democratization in target states on average and also that democratization in target states is not associated with the allocation of NED grants on average.[12] Thus, it is important for

[10] Scott and Steele (2005, 441).
[11] Melia (2006, 129). See also McFaul (2010, 198).
[12] Scott and Steele (2005).

policy-makers and scholars to better understand how and why the NED promotes democracy.

### Why study the National Endowment for Democracy?

The NED is a relatively small American democracy donor. The NED's budget of around $140 million represents about 5 percent of the total democracy assistance budget of the United States. As a quasi-governmental organization, however, the NED offers an excellent test of my argument since it is both a major donor and, in many senses, an organization in the democracy establishment. In other words, the causal argument should operate at multiple levels at the NED. In addition, examining the NED's grants has several other advantages.

First, the NED has cataloged its grants' project descriptions, recipient organizations, target countries, and grant amounts in a thorough, consistent, and transparent way through annual reports. In doing so, the NED is unique in the democracy-assistance field. The USAID democracy and governance aid data reported to the OECD between 1990 and 2003, for example, had only a 0.62 correlation with an internal USAID database kept by two former employees, Andrew Green and John Richter, that staff generally regard as more reliable.[13] That relatively low correlation suggests that there is significant measurement error in officially reported figures on democracy assistance. Achieving the goals of this chapter requires good historical records, which are impossible to obtain from other important democracy donors. To verify the validity of the NED project descriptions, I interviewed people from organizations that implemented NED-funded projects in Jordan. Reassuringly, their descriptions of the projects uniformly matched the NED's descriptions, confirming that the annual reports are accurate records. Indeed, I found no evidence of covert projects that had been omitted from the records.[14]

Second, democracy assistance is usually self-identified by the donors. Whereas all the NED's grants are democracy assistance, by definition, donor governments generally choose how to report and categorize their foreign aid. The new norm of promoting democracy has encouraged new states and international organizations to begin aiding democracy abroad

---

[13] Finkel, Pérez-Liñán, and Seligson (2007, 422). Note that perfect correlation equals 1 and no correlation equals 0.

[14] It is worth noting that the CIA's capacity is widely thought to have declined during the 1990s. See Melia (2005, 22). As such, it is unlikely that any of my findings about the taming of democracy assistance reflect an increase in covert projects since 1985.

each year.[15] That norm has likely also encouraged donors to classify more activities as democracy assistance over time. Thus, it is difficult to compare democracy assistance in 2010 with democracy assistance in 2000 or 1990 across donors.

Third, according to conventional wisdom, the NED's grants represent a hard test for the argument. Experts view the NED as the least bureaucratic and most confrontational American democracy donor. Thomas Carothers describes the NED as "operat[ing] in politically sensitive situations, dispersing financial support to human rights groups, independent newspapers and journals, groups of exiled dissidents, fledgling civil activists, and independent civic education efforts."[16] Political scientist Larry Diamond has also lauded the NED for being nimbler and more risk-taking than USAID.[17] Thus, more so than evidence of the growth of tame democracy assistance at another American donor organization, such evidence from the NED would be surprising.

Finally, the NED – the oldest American democracy donor – is an important organization for both scholars and practitioners. Among scholars, the NED has been the focus of several previous studies of democracy assistance, although the patterns documented here have not been explored.[18] Among practitioners, the organization is also significant. Social power in a network refers to an actor's connectedness to other actors in its network.[19] By that measure, the NED is powerful. In Chapter 6, I will analyze internet connections in the democracy establishment. To preview the findings, the NED received the third most co-links of any organization and the most of any non-governmental organization worldwide. Thus, changes in how the NED promotes democracy matter for the broader practice of democracy assistance.

### A systematic analysis of American government-funded NGOs

The NED is both an agent of Congress (and ultimately the American public) and a principal to its NGO grantees. Therefore, both the NED and the organizations it funds should care about getting government funding and target-country access. I expect both sets of actors to converge on measurable and regime-compatible programs as a consequence of competition and professionalization. At the same time, they should

---

[15] McFaul (2004–5).
[16] Carothers (1999, 95).
[17] Diamond (1997, 22–3).
[18] Guilhot (2005); Scott and Steele (2005).
[19] Kahler (2009, 12–13).

pursue tamer programs when the US government prefers such programs. This section tests the argument by analyzing a new data set of NED projects.

### A new data set of democracy-assistance projects

To test my argument, I analyzed a random sample of 5,000 projects out of the more than 10,000 projects funded by the NED between 1985 and 2009. A sample was used to make the coding task more manageable. I obtained project descriptions from the NED's annual reports.[20] I classified the projects according to the typology described in Chapter 3. Coding was blind with respect to the project year and target country. An undergraduate also coded a sample of the projects, with an agreement rate of 86 percent – a rate that is generally regarded as good for content analysis and thus enhances the reliability of my measures. Figure 5.3 shows the most-funded categories at the NED, which include support to unions, political parties, business, dissidents, and civil society (general category). The average grant in the sample was $90,765, with grants ranging from $2,800 to $14,700,000 in 2010 US dollars.

I then sorted the projects into measurable and regime-compatible groups to create my dependent variables: country–year observations of the proportions of total NED grants that were measurable, regime-compatible, or both. Figure 5.4 reveals the taming of democracy assistance: the proportions of measurable and regime-compatible NED projects have each more than doubled since 1985. Those trends are consistent with my argument that organizations in the democracy establishment have converged on democracy-assistance programs that promote their survival. When the NED began giving out grants in 1985, one of its projects aided Nicaraguan unions that were "resisting government control and repression"; another supported the publication and distribution of *Právo Lidu*, a newspaper associated with the outlawed Czech Social Democratic Party during communist rule. Indeed, democratic activists designed and implemented most NED projects at that time. More typical later activities included CIPE's 2007 effort in China to "encourage better local governance and on-going policy dialogue," and a 2009 initiative that sought to "enable effective communication between parliamentarians and their constituents" in autocratic Azerbaijan.[21]

---

[20] National Endowment for Democracy (1985–2012).
[21] All quotes from National Endowment for Democracy (1985–2012).

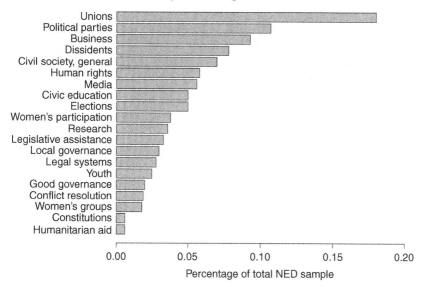

Figure 5.3 NED grant commitments, by category.
*Data sources:* National Endowment for Democracy (1985–2010) and author's coding.

### *What factors influence NED grant-making?*

Figure 5.4 shows that measurable and regime-compatible programs have increased over time. My argument, however, makes more specific claims about how organizations in the democracy establishment should behave. First, when competition is high, I expect organizations to more often select measurable and regime-compatible democracy assistance. Second, owing to professional norms, I expect organizations to converge on measurable and regime-compatible democracy assistance. Finally, I expect organizations to respond to variations in the US government's preferences.

*Competition* First, it is necessary to create an indicator of funding competition for American democracy assistance. It is clear that grant competition is tough in the twenty-first century. In one typical board meeting in 2013, 292 proposals were selected for funding out of around 1,700 NED applicants.[22] Since the NED, like all American democracy donors, does not make application information public, however, it is challenging to create a direct, over-time measure of competition.

[22] Usatin (2013).

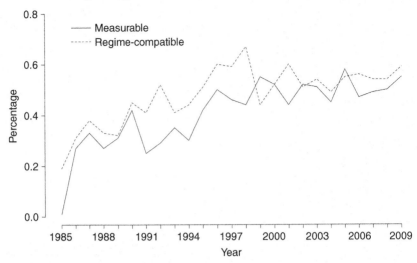

Figure 5.4 The rise of tame democracy assistance.
*Data sources:* National Endowment for Democracy (1985–2010) and author's coding.

Thus, I used the proportion of NED grants in a year that were given to relatively large NGOs (i.e., NGOs that won grants to work in multiple countries in the same year) as a measure for NGO competition. An example of such an NGO is Freedom House. The fewer of the NED's grants that large NGOs win, the more competitive the field. Large NGOs' share of NED grants decreased from 90 percent in 1985 to 50 percent in 2009. This measure squares with the way that previous researchers have conceptualized NGO competition, which is as an "overabundance of organizations" relative to funding.[23] Although the capture of grants by a few organizations could conceivably indicate high competition, in the case of NGO competition for donor aid, that is not normally the case, as qualitative evidence in later chapters further confirms.

It is important to note that alternative measures of NGO funding competition point in the same direction as the measure that I elect to use. The number of NED grantees increased, for example, from eighteen unique grantees in 1985 to more than 800 in 2009. That figure also indicates growing competition in the field. That variable is related, however, to the number of target countries, with more countries enabling

---

[23] Cooley and Ron (2002, 25).

more NGOs to apply. Since the number of target countries has also increased over time, I thus use the large NGOs measure. Notably, *more* NGOs in the twenty-first century are competing for *smaller* grants, with the NED's average grant in the sample shrinking from $306,902 in 1985 to $97,137 in 2009 in 2010 US dollars.

*Professionalism* Next, it is necessary to create an indicator of professionalism in the democracy-assistance field. Professionalism is usually conceptualized in terms of training and formal qualifications. For example, sociologist Harold Wilensky defined professionals as having "systematic knowledge or doctrine acquired only through long prescribed training ... [and] a set of professional norms."[24] I expect professionals to hold common ideas about promoting democracy.

To systematically measure professionalism, I gathered the names of all NED program staff and collected information on their careers from web searches. I considered people with a graduate degree in a related field, for example, a master's degree in international development, and who had worked at another organization in the democracy establishment, for example, CIPE professionals. The proportion of professional staff increased from zero in 1985 to 44 percent in 2004. That trend is consistent with research by Nicolas Guilhot, who conducted a historical case study of the NED and found considerable professionalization at the organization.[25] Professionals should be more likely to fund tame programs because they sympathize with NGOs' survival concerns and view such activities as appropriate. In addition, they should be relatively concerned about the NED's survival, and they should thus view tame programs as a strategy to promote the organization in the same way I argue that other organizations in the democracy establishment do.

In an ideal world, I would also create an NGO-level measure of professionalism. Although it is possible to collect data on NGO staff, that information is better available for NGOs that still exist and are relatively professional, which would bias the results. Since the NED is an organization in the democracy establishment, my measure therefore still offers a reasonable test of the argument about professionalization in the field.

*US government preferences* Finally, the US government's preferences could vary temporally. Indeed, Congress – the NED's

---

[24] Wilensky (1964, 138).
[25] Guilhot (2005, 91–100).

principal – has preferred measurable democracy assistance since the 1990s. Congress called for measurable outputs for government programs with the Government Performance and Results Act (GPRA) in 1993 and the Republican takeover of Congress in 1994. Moreover, the General Accounting Office (later known as the Government Accountability Office, or GAO) issued a report criticizing the NED's monitoring and evaluation systems in 1991.[26] Thus, we would expect the NED's grants to become more measurable in the mid 1990s to help it survive.

In contrast, there is little evidence that Congressional preferences over regime-compatible aid have varied temporally. When I searched the Congressional Record for the NED, I found hundreds of records with various criticisms (for example, that the NED is political pork). In no cases, however, did Congresspeople want the NED to pursue regime-compatible programs. In fact, when the NED is praised, it was often for its confrontational programs that, in the words of Representative David Dreier, helped "people who have been trying to claw their way to self-determination."[27] The absence of obvious support for regime-compatible programs at the NED in Congress is consistent with previous research on American democracy promotion that has found Congress to be more consistently pro-democracy promotion than presidents.[28]

*Other variables* Several other factors that could influence the design of democracy assistance must also be addressed in the analysis. Complete information about the sources and measures that I use for those factors can be found in the data appendix. First, the NED could tailor grants to target countries' characteristics. The NED may support opposition groups in autocracies, offer more regime-compatible programs in states that seem on the verge of democratizing, and support open competition in consolidating democracies.[29] That curvilinear relationship can be empirically modeled by including a measure of a country's democracy level and that measure's square.

Within autocracies, variations in regime type also exist. NGOs may opt for more compatible programs in dictatorships that already allow some competition. I therefore control for the type of authoritarian regime: military, single-party, personalist, or monarchy.

---

[26] United States General Accounting Office (1991).
[27] See Representative Dreier (CA), Congressional Record 150, p. H5250 (July 7, 2004).
[28] Peceny (1999).
[29] Note that the NED has funded untame programs even in highly authoritarian states, such as North Korea. In other words, programs are possible (though not necessarily likely) almost anywhere.

Second, strategies of democracy assistance could vary regionally or with key events. The Middle East, for example, may be exceptional because of the United States' relationships with Arab autocrats. I therefore included regional indicator variables. I also included an indicator for years before the end of the Cold War in 1990 (1992 in robustness checks), since that event is generally regarded as a watershed for US democracy promotion.

Finally, strategically important target countries may receive more regime-compatible aid. A good indicator of strategic importance is the amount of US military aid that the target country received in the previous year. In robustness checks, I instead used the target country's US economic aid and its political affinity with the United States in terms of UN votes as indicators of strategic importance.

### Main results

Table 5.1 presents the baseline models. The estimation technique used in those models – fractional logit models with robust standard errors clustered on country – is one that is designed to accommodate the proportional nature of my dependent variables.[30] First, I used the percentage of NED grants in a year that go to large organizations as a proxy for competition. Second, I used the percentage of NED staff in a year that are professionals as a proxy for the field's professionalization. Both variables are related to the outcomes in the expected directions.[31] I also included several control variables: the target state's lagged military aid receipts, a post-Cold War indicator, and the target state's lagged democracy level and democracy$^2$. Because competition and professionalism are highly correlated ($\rho = -0.87$), I did not include them in the same model.

The substantive effects of competition and professionalism were large. I argued that as fewer NED grants go to large NGOs, competition increases and the proportions of measurable and regime-compatible democracy assistance should rise. As expected, a shift from 69 percent of NED grants going to large donors (25th percentile) to 54 percent (75th percentile) was associated with 8 percent more measurable and 6 percent more regime-compatible democracy assistance. Likewise,

---

[30] Papke and Wooldridge (1996). My findings are robust to including the over-time averages of all right-hand side variables as well as the number of time periods for each target country in fractional probit models with robust standard errors, which accounts for the panel structure of the data. See Papke and Wooldridge (2008, 122).

[31] The results held when I included the total amount of NED funding received by a target country that year and the total amount of funding given globally by the NED that year.

Table 5.1 *How rising NGO competition and professionalism affect NED grants.*

| Variable | DV = % Measurable | | | | DV = % Regime-compatible | | DV = % Both | |
|---|---|---|---|---|---|---|---|---|
| | Model 1 | Model 2 | Model 3 | Model 4 | Model 5 | Model 6 | Model 7 | Model 8 |
| | Competition | Norms | Congress | Congress | Competition | Norms | Competition | Norms |
| % Large NGOs | −2.12*** | | −0.74 | | −1.54** | | −2.22** | |
| | (0.74) | | (0.81) | | (0.74) | | (0.88) | |
| % Professional | | 2.02*** | | 1.24** | | 1.48** | | 2.39*** |
| | | (0.59) | | (0.58) | | (0.58) | | (0.66) |
| Cold War | −0.46* | −0.10 | | | −0.80*** | −0.54** | −0.45 | 0.02 |
| | (0.24) | (0.28) | | | (0.23) | (0.26) | (0.29) | (0.35) |
| Military aid | 0.01 | 0.01 | −0.0 | −0.00 | 0.07*** | 0.07*** | 0.11*** | 0.11*** |
| | (0.03) | (0.03) | (0.03) | (0.03) | (0.03) | (0.03) | (0.03) | (0.03) |
| Democracy | 0.63*** | 0.61*** | 0.64*** | 0.61*** | 0.21 | 0.20 | 0.52* | 0.49* |
| | (0.22) | (0.23) | (0.23) | (0.23) | (0.23) | (0.23) | (0.28) | (0.28) |
| Democracy² | −0.08** | −0.08** | −0.08*** | −0.08** | 0.01 | 0.01 | −0.03 | −0.02 |
| | (0.03) | (0.03) | (0.03) | (0.03) | (0.03) | (0.03) | (0.04) | (0.04) |
| Post-1994 | | | 0.58*** | 0.38* | | | | |
| | | | (0.19) | (0.20) | | | | |
| Constant | 0.09 | −2.04*** | −1.19* | −1.98*** | −0.25 | −1.31*** | −1.37* | −3.71*** |
| | (0.54) | (0.43) | (0.67) | (0.39) | (0.61) | (0.44) | (0.70) | (0.59) |
| N | 1,074 | 1,074 | 1,074 | 1,074 | 1,074 | 1,074 | 1,074 | 1,074 |
| Countries | 113 | 113 | 113 | 113 | 113 | 113 | 113 | 113 |

*Note:* All regressions are fractional logit models. All variables (except year) are lagged by one year. Robust standard errors, clustered on country, are in parentheses. *** denotes $p < 0.01$, ** denotes $p < 0.05$ and * denotes $p < 0.10$.

I argued that as NED staff professionalize, they should select more measurable and regime-compatible programs. They do. A shift from 36 percent professional staff (25th percentile) to 47 percent (75th percentile) was associated with 6 percent more measurable and 4 percent more regime-compatible democracy assistance. Those trends held even though the end of the Cold War was generally associated with less measurable and, especially, regime-compatible democracy aid.

What about the other variables? In general, they explained some variation in the outcomes, but less than competition and professionalism. First, the NED could reward strategically important target countries with regime-compatible aid. Table 5.1 shows that target countries' receipts of US military aid were correlated with regime-compatible programs, although the substantive effect is not very large ($p < 0.01$). A shift from no military aid to \$6.2 million (25th to 75th percentile) was associated with 3 percent more regime-compatible democracy aid in Model 5.[32] Military aid had no relationship with measurable democracy aid, as we would expect.

Second, the NED could tailor democracy assistance to target countries. As Table 5.1 shows, large standard errors prevented me from convincingly establishing a relationship between a country's democracy level and how regime-compatible its aid is. There *was* a clear positive relationship between democracy and measurable democracy assistance ($p < 0.01$). Since I did not predict that relationship, I disaggregated the categories to identify its source. A strong positive relationship between election aid (measurable) and democracy and a strong negative relationship between dissidents aid (non-measurable) and democracy drove the finding.

Of course, democracy levels are not the only indicators of target countries' regimes. I reran the models with indicators for authoritarian regime types (single-party, monarchy, military, and personalist). Non-autocracies were the omitted category. The key independent variables – NGO competition and NED professionalism – retained strong relationships with the outcome variables. Monarchies, single-party, and personalist regimes received somewhat more regime-compatible democracy assistance than non-autocracies, all else being equal. Military regimes did not.

Next, I examined how the NED's grants vary by region. When I introduced regional indicators to the baseline models, the clear effects of

---

[32] That relationship faded when I replaced military aid with total bilateral aid or political affinity. Security hierarchies, not general relationships, are key for democracy assistance.

competition and professionalism remained. Notably, Latin America and
the Middle East received unusually regime-compatible programs. That
finding is consistent with scholars' sharp criticisms of the self-interested
nature of American democracy promotion in those regions.[33] Taken
together with the other results, the evidence shows that NED grants
are unusually "tame" in the United States' Arab allies. That finding is
striking in light of a controversy in February 2012 when the Egyptian
government put staff from American democracy-promotion NGOs on
trial. This book suggests that the Egyptian government's rationale may
have had more to do with the domestic politics of anti-Americanism than
with highly-confrontational democracy assistance.

Finally, I introduced indicator variables for the years after 1994, since
my argument predicts the NED to respond to changes in Congress
preferences. As Table 5.1 shows, that time period was associated with
more measurable aid. The directions of the coefficient estimates for the
competition and professionalism variables remained the same, although
their statistical significance was dampened. The findings suggest that the
rise of measurable programs is linked to changes in Congress, consistent
with my theory. As Congress attempted to promote results-oriented
government programs and monitor government spending, the NED and
its grantees responded accordingly.

### How robust are the results?

Of course, many things change over time. Thus, I consider a battery
of alternative explanations for my findings. First, perhaps only hard
cases are left. Many countries democratized as part of the third wave
in the 1980s and 1990s. As a consequence, the "easy cases" – true
transitioning democracies – may no longer need democracy assistance.
I thus examined democracy assistance just in the seventy countries that
Freedom House classifies as "unfree" throughout the sample. Even
in hard cases, competition and professionalism were correlated with
measurable and regime-compatible democracy assistance ($p < 0.10$).

Second, perhaps target countries became better at denying access to
non-regime-compatible programs. Yet true transitioning democracies –
countries that Freedom House classifies as "free" – should more freely
allow programs supporting elections, political parties, and so on. When
I repeated the baseline models with a sample of free countries, competition and professionalism again were correlated with regime-compatible
democracy assistance ($p < 0.01$).

[33] Brownlee (2012); Robinson (1996).

Third, perhaps September 11, 2001 (9/11), is driving my findings. I thus introduced an indicator for years since 2001 to the baseline models. Doing so altered neither the signs nor the statistical significance of the key variables' coefficient estimates. The taming of democracy assistance also persisted when I excluded projects to Iraq and Afghanistan, two large recipients of post-2001 democracy assistance and possible outliers.

Fourth, perhaps changes at the NED only reflect epistemic learning. It may be the case that democracy-assistance organizations take the long view, pursuing incremental programs that may eventually lead to democratization (and conveniently also promote their own survival). If epistemic learning is the sole driver of change, however, then the NED's "success stories" should have received tamer aid than other countries. One way to think of success stories would be as those countries with more than a two-point increase on the Freedom House scale in one year. Intriguingly, such countries received *less* measurable and regime-compatible democracy aid than other countries, especially between 1985 and 2000, arguably the key learning period. Furthermore, the NED did not send less tame aid to countries that backslid. Thus, the NED did not simply expand effective programs.

Fifth, perhaps presidential partisanship accounts for my findings. I thus include an indicator for presidential administration that takes the value of 1 if the president was a Republican and 0 if he was a Democrat. My key findings remained, and the presidential partisanship indicator variable was not significant.

Finally, I perform two final checks to address concerns about the potential spuriousness of my findings. On the one hand, I restrict my analyses to the post-2001 period, a time during which competition and professionalism vary but there is no overall time trend. On the other hand, I restrict myself to a purely time-series analysis, using the cross-country average for the democracy variable. Doing that greatly reduces the number of observations and creates a hard test, allowing me to see how changes in the market for grants (versus the nature of democracy in the world) matter for the overall composition of aid. In both cases, my key explanatory variables remained statistically significant in the predicted directions.

### *What about information problems at the NED?*

Thus far, the analysis has focused mainly on how increased competition and professionalism have affected aid. That focus was appropriate given the advantages of the chapter's research design. Yet it is also possible to study some limited variations in the NED's information across the different projects it funds because the National Endowment for Democracy monitors its four core organizations less closely than its other grantees. Unfortunately, the NED does not report information about its grantees' further delegation of aid. Yet the NED generally monitors the four core grantees – the Solidarity Center, CIPE, IRI, and NDI – less closely than other NGOs. That is because the core grantees are guaranteed some NED grants each year. Moreover, the core NGOs are larger than the average NED grantee. They are thus more likely to re-delegate aid to other NGOs, which makes it even more difficult for the NED to observe and control projects.[34] For both reasons, the core grantees should pursue more measurable and regime-compatible programs. After all, when donor officials cannot easily observe and control grantees, NGOs are more likely to be rewarded for pursuing measurable programs and less likely to be punished for regime-compatible programs.

In addition, the core grantees are also more professional than the average NED grantee, which is younger, smaller, and less likely to be American. Because the core grantees are more professional, they should prefer measurable and regime-compatible programs more than other NED grantees. According to my argument, professional norms encourage organizations to focus on programs that promote survival and also encourage the belief that such programs are appropriate.

Consistent with those expectations, the core NGOs' programs are indeed more measurable (14 percent) and more regime-compatible (19 percent) than the NED's other programs. Those differences are statistically significant at conventional levels ($p < 0.01$). The core NGOs work in *more* democratic countries than other NED grantees on average – ruling out the possibility that they pursue regime-compatible aid simply because they must. Moreover, the core NGOs have not received more of the NED's grants over time, which suggests that the relationship is not an artifact of the taming of democracy assistance. Thus, evidence from the NED's core grantees seems to support the hypotheses about delegation and professionalization.

## Do trends at the NED represent something broader?

Thus far, the evidence suggests that rising competition and professionalism in the democracy establishment as well as changes in government preferences caused a taming of democracy assistance at the National

---

[34] Bush (2013).

Endowment for Democracy. Although the NED has spent more than one billion dollars promoting democracy around the world and is an influential organization, as noted above, it remains a relatively small donor in dollar terms. Do my findings about the NED reflect a broader trend in democracy assistance?

To answer that question, I explore trends at USAID, which – as the largest donor organization in the largest donor country – is arguably the most important democracy-assistance institution in the world. Indeed, as I will show in Chapter 6, USAID is also the organization that is most linked to online in the democracy establishment. In other words, USAID is a crucial organization to understand for broader trends in democracy assistance. It is important to acknowledge, since USAID is also an American organization, that this chapter's conclusions must be limited to US democracy aid. At the same time, it is worth noting that American democracy assistance is widely thought to put more emphasis on "political" programs, in contrast to European democracy assistance, which is widely thought to put more emphasis on "developmental" or "governance" programs.[35] In other words, non-American democracy assistance today is conventionally thought to be *at least as tame* as American democracy assistance, if not more so, which suggests that the chapter's findings may well explain trends beyond the United States.

USAID was created by the 1961 Foreign Assistance Act. Although there were some early hints at democracy promotion during the administration of President John F. Kennedy, Jr., USAID did not promote democracy in earnest until the 1980s. Then, democracy programming began in the agency's regional bureaus. At the time, President Reagan's administration was seeking to reorient its foreign policy in Latin America and specifically in El Salvador. In 1982, El Salvador held an election as part of a transition from military rule, and USAID provided funding for the State Department to send a group of election monitors there. According to Thomas Carothers, it was a "superficial, highly-politicized observation mission ... which USAID resisted supporting until Secretary of State Alexander Haig insisted."[36] Yet the mission signaled the start of a small wave of USAID democracy programs during the 1980s in Chile, Guatemala, Haiti, Honduras, Paraguay, and the Philippines.

Then the Cold War ended. In 1990, countries in Central and Eastern Europe – as well as in other regions – were embarking on transitions

---

[35] Carothers (2009a); Youngs (2003, 135).
[36] Carothers (1999, 34).

to democracy in the wake of communism's collapse. Looking for help, those countries appealed to Western policy-makers. Although USAID foreign-service officers registered some skepticism about promoting democracy, major bills in Congress, such as the Freedom Support Act of 1991, and pressure from the State Department and the White House forced USAID to expand its mission.[37] In 1990, USAID announced a global "democracy initiative." Several USAID executives at the time were crucial in formulating the organization's vision. In particular, Carol Adelman, an assistant administrator at USAID with ties to the neo-conservative foreign-policy movement, believed that the United States should promote democracy abroad and wanted USAID to play a role.[38]

The atmosphere among many staff was exuberant. One crucial player in the development of USAID's democracy portfolio described the field as follows in an interview:

There was no such thing as democracy promotion classes – the field didn't exist . . . The Europe program dominated everything at the Bureau for a while. It was an eighteen-hour day for me on the democracy side trying to figure out what to do. It didn't exist! I had no idea what I was doing – I'd never even been to Europe. And then over the next few years, democracy became part of the toolkit for US development.[39]

To develop that toolkit, USAID staff first had to establish a work-able definition of democracy. They read various political science and philosophical texts and came up with a five-part definition: elections and political processes; the rule of law; governance; civil society; and media.[40] Although media did not remain its own sub-area because of a bureaucratic reorganization, that general definition has persisted at USAID and continues to provide a framework for its democracy and governance (DG) programs, illustrating the importance of path dependence in the field's development.

During the 1990s, USAID administrator J. Brian Atwood helped professionalize democracy assistance. Atwood was previously NDI's president and was focused, in the words of one of his staff members, on "how we [could] mainstream democracy promotion at USAID."[41]

---

[37] Carothers (1999, 41–2).
[38] Interview 20, with former USAID official, in person, Washington, DC, May 4, 2010. Carol Adelman's husband, Ken Adelman, served on the Board of Trustees at Freedom House starting in the 1990s.
[39] Interview 20, with former USAID official, in person, Washington, DC, May 4, 2010.
[40] Interview 20, with former USAID official, in person, Washington, DC, May 4, 2010.
[41] Interview 4, with former USAID staff member, in person, Princeton, NJ, August 9, 2009.

Atwood's efforts included: making democracy promotion one of the organization's official pillars; creating the Center for Democracy and Governance in 1993; creating a specialist cadre of DG officers; establishing the Office of Transition Initiatives in part to do DG work in transitional and post-conflict countries; and fostering the conduct and dissemination of research on previous USAID DG efforts.[42] By the end of Atwood's tenure in 1999, it was fair to say that democracy assistance at USAID had been institutionalized. As one person who worked at USAID at that time explained, "The late 1990s is when we really started to see 'best practices' come into play for the electoral processes. You come [to a country] with a toolbox of stuff: 'this is how you do it.'"[43]

If the changes I have documented at the NED represent a broader trend in democracy assistance, USAID's programs should have also become tamer over time. Unfortunately, USAID stopped recording project descriptions in the 1990s, so it is not possible to study changes in the fine-grained way I did for the NED. Nevertheless, reliable annual data on USAID outlays between 1990 and 2003 from an internal data set, called the Green–Richter database, are available. USAID staff classified the data using six categories: civil society; elections; good governance; human rights; legal systems; and media.[44] Although those categories lump multiple types of democracy assistance together (for example, business, dissidents, unions, women's groups, and youth groups all fall in the "civil society" category), it is possible to discern some striking trends.

As Figure 5.5 shows, USAID spent relatively more money on good governance as part of its DG activities over time. Out of the six USAID-assigned categories, good governance is the only category that is both measurable and regime-compatible. Its increase over time is thus consistent with my argument about the field's growing competition and professionalization. In contrast, the category of civil society, which is not obviously "tame" since it includes many types of projects, some of which are quite confrontational or hard to measure (for example, aid to dissidents), has declined over time. Although many other things happened between 1990 and 2003, leaving open the question of causality, those trends suggest that USAID's programs did become tamer over time. This trend is consistent with an expanding conceptualization of democracy in democracy promotion to include good governance.

---

[42] Carothers (2009c, 10–11).

[43] Interview 4, with former USAID staff member, in person, Princeton, NJ, August 9, 2009.

[44] Finkel, Pérez-Liñán, and Seligson (2007, 145).

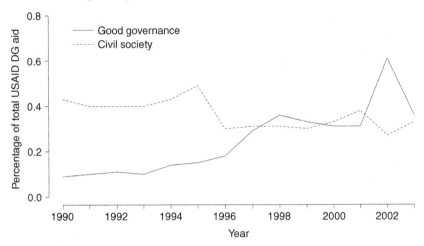

Figure 5.5 Changes in USAID democracy and governance aid.
*Data source:* Green–Richter Database (Finkel, Pérez-Liñán, and Seligson, 2007).

Data limitations and confounding factors make sharp inferences about the existence and sources over time changes in the democracy establishment challenging, especially for donor organizations, such as USAID, that do not offer the researcher the same degree of control that the National Endowment for Democracy does. Still, an examination of the United States Agency for International Development supports a limited but important conclusion: the taming of democracy assistance at the NED has occurred at other major democracy donors. Moreover, the competitive and professional pressures that have significantly affected the NED's approach to democracy assistance operate in the broader profession, which suggests that they are also correlated with changes in other aid programs.

## Conclusions

The National Endowment for Democracy was the United States government's first formal institution of democracy promotion. Even in the twenty-first century, it remains one of the world's most influential democracy-assistance organizations. It has worked in more than one hundred countries over the last three decades to advance democracy. It is clear that the National Endowment for Democracy seeks to, in the words of President Ronald Reagan in the chapter's epigraph, "work hard for democracy and freedom" around the world. But what exactly does that work entail?

The NED is often viewed as a straightforward agent of the United States government, for better or worse.[45] Although this chapter took that claim seriously, it also considered the unique interests of the NED and its grantees. Surprisingly given the common (but false) perception that the NED is fomenting revolutions around the world, I found that competition and professionalism have caused the NED's programs to become tamer over time. The analysis, which examined trends in new data that I collected and coded for this book, controlled for a number of other variables that could also explain the taming of democracy assistance, including changes in the American government, variations in target states, regional variations, the end of the Cold War, September 11, 2001, and outlier cases (Iraq and Afghanistan). Some, but not all, of those factors exerted notable influences on the design of democracy assistance. Yet throughout, competition and professionalization were important predictors of measurable and regime-compatible democracy assistance. The research design ultimately cannot prove that competition and professionalization caused the taming of democracy assistance. But by systematically ruling out plausible alternative explanations and repeatedly showing evidence that is consistent with the argument, this chapter has established that changes within the democracy establishment help explain the taming of democracy assistance in ways that scholars and policy-makers have not recognized until now.

Why do competition and professionalism affect the design of democracy assistance? Unlike most studies of democracy promotion, which largely focus on states, this book brings in the organizations of democracy aid. Those organizations evince a mixture of idealism and self-interest; but the balance between those motives varies temporally. Ideas were crucial in the origins of organizations such as the NED, but the influence of self-interest grew as the field became professional. As of the writing of this book, as the quote in the chapter's epigraph suggests, many professionals in the democracy establishment treat building democracy as they would building a bridge – as technical, portable, step-by-step process. There is some modest evidence that these dynamics take place at multiple American democracy donors.

Another important result was that the NED and its grantees have responded to changes in the US government's preferences. Several events during the early 1990s – a report that criticized the NED, new

---

[45] Guilhot (2005); Robinson (1996).

legislation that sought to make government programs more results-oriented, and the Republican takeover of the House of Representatives – led Congress to value measurable democracy assistance more. Accordingly, the NED's subsequent grants were more measurable. That finding is consistent with my argument that organizations in the democracy establishment want to survive and therefore should respond to variations in donors' preferences. Furthermore, when the United States has a geostrategic relationship with a target state, the NED sent it more regime-compatible programs, despite the organization's purported independence from the government.

One of the chapter's innovations has been to systematically document the rise of funding competition and professionalism in the democracy establishment. It then used those new measures to show how competition and professional norms affect democracy-assistance programs. The research design held constant the institutional setting, although there is some evidence that when the NED can collect better information about its grantees, it funds less tame projects. The chapter's counterfactual inferences about the taming of democracy assistance complement the detailed case studies of organizations that will come in the next chapter, which will focus on causal process observations and detailed measures.

# 6    Creating the democracy establishment

*I had to spend all this time with my staff figuring out from our own beneficiaries how many town hall meetings were held in village X to send to USAID in Macedonia, to send to USAID in Washington, to send to Congress. And you think, "Oh my God, is this really how we measure impact? It's so trivial and silly!" But it's what you have to do.*[1]

In 1941, a group of activists in New York City – Herbert and Eleanor Agar, Dorothy Thompson, George Field, and Ulric Bell – united to form Freedom House at the behest of President Franklin D. Roosevelt. At the time, the United States had no formal involvement in World War II. Given that context, the hawkish activists sought to combat two things: the propaganda emanating from the Nazis' Braunes Haus in Munich and the isolationism of the American public. After the war, Freedom House shifted to supporting the post-war liberal international order and civil rights at home. The organization furthered its agenda through policy statements and research reports, which it financed through membership fees and special events.

By the turn of the twenty-first century, Freedom House was one of the most active, professional organizations in the democracy establishment. It describes itself "an independent watchdog organization that supports the expansion of freedom around the world. Freedom House supports democratic change, monitors freedom, and advocates democracy and human rights."[2] Its 120 staff members in more than one dozen global offices design and implement democracy-assistance projects that are largely funded by the United States government. Such programs support the rule of law, strengthen civil society organizations, and encourage women's political participation, among other things. Staff also advance Freedom House's mission through research, including through creating indices measuring aspects of democracy. The organization's domestic activities ceased long ago, and its international programs have also

[1] Interview 39, with a former director of an INGO, June 14, 2010.
[2] Freedom House (2012).

changed considerably over time. Why did Freedom House's mission and activities change? More broadly, how and why did the democracy establishment emerge?

In Chapter 2, I argued that the government funding structure for democracy assistance rewards organizations in the democracy establishment that pursue programs that have quantitative outcome measures (i.e., measurable programs) and that promote continued access to target countries (i.e., regime-compatible programs). Such programs help organizations obtain donor funding and gain access to target states, but they do not always serve the donor states that hope to effect democratic change abroad by funding programs. Organizations thus prefer to design programs that are relatively tame, but the extent to which they do so depends on donor governments' preferences and abilities to observe and control them.

Organizations in the democracy establishment are not, however, solely driven by material concerns. They are also committed to their principled missions. Interestingly, the way that people in the democracy establishment balance their ideals and self-interests varies over time. As democracy assistance developed as a profession, Chapter 5 showed that organizations in the democracy establishment have become more likely to pursue tame programs, even holding constant donors' preferences and observation abilities. Both professional norms and competition institutionalize tame programs – the former because they foster ideas about the appropriateness of tame programs and the latter because it fosters professionalism and a focus on monitoring and evaluation.

To supplement what scholars refer to as "data set observations" in Chapter 5, this chapter focuses on what are known as "causal process observations."[3] Specifically, it considers the evidence in support of several observable implications of my argument – namely, that competition and professional norms in organizations in the democracy establishment exist, have increased over time, and affect how organizations aid democracy abroad. If my argument is correct, organizations should care about promoting democracy, but they should also care about winning funding and gaining and maintaining access to target countries so that they survive. As the field of democracy assistance becomes more professional, I expect organizations in the democracy establishment to prioritize organizational survival or else to suffer negative consequences in terms of continued funding and access. Those changing preferences should lead organizations to pursue tamer programs (Hypotheses 4 and 5).

---

[3] Brady and Collier (2004).

The effects of professionalization in the democracy establishment were not inevitable. A comparative analysis by political scientist Michael Barnett of humanitarian organizations found, for example, that despite the emergence of a professional field of humanitarianism over time, not all organizations have changed to reflect resource competition. Organizations such as CARE and Médecins Sans Frontières, which have their own resources via individual, corporate, and private donations, adapted less than other agencies, such as the United Nations High Commissioner for Refugees, which rely heavily on government grants. Yet even organizations with similar resource profiles adapted differently due to their organizational cultures and identities.[4] In other words, both funding portfolios and institutional norms can play an important role in determining transnational NGOs' programmatic strategies. Such patterns are precisely what I expect to observe among organizations in the democracy establishment.

This chapter uses several forms of evidence to test the argument's assumptions and observable implications. First, it describes how governments interact with organizations in the democracy establishment, documenting the network structure of the democracy establishment using internet connections and the results from a survey of more than 1,000 practitioners. Second, process-tracing case studies show change in several influential American organizations in the democracy establishment. I compare three historically activist organizations, Freedom House, the Institute for Democracy in Eastern Europe, and the Open Society Foundations (OSF), which varied over time in terms of their resources and professionalism. Freedom House professionalized successfully and thrived; the Institute for Democracy in Eastern Europe did not and shriveled. OSF also professionalized, although its trajectory was shaped by its reliance on private, rather than public, funding (see Hypothesis 7).

Collectively, the evidence supports my account of evolution in the democracy establishment. It also shows that other factors besides professionalization matter. Specifically, the evidence in this chapter highlights the importance of the preferences of donors, which is consistent with Hypothesis 6. It also illustrates how changes in the democracy establishment are linked to the profound political changes brought about by the end of the Cold War. Still, the taming of democracy assistance cannot be fully understood without reference to the competitive and normative changes described in this chapter.

---

[4] Barnett (2009, 654–5).

## The democracy establishment as a network

Examining the networked structure of the democracy establishment can reveal valuable information. First, it should show which organizations are authorities in the network. Second, it should help us understand how practices diffuse across the democracy establishment by depicting the relationships between organizations. One can imagine a variety of networks among organizations in the democracy establishment – regional connections, ideological connections, random connections, center–periphery connections – or even few connections at all. Since my argument involves several testable assumptions and observable implications related to the interactions between governments and organizations in the democracy establishment – as well as the interactions among organizations in the democracy establishment – this examination is important.

Chapter 2 argued that influential norms develop and get transmitted in large part due to the incentives created by the government funding process for democracy assistance. Accordingly, we might expect the network structure of the democracy establishment to involve many connections between donors and organizations and fewer connections among organizations. To assess whether that is the case, we can examine hyperlinks between the websites of organizations in the democracy establishment.[5] Organizations link to each other in the World Wide Web in order to establish and publicize their connections, whether with funders, grantees, or partners. Connections may be aspirational, but research shows that they do tend to reflect real social relationships.[6] Thus, we can identify central actors in networks by seeing which organizations other organizations link to.

To analyze internet connections in the democracy establishment, I fed the web addresses of 150 donors and organizations into the Issue Crawler, a tool that permits the analysis of online networks. Though not comprehensive, that set of donors and organizations represented all donor organizations and all organizations working in democracy assistance in at least three countries. Appendix C contains more information on how I culled the names of organizations from key scholarly sources on democracy assistance. Figure 6.1 presents the results. One limitation of this method of analysis is that it privileges the democracy establishment

---

[5] The Issue Crawler is an online tool that collects links between web pages given by a researcher and graphically represents the resulting connections. I used the "Inter-Actor Analysis" mode, with the maximum number of pages crawled set at 60,000. It is available at https://www.issuecrawler.net/. See also Carpenter (2007, 2011) for other uses.

[6] Carpenter and Jose (2012).

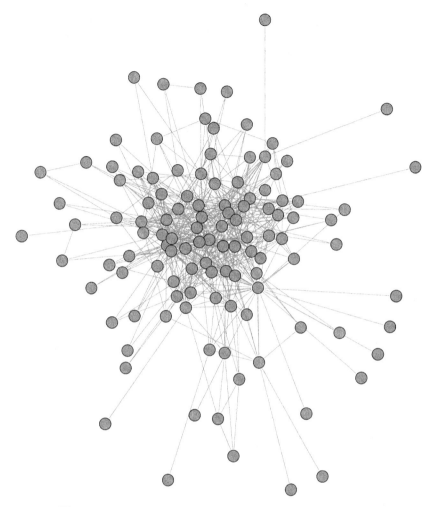

Figure 6.1 Network connections in democracy assistance.
*Note:* This figure was created using websites from 150 major donors and other organizations. The co-link analysis was conducted using the Issue Crawler.

of the twenty-first century over previous iterations, since it relies on websites that were current at the time of the analysis (2012).

Figure 6.1 reveals at least three important features of the democracy establishment's network structure. First, the democracy establishment is a variant of what social network analysts call a scale-free network or hub-and-spoke system. International relations scholars David Lake and Wendy Wong define scale-free networks as having "a small number of nodes that are connected to a large number of other nodes that are not themselves highly connected."[7] They contrast that type of network with random networks in which the nodes are randomly connected with about the same number of other nodes, and with small world networks, in which nodes are connected to neighboring nodes. In a scale-free network, the central nodes wield social and often material power, since they can directly and indirectly structure activity in the network.[8]

Second, the democracy establishment's center consists of not one or two but a few dozen organizations that are tightly connected with other "hubs" in addition to a number of "spokes." Since the center of the network is illegible in Figure 6.1, Table 6.1 lists the number of connections among just the twenty most linked-to actors in the work. All of those actors received at least twenty links from other actors in the network. It confirms that the inner core of the democracy establishment mostly consists of donor governments, multilateral organizations, and large Western NGOs, such as Freedom House and the National Democratic Institute, which themselves act as donors.

It is worth noting that many organizations do not even make it into the periphery of the internet network. Figure 6.1 included nodes for 68 percent of organizations in the democracy establishment because those organizations received at least one link from another organization in the network. In other words, the democracy establishment consists of perhaps twenty core organizations, an additional seventy or eighty peripheral organizations, and many other organizations that compete for funding but that are not truly members of the network. Although there are many organizations that would like to be implementers of government grants and contracts, that finite number of core and peripheral organizations shows that there are limits to how many are able to be major players in the field. It thus substantiates part of my argument, which is that donors may be constrained by the organizations available to them as agents.

Donor–recipient and center–periphery relationships characterize many other transnational networks.[9] But we can imagine alternative network structures within democracy assistance. Core organizations could have sought to increase their bargaining power in the network: for example, creating stables of their own NGOs that they controlled.

---

[7] Lake and Wong (2009). See also Barabasi (2003, 129) for a more general treatment.
[8] Hafner-Burton, Kahler, and Montgomery (2009); Lake and Wong (2009, 132).
[9] Lake and Wong (2009); Stein (2009).

Table 6.1 *The most socially powerful organizations in democracy assistance.*

| Organization | Number of co-links |
| --- | --- |
| 1. USAID | 878 |
| 2. European Commission | 549 |
| 3. NED | 489 |
| 4. Pan American Development Foundation (OAS) | 316 |
| 5. Freedom House | 233 |
| 6. US State Department | 225 |
| 7. EU | 189 |
| 8. Committee to Protect Journalists | 178 |
| 9. UN | 170 |
| 10. OECD | 114 |
| 11. Transparency International | 75 |
| 12. OAS | 56 |
| 13. OSCE | 54 |
| 14. OSF | 53 |
| 14. World Bank | 53 |
| 16. US Institute of Peace | 40 |
| 17. Council of Europe | 34 |
| 18. NDI | 32 |
| 19. International IDEA | 22 |
| 20. UK Department for International Development | 20 |

Such a structure recalls the early days of the NED, which gave most of its initial grants to four core institutes (NDI, IRI, CIPE, and the Solidarity Center). Yet most of today's democracy-assistance NGOs are funded by multiple centrally positioned donors. The NED's core institutes seek grants from other sources. Donor governments may prefer to fund NGOs that other donors have also worked with because doing so enhances the credibility of the enterprise.

Finally, material and social power overlap, but not entirely, in the democracy establishment. The most-linked-to organizations in Table 6.1 are USAID and the European Commission, which are the two largest democracy donors in dollar terms. But the third most linked-to organization is the NED, a comparatively modest donor. The NED's many connections to other nodes in cyber space indicate that it is socially powerful.[10] The NED's social power may derive from its early entrance into the field of democracy assistance in 1985 as well as its relatively narrow mission, which focuses exclusively on democracy promotion rather than on a variety of forms of foreign aid. The NED's social power

---

[10] Kahler (2009, 19).

online is consistent with its role in the real world as a model for other democracy-assistance organizations, such as the European Endowment of Democracy (created in 2013), the Taiwan Foundation for Democracy (created in 2003), and the Westminster Foundation for Democracy in the United Kingdom (created in 1992).

The democracy establishment's network structure should affect the organizations within it. Since the democracy establishment is a scale-free network, I hypothesize that convergence within the network is most likely to have occurred through the peripheral organizations' interactions with the core organizations. Yet because the core organizations are tightly connected to each other, we can expect practices and professional norms to quickly diffuse across donor-government agencies and large NGOs and then out to their grantees.

### The network in practitioners' eyes

Another way to understand the democracy establishment as a network is by analyzing data from a survey of 1,473 high-level practitioners involved in democracy assistance.[11] This unique survey was conducted by Joel Barkan on behalf of the NED's World Movement for Democracy between November 2009 and August 2010. Fourteen donor agencies from a variety of countries cooperated in the project by contacting the leaders of the organizations to which they had given money since January 2008. Although the survey did not involve a random sample of practitioners, it did create a fairly representative sample, with respondents working in 116 countries, including countries in all regions of the world and at all levels of freedom.

The survey reveals a number of interesting characteristics about the democracy establishment. As the previous section's findings might imply, the surveyed organizations were highly dependent on donor funding for their survival. On average, 63 percent of the organizations' budgets were reported as coming from international funding. Most organizations had received funding from at least two foreign donors, with one respondent having reported receiving funding from as many

---

[11] The author acknowledges the assistance of Joel D. Barkan for access to the data set derived from the surveys he conducted of recipients of democratic assistance for the World Movement for Democracy in 2009 and 2010. Responsibility for the analysis of the data presented in this publication lies solely with the author. Her views and analysis do not represent any official or unofficial position taken by Joel D. Barkan, the National Endowment for Democracy, or the World Movement for Democracy. Barkan's published report for the World Movement for Democracy, *Perceptions of Democracy Assistance* (May, 2011) can be accessed at www.wmd.org/documents/perceptions-final-report.pdf. See also Barkan (2012).

as twenty donors. Beyond the NED, which funded 41 percent of the surveyed organizations, USAID (26 percent), the UN (20 percent), and the EU (18 percent) were the largest funders.

Many, but not all, of the high-level staff members could be considered professionals on the basis of their educational and work histories. Most staff members (67 percent) had completed some graduate or postgraduate training or had obtained a graduate or postgraduate degree. An additional 25 percent had graduated from college. Since most of the people surveyed reside in low-income or lower-middle-income countries according to the World Bank's categories, those education levels are notably high.[12] In addition, 64 percent of the staff members surveyed had worked for other organizations that promote democracy during their careers. Of those people, the average person had worked for three other organizations over twelve years. The average length of time that staff members had spent with their current organizations was eight years.

The professionals that were surveyed had markedly different attitudes about democracy assistance to non-professionals. One question asked the respondents to name the "two aspects of democracy assistance [they] liked best." As Table 6.2 shows, the responses of professionals and non-professionals differed on a number of dimensions. For example, almost 20 percent more professionals than non-professionals valued financial assistance. Part of my argument about the professionalization of democracy assistance is that professionals should prioritize organizational survival, and thus tamer forms of democracy assistance, more than non-professionals. Although I argue that professionals value certain types of tame programs as ends in and of themselves due to their training and experiences, I also expect them to value tame programs because they care more about the preservation of their jobs and thus the survival of their organizations. As such, it makes sense that professionals would prioritize the financial aspects of democracy assistance over some of its other purported benefits, such as ties to like-minded organizations. Interestingly, relatively few staff members (of either the professional or non-professional varieties) prioritized other types of democracy promotion, such as donors' statements of political support and the often-vaunted international network ties to other organizations involved in democracy aid.

But how did professionalism come to pass in the democracy establishment? What are the tangible consequences of it in terms of organizational structure and programs? The next section turns to those questions.

---

[12] The median GDP per capita in 2008 US dollars was $1,786.

Table 6.2 *Perceptions of the main benefits of democracy assistance.*

| Main benefit | Professionals | Non-professionals |
| --- | --- | --- |
| Financial assistance*** | 74% | 56% |
| Technical assistance | 28% | 26% |
| Capacity building*** | 15% | 10% |
| Political support** | 12% | 8% |
| Overseas examples*** | 19% | 13% |
| Network ties*** | 25% | 17% |

*Notes:* Professionals worked at other democracy-promotion organizations and had graduate training. ** denotes $p < 0.05$ and *** denotes $p < 0.01$ associated with a $\chi^2$ test of independence or analysis of variance.
*Data source:* Barkan (2012).

## The evolution of aiding democracy

In this section, I focus on the history of three organizations that have aided democracy abroad: Freedom House; the Institute for Democracy in Eastern Europe (IDEE); and the Open Society Foundations (OSF; known as the Open Society Institute, or OSI, until 2011).[13] Why choose those cases? Freedom House, the main case study in this chapter represents a typical case in terms of the causal relationships that I am interested in. Several texts on case selection argue that such a case, which typically has low residuals, is useful for confirmatory analysis.[14] Specifically, it can probe causal mechanisms and ensure that quantitative findings are not spurious.

As discussed in the introduction to this chapter, Freedom House has undergone a remarkable transformation. In its earliest days as an activist organization, it focused largely on domestic issues, but as time passed, it shifted toward an international focus as a consequence of ideological shifts and new funding opportunities. By the mid 1990s, Freedom House started to become a much more professional organization, and with that change designed its programs differently. The book's transnational argument about democracy assistance implies that the organization's transformation should have had its roots at least partially in the rise of funding competition and professional norms.

The Institute for Democracy in Eastern Europe and the Open Society offer more cursory, and yet still important, cases. Like Freedom House,

[13] Note that for ease of exposition, I refer to the Soros Foundations throughout their history as the OSF.
[14] Lieberman (2005, 444); Seawright and Gerring (2008, 299–300).

both organizations are based in the United States and started promoting democracy abroad in the 1980s using fairly activist approaches and untame programs. Unlike Freedom House, however, the other organizations have not professionalized to such a degree, and so I hypothesize that their programs should not have been tamed as much (Hypotheses 4 and 5). Moreover, while the OSF remain key players in democracy assistance, as evidenced by Table 6.1, IDEE has come to occupy a less prominent role in the democracy establishment. Why did IDEE and OSF follow different trajectories as organizations than Freedom House? I argue that their different trajectories can be explained, at least in part, by their different exposures to funding competition and professional norms.

### The transformation of Freedom House

Freedom House is arguably the oldest American human rights organization.[15] Furthermore, as Table 6.1 demonstrated, it is a socially influential actor in the democracy establishment. Yet Freedom House has not always promoted democracy, at least not in the sense in which we use the phrase today. Indeed, from its founding in 1941 to the present day, Freedom House has undergone a remarkable transformation – expanding its size, shifting from domestic to international issues, moving its locus of operations from New York City to Washington, DC, opening more than one dozen overseas offices, and evolving from an activist to a professional orientation. That evolution is consistent, I argue, with the book's transnational argument and, in particular, with its claims about the importance of competition and professional norms.

In the next section, I examine several additional organizations in short case studies using interview data, organizational documents, and secondary sources. This section uses such material, too, but it also draws on extensive archival material because Freedom House houses its administrative records at Princeton University. The archive contains, among other things, minutes and supplementary materials from all meetings of the boards of trustees, policy statements, the personal papers of executive directors, financial records, and extensive documentation of Freedom House's programs, press releases, and press clippings.

Beyond the availability of those records, one other valuable aspect of studying Freedom House is that it is an organization in which the effects of professionalization may be underestimated. Like the NED, Freedom House is often portrayed as a direct agent of the US government and as a

---

[15] Korey (1998, 443).

highly ideological and political organization.[16] For that reason, we might expect it to be relatively impervious to the sorts of professionalizing pressures that could more easily shape other NGOs with different organizational cultures.

*Activist origins (1941–1993)* At the request of President Franklin D. Roosevelt, a group of Americans established Freedom House in 1941 to support the United States' involvement in World War II. The resulting membership organization was based in New York City and was led for years by a single person – founding executive director George Field – and his assistant. After World War II, the organization supported the emerging liberal international order and civil rights in the United States.[17]

Gradually, the organization transitioned to international issues. One of its major early initiatives occurred in 1982, when Freedom House monitored elections in Cambodia. As was typical of the organization's decision-making at the time, the board carefully debated the decision to monitor elections. At a board meeting, the labor leader Norman Hill noted "that there had been questions raised about the urgency with which the mission was undertaken, and the financing secured to mount it. He recommended that some sub-group of the Board be mandated to examine future situations."[18] That the activist-heavy board of trustees was involved in the daily running of Freedom House, rather than staff members with technical expertise, illustrates the organization's non-professional orientation in the early 1980s. The board's wide-ranging discussions even included philosophical debates on questions such as "What is Freedom?" – in contrast to the financial and governance issues that would later dominate meetings.[19]

The organization's survival started to preoccupy the organization in the 1980s. Its New York building was expensive to maintain, and when Freedom House sold the property in 1985, its former tenants sued. To cope, Freedom House pursued new democracy grants from the US government. Notably, the board was heavily involved in the application processes. Later, staff would compose and submit funding proposals without board approval since they had the requisite expertise to

---

[16] Giannone (2010).

[17] Korey (1998, 444–6).

[18] Meeting Minutes, Board of Trustees, taken by John W. Riehm, p. 3, April 19, 1982; Freedom House Records, Box 1, Folder 13; Public Policy Papers, Department of Rare Books and Special Collections, Princeton University. Hereafter referred to as "Freedom House Records."

[19] Freedom House Records, Box 21, various folders.

successfully navigate the aid bureaucracy. But in 1984, the board reviewed nine potential proposals to the NED. No programs or strategies were taken for granted as appropriate at the time. From the start, the board wanted to identify proposals that were "designed to produce visible results," rejecting one – "Can New Communications Technologies Be Placed in the Service of Democracies?" – because "no short-term results can be expected."[20] Visible results are a way of signaling success to funders and, as such, that comment is consistent with my argument that NGOs pursue measurable projects as a strategy for securing government funding. Indeed, survival via securing government money was the organization's growing focus at the time. Given its grave financial situation, executive director Adrian Karatnycky would later reflect that Freedom House "could not have weathered the transition period without [government] contracts."[21]

Yet despite its early interest in results, most of Freedom House's first NED (and other) grants fell into categories that were not associated with quantitative outcomes and directly confronted dictators. In other words, the programs were not tame. Consider a typical NED grant to Freedom House supporting dissidents in Yugoslavia: "To enable the Committee to Aid Democratic Dissidents in Yugoslavia to continue publishing its Bulletin. Distributed in Yugoslavia and the West, the Bulletin publicizes activities of and repressions against independent intellectuals and dissidents."[22] Twenty-six out of thirty-four of Freedom House's 1980s NED grants aided dissidents. Recall that the NED's calls for proposals do not have any requirements in terms of programs' content, suggesting that organizations had considerable discretion in terms of their activities. My argument predicted those outcomes due to the relatively low competition and professionalism in the democracy establishment at the time.

In the absence of strong professional norms or competitive pressures, ideological concerns were major motivators for strategic decisions in the organization. Based on my reading of the archival record, the last major internal debate about the organization's direction and the meaning of advancing freedom came in 1991. It occurred during a board meeting at the end of the Cold War, as the organization was celebrating its fiftieth anniversary. The timing highlights the importance of shifts in international politics, which were also significant in the quantitative analysis.

[20] Meeting Minutes, Board of Trustees, p. 1, May 2, 1984; Freedom House Records, Box 1, Folder 15.
[21] Meeting Minutes, Board of Trustees, New York, Notes by Angier Biddle Duke, p. 6, September 20, 1994; Freedom House Records, Box 180.
[22] National Endowment for Democracy (1988, 25).

During the meeting, longtime board member and former ambassador Max Kampelman "spoke on his view that Freedom House should concern itself much more strongly with American domestic issues." Yet the board decided to pursue foreign issues for both ideological and practical reasons. On the one hand, Gerald Steibel said that foreign issues "presented clear good-vs.-evil lines."[23] On the other hand, Jeane Kirkpatrick, a member of President Ronald Reagan's National Security Council, emphasized the pragmatic benefits for the organization that could come from specializing in overseas programs. She stated that she felt "strongly that Freedom House can do useful work in foreign affairs, [and] should leave domestic [*sic*] to others."[24] And so it did.

*An increasingly professional organization (1993–present)* A key turning point in terms of the professionalization of Freedom House came in 1993. Some of the changes related to the organization's governance. Former executive director Leonard Sussman wrote, for example, "Freedom House's new era began in 1993 with the election of Bette Bao Lord as chair of the Board of Trustees." A novelist and human rights activist in China, Lord oversaw Freedom House's transition during the mid 1990s when it started to become a fully professional organization.[25]

During this time, Freedom House became more bureaucratic, which is a hallmark of professionalization. The staff no longer relied on the board for programmatic advice. Freedom House expanded its reports quantifying democracy from its flagship *Freedom in the World* reports to new areas, which today include press freedom, internet freedom, women's rights in the Middle East, governance, and reform in the former Soviet bloc. The indices helped the organization assess its programs and establish credibility in the eyes of US government officials. In addition to the expansion of those ranking systems, Freedom House also made some subtle revisions to the criteria of the *Freedom in the World* reports. The organization, which has long viewed these rankings as measures of democracy, started to include assessments of the degree of corruption, rule of law, and transparency in government after 2002.[26] Those changes were consistent with the broader reconceptualization of democracy to include good governance that I discussed in Chapter 5.

[23] Special Meeting of the Executive Committee Plus Other Board Members, Washington, DC, notes taken by Gerald L. Steibel, p. 1, August 3, 1991; Freedom House Records, Box 148.
[24] Summary of Board Responses to Freedom House Statement on the 50th Anniversary of Freedom House and on the Future; Freedom House Records, Box 148.
[25] Sussman (2009).
[26] Giannone (2010, 76, 87, 89).

By the mid 1990s, it was important for Freedom House to compete against other organizations in the field that were also professionalizing and developing technical skills. Around that time, the National Democratic Institute, for example, was emerging as a pioneer in election-monitoring, despite the initial reticence of the organization's president, Brian Atwood. According to one former NDI staff member, "election-monitoring basically made NDI. NDI thought you could have people that are technically qualified – who can do more than the media or the government – who can do election observation and make the field much more professional."[27] It is worth noting that NDI eventually found a place in Table 6.1 as one of the most socially powerful organizations in the democracy establishment, whereas IRI did not – even though both organizations started out with similar visions and funding sources. NDI distinguished itself in part through its pioneering election-monitoring programs. Freedom House needed to keep up.

The background of Freedom House's staff soon reflected its transformation. Jennifer Windsor, the former head of USAID's Center for Democracy and Governance and a graduate of Princeton University's Woodrow Wilson School, became the executive director in 2001. Her successor, David Kramer, also served in government as the Assistant Secretary of State for Democracy, Human Rights, and Labor (DRL). Their backgrounds contrast with the activist orientations of their predecessors; Leonard Sussman, for example, led the organization for twenty-one years and previously worked in journalism and for the American Council for Judaism.

As Freedom House's professionalism increased, so too did its concerns about survival. Increased funding competition fostered that survivalist focus. At the time, staff and board members debated how to position Freedom House vis-à-vis USAID, NED, and the State Department in the search for grants and sought to develop administrative systems to enhance the organization's standing.[28] Other NGOs, such as the German Marshall Fund, were also encroaching on Freedom House's analytical and grant-making turf. Although it is important to note that more government agencies were now funding democracy aid, Freedom House's NED grants dropped from thirty-four in the 1980s to thirty-one in the 1990s to only thirteen in the 2000s. Over that time period, the programs aiding dissidents that were so common in the 1980s were

---

[27] Interview 47, with a director of a democracy-assistance NGO, in person, Washington, DC, April 30, 2010.
[28] Meeting of the Board of Trustees, Freedom House, Washington, DC, notes taken by Gerald L. Steibel, p. 3, January 14, 1991; Freedom House Records, Box 148.

replaced at Freedom House, as was the case elsewhere in the democracy establishment. None of Freedom House's NED grants between 2000 and 2009 aided dissidents. Such trends are striking, since Freedom House justifiably has a reputation as a major democracy-assistance organization that is relatively likely to directly challenge overseas regimes.

In response to the growing competition, Freedom House sought to establish more of an overseas presence. In 1994, Freedom House opened its first overseas office in Kiev. It subsequently opened offices in Russia, Serbia, Nigeria, Jordan, Tunisia, Mexico, Southern Africa, and Central Asia. In 1997, Freedom House increased its overseas capabilities by merging with the National Forum Foundation, an organization that relied even more on US government democracy grants than Freedom House. One former Freedom House country director described the organization as trying to "muscle in" on other organizations' territory via this strategy, becoming more of a "Beltway bandit" than an activist NGO. Practitioners note that when American NGOs such as Freedom House maintain overseas offices, that they are forced to pursue less confrontational activities because of heightened access concerns.[29] In other words, this shift toward overseas offices was a significant moment for Freedom House's programmatic activities.

As expected, Freedom House's reactions to competition were not confined to changes in its programs, although such changes are my main focus in this book. In one bold move, Freedom House sought unsuccessfully to take over the NED's World Movement for Democracy, because its leaders thought doing so would help them organizationally. In another instance, Freedom House staff opened an office in an East European city at their own cost "to make themselves more competitive for future USAID contracts."[30] The organization's forward thinking included involving high-profile political leaders on its board, which helped the organization lobby for its interests in Washington. Freedom House's connections served as a bulwark against funding cuts.

Diversifying Freedom House's funding was also a strategy considered. By 2002, at least 80 percent of the organization's revenues came from US government grants, whereas just five years earlier that proportion had been 70 percent. The organization's concentrated funding sources encouraged it to highly value new opportunities. At a 2003 board meeting, for example, diplomat Mark Palmer objected to Freedom House funding some of its programs with money from tobacco companies.

[29] Haring (2013).
[30] Author's interview with a former Freedom House staff member, by telephone, October 18, 2012.

But according to the meeting minutes, "Other Board Members noted that many companies could be ruled out in a similar fashion, and that by doing so Freedom House [would] eliminat[e] potential sources of support."[31] After all, in the hunt for funding, compromises must be made.

Of course, principles continued to affect Freedom House's programs. Although the organization benefited from new funding opportunities after September 11, 2001, staff avoided working in the controversial main targets of democracy aid: Afghanistan and Iraq. Yet their principled decisions were tempered by what maintaining funding and access required. The organization issued a statement in March 2003 in support of the Iraq War that stated, "The building of a democratic Iraq will require a serious long-term commitment of time and resources. Freedom House will do its part to press our government and other governments to make a serious commitment to this effort."[32] As Chapter 7 discusses in more detail, my interviews with staff in Jordan, where Freedom House maintained a Middle East regional office, suggest that relatively tame women's political participation programs dominated the organization's efforts in the wake of the Iraq War, since such activities were popular with US government donors and local governments alike. An example of such a program is the Freedom House-supported documentary, *A Badia Worthy of its Women*, about Bedouin women in rural parts of the country.

Such calculations were not unique to the Middle East. In an interview, a staff member bluntly discussed the challenges of working in closed regimes: "One of our problems is that the Russian government is sure as hell not going to invite us to come in."[33] But because Russia is "central for democracy in the region and even in the world," it was considered important for a leading democracy-promotion NGO to have some presence there in terms of maintaining its reputation. Freedom House thus opted to support some relatively anodyne legal aid programs in Russia in the 2000s.

It is also worth noting the alternative explanations of the taming of democracy assistance that the evolution of Freedom House does not support. Little high-level energy at board meetings was devoted to discussing best practices or effective programs, for example, which suggests that epistemic changes were not key to the organization's transformation.

[31] Summary of Freedom House Board of Trustees Meeting, New York City, p. 3, October 21, 2003; Freedom House Records, Box 181.
[32] Freedom House (2003).
[33] Author's interview with a Freedom House staff member, by telephone, June 22, 2010.

Additionally, the organization's internal documents include few discussions about which overseas NGOs to fund or how to monitor them, even though Freedom House's grants were often "passed through" to other organizations. That omission highlights the information problems in democracy aid emphasized in my argument.

In sum, this case study of Freedom House showed how the NGO changed its programs as it tried to survive and thrive as an organization. That evolution caused some tension and internal debate, but eventually became taken for granted. Professional leaders worried more than activist leaders about getting grants and improving the organization and less about ideology or the organization's mission. Pursuing more measurable and regime-compatible programs was the strategy those professional leaders used to promote survival.

### Institute for Democracy in Eastern Europe (IDEE)

The Institute for Democracy in Eastern Europe was created in 1985 to support dissidents seeking to bring down communist regimes in Eastern Europe. The organization grew out of the Committee in Support of Solidarity, another American NGO. That organization, which sought to aid the anti-Soviet Polish trade union Solidarity (Solidarność), was founded in 1981, in response to General Wojciech Jaruzelski's declaration of martial law. IDEE's founding president and later co-director, Irena Lasota, was a Polish political activist; its founding director and later co-director, Eric Chenoweth, was an American labor activist.

IDEE's initial activities concentrated on supporting Solidarity in communist Poland. With some of the NED's early direct grants as well as NED funding passed through from the Free Trade Union Institute (an offshoot of the AFL–CIO), IDEE supported local trade union structures, published materials for Solidarity, and aided the intellectual and cultural aspects of Solidarity's movement.[34] Indeed, IDEE's confrontational programs were anything but tame and its organization was far from professional. Like its predecessor, IDEE sprang in large part from young labor activists' passion for helping a like-minded social movement overseas.

It is worth noting that, as is the case with other democracy-assistance programs, IDEE's early efforts sometimes worked at cross-purposes to official American government policy at the time. When, for example, Fighting Solidarity (Solidarność Walcząca), a radical group opposed to

---

[34] Interview 30, with a democracy-assistance practitioner, in person, Washington, DC, September 16, 2009.

continued Soviet rule, split off from the Solidarity movement, NED and IDEE supported it even though doing so explicitly contradicted the State Department's policy of working with moderate unions in Poland.[35] The democracy promoters justified their decisions with the logic that empowering more extreme groups would encourage the Polish government to compromise with Solidarity.

IDEE's work with Solidarity in Poland gradually won it notice from dissidents throughout Eastern and Central Europe. After all, the Polish transition was an inspirational case for activists worldwide. Lech Wałęsa, Solidarity's founder, had won the 1983 Nobel Peace Prize and helped broker the Polish Round Table Talks in April 1989 that led to partly free parliamentary elections later that year. Buoyed by its association with that success, IDEE started to conduct similar work with dissidents in Hungary and Czechoslovakia, not only providing organizational and intellectual support but now also giving dissidents concrete assistance, equipment, and money. IDEE, for example, delivered a fax machine to civil society activists in Czechoslovakia that they used to organize and publicize their work, which eventually contributed to the Velvet Revolution in 1989.

Various funders supported IDEE's expanding programs and growing reach. Grants came not only from the NED but also from USAID, the State Department, Freedom House, the German Marshall Fund, and the United States Institute for Peace, among other funders.[36] Despite its name, the Institute for Democracy in Eastern Europe also expanded geographically, eventually reaching twenty-nine countries, including Cuba and various countries in Central Europe and Asia. Although the democratization of Eastern Europe was therefore a change that undoubtedly affected IDEE, it did not spell the organization's immediate death. The organization widened its mission and pursued funding opportunities accordingly.

Notably, IDEE did not abandon its confrontational, untame approach in the 1990s, even as the broader field was changing. From 1988 until 1998 it published a journal, *Uncaptive Minds*, that contained political analysis. With NED funding, IDEE created the Centers for Pluralism in 1992 to create a network of dissidents across countries and to coordinate its election-monitoring efforts. Few of its programs at the time beyond those electoral programs were associated with quantitative outcome measures. Although IDEE's good reputation from its work with Solidarity and other dissidents opposing communist rule gave it some

---

[35] Thiel (2010, 210).
[36] Institute for Democracy in Eastern Europe (2001).

renown, the success of its programs was hard to ascertain short of further democratic breakthroughs.

Perhaps unsurprisingly, IDEE gradually became less effective at winning grants from the United States government, its primary funder. IDEE's last NED grants came in 2002, prompting the organization to abandon its flagship Centers for Pluralism initiative. According to one insider, IDEE's program struggled to win funding because the NED viewed it as competing with its own World Movement for Democracy. Although other factors, such as the organization's leadership, surely affected its changing prospects, too, growing competition from other, more professional organizations appears to have made it harder for IDEE to get funding.

The organization's leaders, steeped in the activist tradition, did not abandon their unique approach to democracy assistance in the face of such problems. Indeed, they seemed to balk at the corporatization of democracy assistance. Irena Lasota praised the old model of internationally-supported elections in Georgia, for example, for being effective in terms of democratization as well as in terms of cost. Referring to Georgia, where her organization had been working since 1989, she wrote, "I would estimate that the cost per registered voter remained roughly $0.10 at the most (as compared with $11.34 in South Africa in 1994). In the Republic of Georgia, the elections of October 1989 were free and pluralistic and attracted a turnout of over 70 percent, despite Soviet laws, Soviet pressure, and a lack of money, both local and foreign."[37]

In keeping with Lasota's praise for "old school" democracy programs, the Institute for Democracy in Eastern Europe has continued to pursue its model of support to dissidents overseas. In fact, on the organization's website, IDEE's programs and activities between 2010 and 2012 were described as focusing on a "handful of 'hard case' countries – Belarus, Cuba, and Georgia."[38] But although IDEE's programs supporting dissidents, elections, and civil society over that time period were funded by the US State Department's DRL Bureau, the organization's website indicated that it had eventually lost that funding, too. Many of its long-standing programs were being discontinued. That is an important development for the purposes of testing my theory, since Chapter 5 showed trends in programs rather than providing direct evidence of the death of organizations.

---

[37] Lasota (1999, 126).
[38] Institute for Democracy in Eastern Europe (2012).

Notably, IDEE continued to run its programs without opening potentially lucrative field offices, as many other American NGOs, such as Freedom House and NDI, did. It is worth underscoring that Freedom House and NDI never originally intended to open such offices. Much like IDEE, the original conception of NDI, as described in the minutes of an early board meeting, did not include any overseas work. Instead, the organization sought to conduct exchanges, bringing democrats from overseas to the United States on educational trips.[39] In contrast, as of 2005, NDI had field offices in more than sixty countries, which contain a staff of more than a thousand people, and over the course of its history NDI has operated in approximately 125 countries.[40]

In contrast, IDEE struggled to find other funders to fill the gap left by dwindling US government grants. The organization's lack of adaptation to changing professional norms and growing competition intensified its problems obtaining funding. People affiliated with IDEE pinpointed the organization's problems as being caused by changes in the democracy-assistance field that IDEE had resisted. One interviewee said, for example, "Democracy assistance became very institutionalized, and then hand-in-hand with that, IDEE became *persona non grata*."[41]

Of course, the decline of the Institute for Democracy in Eastern Europe as a leading organization in the democracy establishment had multiple sources. One was that its brand of programming may be less relevant in today's world, although the organization's continued desire to run programs in countries such as Belarus, Cuba, and Georgia belies that hunch. Another explanation of its struggles to attract and retain American government funding was that its approach may have been deemed to be a failure. It is certainly the case that it is difficult to assess the causal impact of IDEE's programs, and attempting to do so is beyond the scope of this book. Yet, as discussed earlier, evidence about democracy-assistance programs' effects is not readily available – and IDEE's programs were deemed at least sufficiently successful that the organization was able to expand its programs well beyond its initial regional expertise with US government and private foundation support. Thus, new ideas about what type of programs were appropriate – alongside growing competition from other NGOs more focused on how to play the funding game – accounted for at least some of the organization's decline. Greater adaptation of the sort that Freedom

[39] National Democratic Institute (2010, 7).
[40] Melia (2005, 5).
[41] Interview 30, with a democracy-assistance practitioner, in person, Washington, DC, September 16, 2009.

House engaged in may have helped the organization survive, although doing so may have involved surrendering some of its unique vision.

### Open Society Foundations

The Open Society Foundations are the creation of financier George Soros. Soros was born in Budapest, Hungary in 1930. After his Jewish family survived Nazi Germany's occupation of Hungary during World War II, Soros moved to Great Britain, where he studied at the London School of Economics. There he read the writings of philosopher Karl Popper, which would influence Soros's subsequent investment strategies as well as his political ideals.[42] After completing his degree, George Soros moved to New York, where he began a career as one of the twentieth century's most successful investors. According to one biography, "He managed his funds in a style later characteristic of his human rights efforts: he was directly involved in their operations; he took large risks, based, however, on his own careful analysis of situations; and he acted boldly and quickly to invest for gain and to retreat to cut losses."[43]

Drawing on his personal fortune, Soros began promoting human rights and democracy abroad in a concentrated way, first in 1979 in South Africa via the University of Cape Town, in 1984 with the Hungarian Academy of Sciences (or George Soros Foundation) in Budapest, and then in 1986 with the Fund for the Reform and Opening of China in Beijing. Soros's early efforts directly confronted the world's dictators, distributing copying machines to Hungarian dissidents and sponsoring various activities in China that were so threatening to the communist regime that the government's secret police infiltrated the Soros Foundation's office there. Throughout the 1980s, Soros continued to support dissidents overseas, including in Russia, the Philippines, South Africa, Guatemala, and Chile. At the time, the foundation was run out of Soros's home by his wife, Susan.[44] Although it would be wrong to label such efforts as "grassroots," they were hardly professional in the sense of resulting from specialized training or expertise.

In 1993, contemplating political openings in Central and Eastern Europe, Soros united the various groups and institutions that he had funded in more than thirty-four countries under the umbrella of the Open Society Foundations. The OSF were directed by former Human Rights Watch executive director Aryeh Neier and headquartered in New

---

[42] For a more in-depth discussion of Soros's intellectual roots, see Guilhot (2007, 458–64).
[43] Krisch (2009).
[44] Soros (1995, 117).

York and Budapest. Neier stepped down in 2012 and was replaced by Chris Stone, an expert on non-profit organizations from Harvard University. The OSF's initial funding allocation was $300 million. The OSF model involved creating and then supporting overseas Soros foundations, run by local boards, in addition to funding overseas projects directly from New York. The organization's mission, as described on its website, was laid out as follows: "The Open Society Foundations work to build vibrant and tolerant democracies whose governments are accountable to their citizens."[45] Soros's foundations spent more than $8 billion over their first thirty years, of which around $3 billion went to support democratic development and human rights abroad, making the OSF a larger democracy donor than many of the state governments discussed in Chapter 4.[46]

The organization initially placed less value on the emerging professional expertise of the democracy establishment than did Freedom House and many other organizations. Even in the twenty-first century, staff members working at the OSF headquarters were more often chosen for regional expertise (for example, a background in Russian culture and history) than substantive expertise (for example, knowledge about elections). In that way, the OSF's staff were similar to most of the people hired in other organizations in the democracy establishment in the 1980s and early 1990s. Staff members at local foundations, who were often intellectuals and former dissidents, were also removed from the mainstream of the democracy establishment.

As my argument would predict given that lack of professionalism, the OSF have been unique in their relative disdain for measurable programs. That preference also related to Soros's general lack of patience with bureaucracy. For both reasons, the OSF held their aid recipients accountable through mechanisms such as rewarding low overheads and not examining measurable outcomes.[47] Once funded by the OSF, aid-recipient organizations rarely had to compete hard against other organizations for funding; they could apply to the OSF on a rolling basis for renewals that they usually won, so long as the advisory boards of their local foundations approved.[48] George Soros and Aryeh Neier were involved in specific programming decisions, exercising a high degree of executive oversight. A former staff member described how George Soros, on one of his many travels overseas, had met a Russian journalist

---

[45] Open Society Foundations (2012a).
[46] Open Society Foundations (2012b).
[47] Soros (1995, 126).
[48] Interview 12, with a former democracy-assistance practitioner, in person, Washington, DC, May 2, 2010.

who wanted to film a political documentary. The New York office consequently funded that project.[49] In such a case, a much shorter delegation chain implies greater ease of observation and control from the perspective of the donor.

Under the circumstances, it should perhaps come as no surprise that the OSF are regarded as one of the least tame democracy-assistance donors in the business. Without the severe problems of observation and control that plague many other donors, grant-makers at the OSF have less reason to reward measurable programs that are associated with quantitative outcomes but that do not necessarily lead to democratization. Moreover, they are more likely to punish regime-compatible programs that do not directly confront dictators. The less-entrenched professional norms at the organization only reinforce those trends. Of course, George Soros's distaste for bureaucracy and his bold politics have also shaped the organization's preferences and thus the untame programs that result.

Most evidence bears out the argument's predictions about the type of programs that the OSF ought to fund. The leading democracy-assistance expert Thomas Carothers, for example, has harshly criticized many programs, yet he has praised the Open Society Foundations' confrontational and unbureaucratic efforts, even going so far as to join the OSF board of directors in Budapest for a number of years starting in 1999.[50] Earlier, Carothers had compared American government efforts in post-revolution Romania with the Soros Foundation's and found them wanting. He observed that USAID's office had spent more than three times the amount of annual money spent by the Soros Foundation and yet had hired fewer than one-third of its employees. According to Carothers, "The much larger number of employees at Soros Romania reflects its much greater level of responsibility with regard to programming and its much lesser reliance on managerial and technical support from external Soros institutions. It is also related to Soros's much more labor-intensive assistance methods."[51] USAID's approach emphasized results; the OSF's emphasized process.[52] The consequence was a difference in programs. Whereas USAID's programs focused on good governance, legislative aid, and the rule of law, the OSF's programs focused more on civic education, civil society, and dissidents.

[49] Interview 12, with a former democracy-assistance practitioner, in person, Washington, DC, May 2, 2010.
[50] Carothers (1999, 273–4).
[51] Carothers (1996, 19).
[52] Carothers (1996, 20).

Perhaps unsurprisingly, critics and supporters alike have singled out the Soros Foundations as particularly important players in assisting dissidents during the Colored Revolutions.[53] In fact, amidst the protests that would eventually lead to his ouster, President Eduard Shevardnadze was quoted as fuming, "What does Soros want? I am declaring a categorical protest against the actions of Soros. Everyone should know their place."[54] Among the contributions that the OSF made to Georgia's Rose Revolution were sending local dissidents to Belgrade to meet with Otpor! (Resistance!), the successful youth resistance movement from Serbia, and sponsoring election programs that revealed that Shevardnadze had stolen the November 2, 2003, elections and thus mobilized protesters.[55] Such confrontational programs were distinctive and, according to some observers, effective. Comparing the OSF's efforts to USAID's, political scientists Valerie Bunce and Sharon Wolchik praised the Soros Foundation's civil society programs, writing, "The ability to move quickly [possessed by the OSF] was critical in the Georgian context, because getting rid of Shevardnadze was less about governance and capacity building, which was a major concern of USAID (and especially of the European Union), than about short-term politics."[56]

Yet the Open Society Foundations have not been immune from the broader forces that have affected organizations in the democracy establishment. As argued in Chapter 2, professionalization can result from greater competition among organizations, but it can also result from changes in education, non-profit management, and other society-wide changes. The latter forces – along with changing donor preferences – have been drivers of professionalization in the case of the OSF. The organization's reliance on donations from George Soros insulates it from some of the pressures to document quantitative results that affect governmental programs that rely on maintaining voters' goodwill. But Soros has become a more distracted donor, turning his attention to other issues and challenges, such as American domestic politics and the global financial crisis. As he has turned away from the OSF, Soros has also sought to professionalize the organization. That professionalization was foreshadowed by Soros in a 1995 interview, in which he said:

In the beginning, I wanted to have an anti-foundation foundation, and for a time I succeeded ... Yet to continue without becoming an institution would

---

[53] Beissinger (2007, 270).
[54] Chikhladze and Chikhladze (2005, 8).
[55] Mitchell (2009, 5).
[56] Bunce and Wolchik (2011, 162–3).

be very detrimental. To operate without bureaucracy would render us wasteful and capricious. I have come to realize that we require a solid organization, a bureaucracy if you will. I have become reconciled to the fact that we must switch from a sprint to long distance running.[57]

As Soros's comments indicate, his foundation's transformation mirrors the transformations that all lasting and successful organizations experience. Therefore, although it is still unique, the Soros Foundation is becoming more similar to other organizations in the democracy establishment. That the OSF's staff members increasingly move on to work at other organizations or donors in the democracy establishment, and vice versa, only furthers the organization's isomorphism.

Today, the OSF do have some bureaucracy. Academic Diane Stone, who conducted interviews with a number of the OSF headquarters staff, characterized the organization as moving toward "a 'top-down' professionalised dynamic of policy interaction with decision makers."[58] A staff member told her that the organization was now "more like a traditional foundation with programme officers in New York."[59] As a consequence, hierarchical relationships between the OSF and grantees, many of which are funded repeatedly, increasingly characterize the OSF, rather than the more horizontal relationships for which the organization was once known. In that way, the OSF's social ties resemble those of other organizations in the democracy establishment. In the words of one former staff member, "OSI has gotten more serious over time in terms of impact."[60] At the same time, top-down efforts to promote greater monitoring and evaluation, such as those led by former ActionAid CEO Ramesh Singh, when he worked as OSF director of learning, monitoring, and evaluation, met with some resistance from the OSF's overseas offices – reflecting the controversy that can accompany major changes within an organization. In the midst of those changes, it remains to be seen how successful the OSF will be going forward in terms of securing democracy assistance and promoting democracy effectively.

The field research presented in later chapters suggests that the OSF's projects have remained less tame than many other projects in the 2010s. But even the OSF's programs have become more measurable, suggesting the importance of broader professional norms on the design of the organization's programs. Viewed alongside the other organizational transformations described in this chapter, we can see that that evolution

---

[57] Soros (1995, 147).
[58] Stone (2010, 277).
[59] Quoted in Stone (2010, 277).
[60] Interview 11, with a practitioner at a democracy NGO, by telephone, June 22, 2010.

is in response to the OSF leaders' increasing commitment, encouraged through social network ties, to monitoring and evaluation.

## Conclusions

When the National Democratic Institute was founded in 1983, it faced a wide-open world of possibilities. In the words of one person who worked at NDI in its early years, "A few people had a little tiny bit of money, a lot of idealism, a lot of energy, a lot of creativity, and they just started making things like election monitoring up."[61] Another longtime staff member characterized the organization as "informal, slightly funky, youthful, risk taking, with an attitude, creative, energetic, non-bureaucratic."[62] Eventually, the organization would change sufficiently in the late 1990s and early 2000s that that description was no longer so apt. First, geographic divisions were created within the Washington, DC, headquarters of NDI, followed by thematic divisions (for example, on political parties) and eventually support teams (for example, on evaluation). The more the money flowed in and the organization grew, the more hierarchical and specialized it became. Professional staff members came to see themselves "as a permanent fixture in a country's hopefully long-term liberalization," and they adopted the programs that would help them remain permanent fixtures.[63] Doing so involved pursuing measurable programs that would lead to continued government grants as well as regime-compatible programs that would lead to continued target-country access.

Such a transformation is characteristic of the democracy establishment. Freedom House transitioned into a highly credible and professional organization in the mid to late 1990s, and that transformation was linked to its strategy of pursuing tamer democracy-assistance programs. In contrast, due to its leaders' ideological commitments, IDEE retained its confrontational and untame approach to democracy assistance. Yet as a consequence of its lack of adaptation, it gradually ceased to be competitive. The OSF's history fell somewhere in between the experiences of Freedom House and IDEE, adapting somewhat over time due to changing preferences and norms, but remaining relatively untame, in part thanks to its private funding source. In sum, the evidence supports the book's argument about rising competition and

---

[61] Interview 47, with a director of a democracy-assistance NGO, in person, Washington, DC, April 30, 2010.
[62] Email from former NDI staff member to other staff members, August 19, 1998.
[63] Interview 40, with a former director of a democracy-assistance NGO, in person, New York, May 26, 2010.

professionalism over time in the democracy establishment and how those forces encourage organizations to pursue tamer approaches to democracy assistance (Hypotheses 3–5).

That analysis was situated within a broader examination of the network structure of the democracy establishment. Using hyperlink analysis tools that collect and depict connections across organizations' websites, I found that the democracy establishment as a network is dominated and linked together by a few key donor organizations. This finding was consistent with an argument that suggests that convergence in the democracy establishment ought to occur through peripheral organizations' interactions with core donor organizations, rather than through regional or programmatic diffusion patterns. Moreover, a survey of democracy-assistance practitioners confirmed the financial importance of international aid in the eyes of recipients, especially professional ones.

The collected evidence in this chapter supports the transnational approach to democracy assistance. Democracy-assistance organizations behave like "regular" organizations in their search for funding, despite their ideological roots. The extent to which they behave like regular organizations, however, depends on the funding environment as well as on the nature of the organization and its particular culture and norms. The findings in Chapter 5 suggest that the evolutions that it documents in organizations in the democracy establishment are representative of a broader trend in the field. To see how well the evolutions track variations within non-American organizations, I now turn to case studies of democracy assistance in the Middle East.

# 7    Jordan: aid in the shadow of geopolitics

> *[We must] be discerningly aware of the difference between the required democratic transformations and achievable ones on the one hand, and the risks of chaos and* fitna *[sedition] on the other.*[1]

> *We can't have a strategy as an NGO because we're just trying to survive in a situation with a lot of pressures. We can't plan if we don't know what our funding opportunities will be in the future. And we can't plan if we don't know what the government will allow.*[2]

According to Steven Heydemann at the United States Institute of Peace, who was writing prior to the Arab uprisings, democracy assistance in the Middle East has failed. Instead of promoting reform, he argues that international efforts have shaped strategies of authoritarian survival, creating a situation in which rulers adopt the language but not the substance of democracy.[3] King Abdullah of Jordan, who held onto power more easily than other Arab leaders during the upheavals of 2011, has been especially adept at this strategy. His approach blended promises to reform and government shake-ups at home with pleas for more aid to sustain his regime abroad.

Heydemann is not alone in his pessimistic assessments of democracy aid in the Middle East.[4] But why have external actors promoted democracy in the ways they have if Arab dictators know how to use elections and other seemingly democratic institutions to their advantage? To design more effective democracy assistance, it is important to understand what factors cause democracy promoters to select certain programs and not others in the first place.

To understand the factors that shape democracy assistance in the Middle East and beyond, this chapter presents a case study of Jordan between 2008 and 2012. It tests the theory I laid out in Chapter 2

---

[1] Ibn Al Hussein (2011).
[2] Interview 66, with a director of a Jordanian NGO, in person, Amman, October 29, 2009.
[3] Heydemann (2007).
[4] Brownlee (2012); Carapico (2002); Vitalis (1994); Wittes (2008).

Table 7.1 *Summary of variables in Jordan.*

| Years | Competition | Professional norms | Strategic importance | Freedom House rating | Expected aid |
|---|---|---|---|---|---|
| 2008–9 | High | High | High | Partly free | Tame–very tame (varies by delegation relationship) |
| 2010–12 | High | High | High | Not free | Tame–very tame (varies by delegation relationship) |

*Note:* Details about coding the variables are in the text.

using evidence drawn from more than seventy-five semi-structured interviews, participant observation, organizational materials, news articles, and secondary research. To assess the empirical support for my hypotheses, my first objective is to evaluate the values of the key variables, which are laid out in Table 7.1. This chapter's main emphasis is on testing the hypotheses about how delegation relationships affect the design and implementation of democracy assistance (Hypothesis 2); the main emphasis of Chapter 8 will be testing the hypotheses about professionalization (Hypotheses 3–5). One of the advantages of this chapter's qualitative approach is that it relies on more fine-grained data than previous chapters. I am thus able to explore delegation farther down the chain – for example, from NGO to NGO. Another advantage is that this chapter examines patterns using complete data on foreign-funded projects during the period of study. Even the best official multi-country data sources on democracy assistance usually suffer from some omissions and mistakes, which my in-depth field research in a single country can overcome.

My second goal is to evaluate the evidence in support of the hypothesized causal mechanisms. First, when donors have a relatively difficult time observing their grantees, organizations should pursue more measurable programs. They should do that to promote their survival and, in particular, to secure future funding. Second, when donors have a relatively difficult time observing their grantees, organizations should pursue more regime-compatible programs. They should do that because they are less likely to be punished and because that strategy promotes their survival and, in particular, their continued access to Jordan. Finally, because organizations want to win funding from government donors, they should respond with their programs to donor officials' preferences.

The chapter proceeds in four sections. The first section describes the domestic and international context. The second section presents and challenges the conventional wisdom about democracy promotion in Jordan: donor governments' strategic interests alone shape democracy assistance. The third section develops a fuller explanation for the design of democracy assistance in Jordan that builds on the previous chapters' transnational approach. It shows the importance of organizational survival, both in terms of funding and access, and professional norms for the design and implementation of democracy assistance. The final section concludes.

## Context for the case study

Because this chapter seeks to explain the design and implementation of democracy assistance in Jordan between 2008 and 2012, it is important to understand the domestic and international context there. One relevant point was Jordan's robustness as an authoritarian regime. Another was the interest of Western, and especially, American, policy-makers in the stability of the regime. Those factors could significantly affect the design and implementation of democracy assistance in Jordan.

### *The domestic context*

Jordan is a small country in a bad neighborhood. Bordered by Saudi Arabia, Iraq, Syria, and Israel and the Palestinian Territories, Jordan has been involved in most of the Middle East's post-World War II conflagrations, from the Arab–Israeli conflict to the 2003 Iraq War. Once a British protectorate known as Transjordan, Jordan gained independence in 1946. Its first post-independence king, Abdullah I, was assassinated by a Palestinian nationalist in Jerusalem at the Al Aqsa Mosque in 1951. His son, King Talal, led the country for just thirteen months before abdicating due to poor mental health. King Hussein Ibn Talal, known as Hussein and Abdullah I's young grandson, then took office in 1952 and led the country over five decades. After Hussein's death from cancer in 1999, his son, King Abdullah II, assumed the throne and has ruled ever since.

King Hussein's long rule was turbulent. He survived coup and assassination attempts by Arab nationalists as well as the Arab–Israeli War, which led to the loss of Jordan's territory in the West Bank in 1967. To maintain order, Hussein sharply limited political freedom, including banning political parties in 1956 and introducing martial law in 1967. Foreign aid from the British government and neighboring Arab states helped sustain the Hashemite regime during those troubled times. Since 1964, foreign aid as a percentage of the central government's budget expenses has hovered at around 25 percent and never fallen below 10 percent.[5]

Hussein oversaw a temporary political opening in 1989 after a decade of economic crisis. Ructions in the global oil market had led to fewer remittances from Jordanians working abroad, as well as a decline in foreign aid from Arab states. As a consequence, in 1989, Jordan could no longer make payments on its debts, prompting it to implement an economic adjustment and austerity plan so that it could access a loan from the International Monetary Fund.[6] The austerity plan sparked a political crisis when riots spread from the south of the country to Amman, the country's centrally located capital. To cope, Hussein embarked on a strategy of "defensive democratization": in 1989, he suspended martial law, held legislative elections for the first time in more than two decades, and allowed political parties to legally organize.[7]

Yet since then, authoritarianism in Jordan has intensified. As Figure 7.1 shows, since 1989, freedom in Jordan has declined despite its steady global rise. New sources of foreign aid from the West allowed the monarchy to entrench in the 1990s. Despite the West's democratic triumphalism after the end of the Cold War, Jordan, like some other Arab countries, successfully maintained and even increased its international patronage networks.[8] Crucial to solidifying those patronage networks was Jordan's peace treaty with Israel in 1994. More recently, Jordan's status as an American ally in the Iraq War and broader "war on terror" has promoted its claims for foreign aid. Thanks to foreign economic and military aid, Abdullah does not need to rely as heavily on the public for taxes, which reduces citizens' demands for democracy. Instead, he can distribute "rents," or political bonuses, to his key supporters, the Transjordanian tribes, and hang onto power.[9]

Like any autocratic regime, the Hashemite dynasty in Jordan uses various strategies to maintain its rule. In 1993, for example, Jordan's election law was amended to reduce the influence of the monarchy's opponents.[10] In protest, the main opposition party, the Islamic Action Front, has often boycotted elections. The king can dissolve parliament at will (as he did in 2001 and 2009) and delay elections indefinitely, gives

---

[5] Peters and Moore (2009, 269, 272).
[6] Ryan (1998).
[7] Robinson (1998).
[8] Bellin (2004, 148–9).
[9] Lust-Okar (2009). For a more general treatment, see Morrison (2009).
[10] Lust-Okar and Jamal (2002, 358).

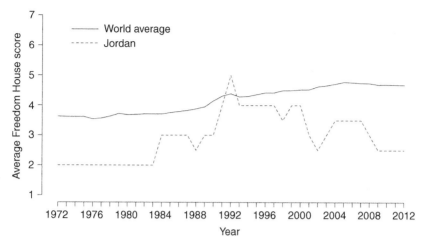

Figure 7.1 Freedom in the world and in Jordan, 1972–2012.
*Note:* I averaged countries' political liberty and civil rights scores, which were rescaled so that 1 represents the least democracy and 7 the most.
*Data source:* Freedom House (1973–2013).

parliament little authority to make laws, and he retains (and uses) the right to issue temporary laws by decree without parliamentary consent. Furthermore, he sharply restricts freedom of expression and assembly. Between 75 and 80 percent of the respondents in an annual survey run in Jordan since 2001 have stated that they are afraid to criticize their government.[11] Those domestic constraints are important to bear in mind when considering what local and international organizations want to and are able to do in Jordan under the umbrella of democracy assistance, as are several international factors.

### The international context

Even as its freedom declined, Jordan adopted certain democratic institutions and practices in an attempt to establish its liberal bona fides. In addition to holding parliamentary elections, Jordan invited international election monitors to observe its elections in 2010 and 2013, adopted a quota for women in parliament in 2003, doubling that quota in 2010, and created prominent government-tied human rights and women's empowerment organizations. Such practices amount to performing democracy according to an internationally legitimate script. In the words of political scientist Sean Yom, the Jordanian government

[11] Yom (2009, 161).

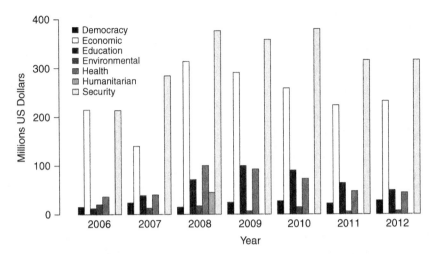

Figure 7.2 American aid to Jordan, by sector, 2006–2012.
*Note:* Aid is in constant US dollars.
*Data source:* ForeignAssistance.gov.

has pursued "reform" to court foreign approval, "maintain[ing] a veneer of political openness and moderation that allows Jordan to pose (with a special eye on Western donor countries) as a modern and relatively progressive polity amid the surrounding turmoil of the troubled Middle East."[12]

King Abdullah II's efforts have paid off. In 2010, the United States awarded Jordan a $275 million grant through the Millennium Challenge Corporation (MCC) – an aid initiative created by President George W. Bush to reward well-governed countries – after Jordan passed through a $25 million MCC Threshold Program aimed at strengthening Jordan's democratic institutions. Meanwhile, after judging Jordan to have made "significant progress in the area of governance and transparency," the European Union rewarded it with "advanced status" in 2010 and a €223 million aid package.[13] As Figure 7.2 shows, in 2010, the US State Department and USAID together gave Jordan $258 million in economic aid and $380 million in military aid – figures that dwarfed the $26 million in democracy aid the US government gave that year.

It is in that inauspicious context that the international community has sought to promote democracy. Democracy assistance in Jordan is relatively new: it began in earnest not when the Cold War ended, as in

[12] Yom (2009, 152).
[13] Hazaimeh (2010); *Jordan Times* (2010).

many parts of the world, but later, after Jordan signed the peace treaty with Israel. Democracy aid then increased markedly during and after the 2003 Iraq War. Although most democracy assistance in Jordan comes from the United States, non-American sources of democracy assistance have become more prevalent. The 1995 European–Mediterranean Partnership and 2005 European Neighbourhood Policy have been the key European financial instruments.

Jordan's success in winning foreign economic aid has continued, even after the Arab uprisings shifted some international attention to other countries in the region. In May 2011, for example, the Group of Eight met in Deauville, France, and promised around $40 billion in direct aid and development loans to support the transitions in Egypt and Tunisia. By July 2012, only $18 billion had been dispersed, $4.9 billion of which ended up going to Jordan, a country that was belatedly added to the initiative due to its strategic relationships with donors.[14]

We can thus conclude that geopolitics influence democracy-assistance *aid flows* in Jordan. But how does geopolitics influence the *design and implementation* of democracy assistance there? And what other factors, if any, also influence those outcomes? It is to those questions that I now turn.

### A partial explanation: donor states' preferences

Given the domestic and international context in Jordan, democracy donors may prefer stability in Jordan to democratization. As a consequence, we might expect Jordan to receive little democracy aid. As discussed above, that is not the case. Alternatively, we might expect democracy assistance in Jordan to be more regime-compatible than in other states. Since Jordan is a country that is a close autocratic ally of the United States, it is a likely case for the power of the donor preferences approach.

At first blush, there is ample support in Jordan for that perspective. As Figure 7.3 shows, most programs (64 percent) in 2009 were regime-compatible. That proportion is 4 percent greater than in other countries that year on average and 6 percent greater than in other countries that year at the same level of freedom. Programs in relatively tame categories such as governance, legislative aid, and women's groups and participation were particularly common in Jordan.

To get a sense of such programs, consider a legislative-assistance program that I classify as not measurable but as regime-compatible. USAID

[14] Khalaf (2012).

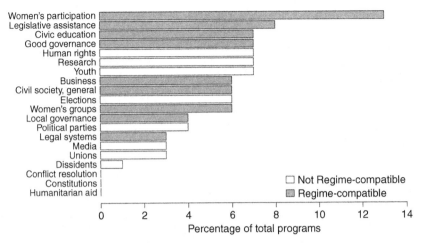

Figure 7.3 Democracy assistance in Jordan, 2009, by category.
*Data source:* Author's coding based on interviews and organizations' materials.

funded a five-year, $8.7 million legislative-strengthening program in Jordan that was implemented by the State University of New York's Center for International Development (SUNY CID) between 2005 and 2010. According to the SUNY CID website, "The central objectives of the program [were] to assist the Parliament of Jordan in strengthening its legislative, budgetary, and oversight capacities; increase the institution's transparency and accountability; and promote citizen participation and improve the public understanding of Parliament."[15] By design, the program was technical, not political. When the king dissolved parliament in 2009 and did not hold elections for months, the program continued as planned since it involved collaboration with permanent parliamentary staff. The existence of MPs was irrelevant. As such, SUNY CID was often viewed locally as siding with the status quo.

Although foreign-funded efforts rarely fell into non-measurable, non-regime-compatible categories such as dissidents, political parties, and unions, it is hard to argue that those categories were ignored because of a lack of need. Political parties in Jordan existed, but they were feeble, which made them potentially good targets for foreign support.[16] Dissidents in Jordan existed, too, sometimes expressing their

[15] State University of New York's Center for International Development (2010).
[16] Lust-Okar (2009).

opposition via protests and demonstrations.[17] In other words, the "ripeness" argument – that regime-compatible aid is only needed under certain conditions that are no longer met in the twenty-first century – does not fully explain aid patterns in Jordan.

Those initial patterns therefore suggest a relationship between donor states' strategic interests and the design of democracy assistance. There are, however, at least four limits to that perspective as a complete explanation of variations in democracy assistance in Jordan. First, there was some genuinely non-regime-compatible aid in Jordan, which is hard to square with a perspective that only recognizes donors' preferences for stability. Second, regime-compatible programs in Jordan were very similar to programs in countries that were not strategically important, which challenges the idea that strategic value is a necessary condition for regime-compatible aid. Third, donors did little to ensure that programs did not confront the Jordanian regime, which is how donors that highly value stability would probably behave. Relatedly, donors did not have uniform preferences for stability in Jordan. Finally, donors' preferences for stability cannot account for other salient variations in democracy assistance in Jordan, such as the extent of measurable programs. I discuss each point in more detail below.

First, although aid in non-regime-compatible categories was relatively rare, it did exist, as Figure 7.3 shows. To give one example, a media program funded by the US government led to an on-air radio revelation in 2009 that twelve MPs had not spoken in parliament in over four months. That information contributed to a delegitimization of the parliament, an institution that supports the monarchy's survival. The existence of such a program is puzzling from the perspective that donors' preferences for stability completely explain the relative timidity of aid in Jordan.

Second, regime-compatible programs in Jordan were modeled on programs from other countries that had less strategic importance. Interviewees working for the SUNY CID effort, for example, explained that their program was modeled on previous USAID-funded legislative-assistance projects. Competitive or fully authoritarian regimes such as Benin (2000–2), Zimbabwe (1999–2003), and Kenya (2007–9) hosted similar USAID programs, implemented by SUNY CID, despite those countries' far different security relationships with the United States. Strategic interests could be sufficient for such programs to exist in a setting such as Jordan. But if the programs are occurring in Jordan due to US strategic interests, then the causal mechanism does not involve

---

[17] Ottaway and Hamzawy (2011, 4); Schwedler (2003).

policy-makers directly observing or controlling aid agencies. When I discussed the program with Congressional staff in Washington who were involved in aid appropriation, interviewees expressed surprise that such a program existed, telling me that they considered it wasteful.[18]

Third, if donors were worried about democracy assistance destabilizing Jordan, then we would expect them to have been closely monitoring it. Yet none of my interviewees in Jordan expressed worries about upsetting donors due to programs that were too confrontational. That was not because their programs never generated local controversy. Indeed, even the seemingly anodyne USAID-funded SUNY CID program discussed above managed to provoke the Jordanian government's suspicion. One staff member explained the situation to me as follows: "On the visible level, they [the government] are really supportive of our work, but they don't really support us and they do everything in their power to undermine reform. … You ask if you can show the MPs how to ask a good question, but they don't let you do it."[19] Donor officials who were deeply worried about destabilizing the Jordanian monarchy – or destabilizing their relationships with the Jordanian monarchy – should care if a USAID-funded program is approaching the Jordanian government's red lines. In my interviews with grantees, I asked questions about whether donor officials were behaving in that way. No interviewee could provide evidence that they were being controlled.

A related challenge to the donor preferences' approach as a complete explanation is that donors' preferences about democracy in Jordan are not always clear. As more than half of the grantees I spoke to noted, the United States government is not monolithic on issues of democracy promotion. Indeed, it contains at least some influential people who prioritize democratic reform in Jordan. My conversations with government officials – including different people in the same positions over time – confirm that some of them strongly advocate change in Jordan. In an interview at the NED, for example, a grant-maker made clear that it was the confrontational approach of a funded NGO that had won it NED grants for over a decade.[20]

Indeed, democracy assistance can often become disconnected from other aspects of foreign policy. At the same time as the United States was expressing a firm commitment to supporting democratic and just government in Jordan via democracy assistance, it was also continuing

---

[18] Interviews 157 and 158, with staff at US House of Representatives, March 12 and 13, 2013.

[19] Interview 21, with a director of an INGO, in person, Amman, October 5, 2009.

[20] Interview 6, with an international donor representative, in person, Washington, DC, September 19, 2009.

its policy of close cooperation with the authoritarian regime. One former US government grant-maker based in Jordan wished for more consistent democracy promotion on the part of government officials and explained the foreign-policy disconnect thus: "One thing that I always felt was that diplomacy and democracy-assistance programs were not happening in tandem."[21]

Finally, a limitation of an approach to explaining democracy assistance that just emphasizes donor officials' preferences for stability in Jordan is that it can only explain how regime-compatible Jordan's aid is when compared to other countries. It does not offer insight into variations within democracy assistance in Jordan when its relationships with external actors are held constant. And during the period under study, those relationships did not change (recall Table 7.1). Yet there is a wide variety of democracy-assistance programs in Jordan, including some that emphasize measurable outputs and some that do not. Donor governments did not undergo any major changes during the time period of study in terms of preferences for measurable programs. So what explains the conditions under which relatively tame programs are more likely? It is necessary to develop some additional theory to answer that question.

Given the limitations of an explanation of democracy assistance in Jordan that only relies on donor officials' preferences, in the next section, I introduce organizations in the democracy establishment in Jordan to create a fuller explanation. My point is not that donor interests play no role in shaping democracy assistance – they do. Rather, I argue that those preferences set some of the broad parameters for the work of organizations in the democracy establishment and that those organizations' concerns about survival help account for unexplained variations in programs.

### Bringing in the democracy establishment

As laid out in Chapter 2, donor states' visions must be implemented by organizations in the democracy establishment. Donors cannot perfectly observe those organizations. Information problems result for various reasons discussed previously: long delegation chains; incomplete feedback loops; uncertainty over outcomes; collective principals; and multiple principals. As a consequence, organizations in the democracy establishment have an opportunity to influence programs' design and implementation by choosing the foreign partners and activities closest to their preferences.

[21] Interview 71, with a former officer at an international donor, in person, Amman, July 1, 2010.

That opportunity is significant because organizations in the democracy establishment have preferences that differ from donors' preferences. As I have already argued, organizations in the democracy establishment want to survive and thrive as organizations in addition to wanting to advance democracy. They also are guided by professional norms. Whereas donors are primarily concerned with effective programs – and meeting other foreign-policy objectives – organizations are sometimes willing to trade off efficacy in favor of programs that help them survive. As such, organizations may want to continue programs that no longer make sense due to political changes, perhaps such as legislative assistance after the parliament no longer exists, whereas donors may prefer that such a program be suspended or amended. This section explores how organizational survival and professionalization play out in contemporary Jordan.

During my period of field research, the field of democracy assistance in Jordan consisted of both Jordanian and international (i.e., non-Jordanian) organizations working on issues related to democracy and political reform.[22] The INGOs, which totaled fourteen, were mostly American non-profit organizations (for example, IRI and NDI), but also included for-profit companies (for example, ARD) and non-American NGOs (for example, People in Need, a Czech NGO). The Jordanian NGOs, which totaled forty-three, ranged from small organizations with only two or three full-time employees to large organizations with dozens of full-time staff members and offices across multiple buildings. Several royal non-governmental organizations (RONGOs) also received democracy assistance. Although RONGOs were clearly not sincere democratizers in the sense of promoting electoral democracy, they worked on internationally supported objectives such as advancing women's participation on municipal councils. All of these groups were funded by a panoply of foreign government agencies. Every international donor that included the Middle East as part of its purview funded at least some activities in Jordan.

### The fight for organizational survival

Promoting democracy in an autocracy involves many risks and few rewards in terms of reform. The people that nonetheless seek democratic

---

[22] Other organizations in Jordan worked on issues that could contribute to democracy in Jordan in the long run, such as through an education program with no civic education component. Since I am interested in testing the argument about democracy assistance from Chapter 2, I do not discuss such organizations in the case studies.

change usually believe ardently in democracy. Mohammad founded an organization to promote media freedom in Jordan because he believed "freedom of the press is the cornerstone of democracy and human rights ... [and, in Jordan,] the freedom of the press was very bad."[23] Lama, a Jordanian working for an INGO, told me how she more or less stopped working during January and February 2011 because she was so gripped by news of revolutions from Tunisia and Egypt. But she only shared her passion for democracy with colleagues and foreigners – not her family or friends – because she was afraid to do so.[24] All of my interviewees in Jordan indicated that principles drew them to their work. As one person put it: "How did I come to work here? I have always been passionate about reform."[25]

But professionals cannot advance democracy without helping their organizations survive. Sometimes the pressures of organizational survival encouraged practitioners to engage in activities that they would not have pursued in terms of purely principled or pro-democracy grounds. As one practitioner, Robert, asked rhetorically about his organization, "At what stage do we decide not to work in a particular environment? Would we provide assistance for elections in Syria right now if they invited us? I would say, 'No.' But the field is a business in some sense. Whether or not we can realistically make a difference should always be part of the discussion inside our organizations, and I don't know if it is."[26]

Many Jordanian professionals echoed Robert's characterization of democracy assistance as a business. In around half of my interviews, practitioners accused other organizations specifically of being *dakakin* – the word for "shops" in Arabic. Calling NGOs shops was an insult because it conveyed the sense that the organizations were in the field to earn money, not to sincerely promote democracy. A program director at a Jordanian human rights NGO put it this way: "An organization on youth will apply for a grant on torture just because it is available."[27] Waleed, who had worked for both international and domestic NGOs in the democracy establishment, further elaborated, "The democracy NGOs want to earn money – and some of them want to drive a Mercedes

---

[23] Interview 66, with a director of a Jordanian NGO, in person, Amman, October 15, 2009.

[24] Interview 102, with a staff member of an INGO, in person, Amman, May 23, 2012.

[25] Interview 71, with a former officer at an international donor, in person, Amman, July 1, 2011.

[26] Interview 149, with a director of an INGO, in person, Amman, May 23, 2012.

[27] Interview 82, with a program director of a Jordanian NGO, in person, Amman, November 11, 2009.

or BMW – and since the country depends so much on foreign aid, starting up an NGO is the way to do that."[28]

Government donors reported that one of their priorities was avoiding funding NGOs that over-emphasized organizational survival. The director of a USAID project that gave out many grants to Jordanian NGOs said, for example, "The challenge in Jordan is to make sure that we're not reinforcing the NGO business."[29] Maryam, a former grant-maker at an American government donor likewise exclaimed in frustration: "Civil society organizations may have only five people – and they're all working to get funding! They don't have a constituency or a presence or any visibility."[30] In fact, several government officials turned the tables during research interviews to ask me which NGOs I thought were most sincere and least business-like. Their desire not to fund NGOs that prioritized survival over democracy illustrates how, if donors could perfectly observe and control grantees, grantees would have less slack to pursue programs that support their survival. Indeed, at least some donors in Jordan viewed such a pursuit as in conflict with their goals.

As expected, professionals concerned with organizational survival worried specifically about interacting with Western government donors and the Hashemite monarchy. Continuing to work in the democracy field in Amman required that NGOs win government grants and maintain access to Jordan. I discuss each imperative in turn below. As we shall see, organizations pursued measurable and regime-compatible democracy assistance as strategies to achieve their organizational goals.

*Getting funding and measurable programs* In terms of their strategies for financial survival, organizations in the democracy establishment focused on getting foreign government funding because doing so was lucrative. The vast majority (91 percent) of NGOs working on political reform in Jordan received at least some foreign government funding, with about three-quarters of them relying primarily on foreign grants, which is to say that foreign donors usually or always funded them.[31] The average organization received funding from five different international donors. That number is higher than the average number among respondents in Chapter 4's survey of practitioners, showing that Jordan's civil society is

[28] Interview 68, with a program officer at an INGO, in person, Amman, November 18, 2009.
[29] Interview 35, with a director of a USAID-funded project, in person, Amman, December 12, 2009.
[30] Interview 71, with a former officer at an international donor, in person, Amman, July 1, 2010.
[31] Sundstrom (2005, 428).

unusually saturated with foreign aid. Because donor governments tend to have strong preferences for measurable – and in the case of Jordan, regime-compatible – programs, those funding patterns are significant. Were alternative funding sources more readily available, civil society organizations in Jordan might approach their work differently.

There is one other notable source of funding for organizations working on political reform in Jordan, although it is not a source likely to support untame programs: the Jordanian government. Some 38 percent of organizations in the democracy field received some direct or in-kind support from the Jordanian government. That figure serves as a further example of the regime's efforts to control civil society, a theme that I return to in more detail below.

Another way to illustrate the importance of foreign government funding to organizational survival is to consider when democracy organizations in Jordan were founded. If NGO leaders were motivated by political opportunities, then they might have created organizations during moments of political opening, such as 1989. Few democracy NGOs in Jordan predate 1995. Freedom has steadily eroded since 1995 (recall Figure 7.1), implying that organizations' creations are not linked to a widening of civic or political space. The mean year of founding for the organizations was 1997, with most organizations being created only since 2003. Organizations' founding dates thus coincide with when democracy assistance spiked.

The importance of winning foreign government funding for Jordanian NGOs is striking because accepting foreign funds has significant draw-backs. Formally, the 2008 Law on Societies (Law 51) prohibits NGOs from accepting foreign funding until they have obtained government approval, which is often a long and uncertain process.[32] Informally, accepting foreign funds may harm an NGO's legitimacy since many citizens (not to mention NGO staff) object to Western countries' foreign policies vis-à-vis Israel and Iraq. According to the Pew Global Attitudes Project, for example, few Jordanians trust the United States, with between just 1 and 25 percent of Jordanians holding a favorable opinion of the United States since 2002.[33] Taking foreign funds can thus involve legal hurdles, reputational costs, and staff members' principled objections.

Around 9 percent of organizations in the democracy field in Jordan did not receive any foreign funding. In some cases, that was because the organizations did not apply. One major NGO that generally eschewed

---

[32] International Center for Not-for-Profit Law (2012).
[33] Pew Global Attitudes Project (2012b).

foreign funding was the Jordanian Women's Union, a left-wing women's group that is regarded as one of the most successful civil society organizations in the country, thanks to its sometimes controversial programs aiding Palestinian refugees and advocating legal equality for women. Yet there was little evidence of a rise in indigenous networks that opted out of international funding despite the high – and rising – levels of suspicion of foreign actors.

The drive to obtain foreign-government grants was not limited to Jordanian NGOs. The Solidarity Center opened a country office in Amman in 2003 to support Iraqi refugees in Jordan, foster a regional network of women workers, monitor labor abuses, and organize workers in Jordan's qualified industrial zones, among other things.[34] The Solidarity Center lost its NED funding in 2009 when the United States reshuffled its funding for Iraqi unions. When a new call for proposals went out via the State Department rather than NED, Relief International won the grant to support Iraqi refugees and unions.[35] Since the aid for Iraqi unions was the organization's primary funding source, from which staff siphoned off resources to support their Jordanian efforts, the Solidarity Center's office in Jordan closed.

My argument predicts that organizations will pursue measurable programs to appeal to donors when there are problems of observation and control. It is therefore important to think about the conditions under which such problems were stronger or weaker in Jordan. One relevant condition relates to the location of organizations' offices. Donors that had offices in Jordan could more easily observe and control their grant recipients than donors that did not have any long-term local presence. Locally based donors could observe and control grantees by going to observe their events, speaking directly to purported beneficiaries, and so on. I therefore expect overseas donors to be more likely than Amman-based donors to reward measurable programs, which help them gauge effectiveness in the absence of other types of information.

My interview data support that hypothesis, with non-local donors being approximately 8 percent more likely to fund measurable programs and regime-compatible programs than local donors. The qualitative evidence supports my causal logic, as well. I asked Omar, the director of a Jordanian NGO funded by a variety of government donors, to compare the donors' information-gathering techniques. He replied, "There are many similar things about the donors – they all like to monitor. But there

---

[34] Interview 17, with a director of an INGO, by telephone, November 16, 2009.
[35] This anecdote illustrates the advantages core grantees enjoy at the NED versus at other funders and therefore the reduced monitoring that they are subject to at the NED.

are some differences. USAID's office in Amman likes to go to the events and see everything for itself. The NED [not physically present] just likes to get the reports, the receipts, and the numbers."[36] Thus, Omar told me that he saved the quantitative measures and outputs for donors like the NED that were farther away and rewarded him the most for them. Zeid, another NGO director based in Amman, complained mightily about the foreign NGOs, such as Freedom House and NDI, that gave his organization grants and maintained local offices in Jordan. In contrast to his other funders, which included the NED and MEPI, two donors that did not have a physical presence in Amman, he said that the locally based donors were "very difficult for me in terms of interference ... I got $25,000 from [each of] them and if I could have given the money back, I would have."[37] All else being equal, organizations like Zeid's preferred the freedom that comes from obtaining grants given by donors that are farther away and not able to come to their events personally. In such cases, reporting back to donors using quantitative indicators makes sense as a signaling strategy for obtaining future funding.

Consistent with my argument and grant recipients' comments, donors reported that they were less likely to reward measurable programs when they had offices on the ground in Jordan due to the less-severe information problems. In one interview, I asked a donor based in Amman why the programs his office chose to fund seemed to be less frequently associated with quantitative, measurable outputs than those of other donors working in Jordan. He replied:

We know that not everything that counts can be counted. So, for example, if we are working with rights for migrant workers in Jordan, we go talk to the people involved and ask, who established the legal help desk for them – the grantee or us? My objective in giving that grant to the Tamkeen Center [a Jordanian NGO] is achieving the rights of workers. Has this been achieved? It is difficult to answer this question quantifiably. There are some things that can be measured, and others that cannot. We can count the number of legal help desks, but the quality of legal help desks is difficult to count.[38]

His statement is consistent with my argument that measurable programs please donors that face information problems, but involve perceived drawbacks, including that some desirable outcomes are not easily

---

[36] Interview 48, with a director of a Jordanian NGO, in person, Amman, October 26, 2009.
[37] Interview 31, with a director of a Jordanian NGO, in person, Amman, October 15, 2009.
[38] Interview 61, with an international donor representative, in person, Amman, July 1, 2010.

measured. The extent to which rational organizations pursue measurable programs at a given point in time or in a particular place thus depends in part on the preferences and monitoring abilities of their donors.

*Maintaining access and regime-compatible programs* Rana had prepared for her INGO's political-party training for months. She invited all of Jordan's weak political parties. But on the day of the workshop, several men showed up that were not on Rana's participant list. The men sat quietly throughout the workshop, taking notes and observing the day's events but not participating in the activities on crafting messages, developing platforms, and designing voter outreach. As the workshop continued, the other participants became uncomfortable. Although the men had introduced themselves as members of an unspecified political party, it was clear that they were observers from the *mukhabarat*, Jordan's omnipresent and highly professional General Intelligence Directorate (GID).

As Rana's experience suggests, while they must obtain funding from government donors, people working in Jordan's democracy establishment must also worry about maintaining good relations with the Jordanian government. The Hashemite regime carefully monitored democracy assistance in Jordan, threatening (more often covertly than overtly) the people and organizations that approach the unwritten "red lines" of opposition to the king. Between 2008 and 2012, concerns about maintaining access anecdotally mounted, with the Jordanian government appearing to take a harder line against NGOs after the Arab Spring and amid simmering discontent in Jordan.

The Jordanian monarchy threatens organizations working to promote political reform using various methods. As discussed previously, the Jordanian government uses a variety of legal channels to monitor and manipulate foreign attempts to promote democracy. It restricts foreign funding; and it also creates royal non-governmental organizations to gain a foothold in civil society.

In addition, the royal court and the GID use extralegal and informal tactics – as with Rana's political-party workshop – to thwart democracy assistance. The government inexplicably barred the director of a local NGO, for example, from implementing a previously planned, foreign-funded program in cooperation with the Anti-Corruption Commission in 2009. The director guessed that the government was retaliating for the NGO's publication of a study that documented corruption, an explosive political issue in the country.[39] An employee of an INGO similarly told

---

[39] Interview 77, with the director of a Jordanian NGO, in person, Amman, October 18, 2009.

me that the GID monitors Jordanians who work for INGOs and bans them from holding sensitive positions in the government. He described the regime as Janus-faced: "On the one hand, they want to work really closely with the United States and USAID. On the other hand, they try to do everything in their power to dictate their own agenda to USAID and to undermine Jordanians who work closely with American organizations."[40] Other interviewees from INGOs told me that the *mukhabarat* had planted false stories about them in student newspapers and on Facebook, hoping to stir up sovereign–nationalist sentiments that could delegitimize and even shut down their activities. Even if such allegations are false, they establish that fear of the government pervades the field of democracy assistance.

Since NGOs in Jordan's democracy establishment worried about maintaining access, I expected most of them to prefer regime-compatible programs to avoid confrontation with the monarchy, all else being equal. Moreover, I predicted that when government funders found it more difficult to monitor grantees, they should have been more likely to pursue regime-compatible programs. Confrontational programs jeopardize organizations' survival, making many organizations less willing to pursue them unless forced to do by donor governments.

There are some relevant sources of variation in the degree to which organizations need to maintain access to do their work, which I can leverage to test my theory. One relevant source of variation in access problems has to do with organizations' nationalities. Organizations that are Jordanian should face more acute access problems than non-Jordanian organizations, which can leave the country and work elsewhere, if necessary. Consistent with that expectation, Jordanian organizations pursue 8 percent more regime-compatible programs on average than non-Jordanian organizations. That difference is striking because Jordanian NGOs are less professional than non-Jordanian INGOs on average, which I expect should make them less likely to pursue regime-compatible programs, all else being equal. That difference is also consistent with my findings from Chapter 4, which presented evidence in support of the idea that donors have more difficulty observing and controlling target-state NGOs than donor-state NGOs. One reason why donors find it difficult to control target-state NGOs is that their preferences should be farther away from donors' preferences on average. Because target-state NGOs have to live with the consequences of directly confronting their governments, they may be hesitant to pursue certain types of programs, even though they would also benefit most from political change. It therefore

---

[40] Interview 78, with the program officer at an INGO, in person, Amman, December 8, 2009.

makes sense from a survivalist perspective that Jordanian organizations would pursue more regime-compatible programs than non-Jordanian organizations.

Another relevant source of variation in access problems has to do with where organizations implement programs. Non-Jordanian organizations that are based in Jordan but that also conduct work in other Arab countries from there should be more likely to pursue regime-compatible programs in Jordan than elsewhere in the region. The logic is that they can exit various overseas operations, if necessary, but that it would be more difficult to move their permanent offices. The number of non-Jordanian organizations with regional headquarters in Amman is too small to enable meaningful quantitative comparisons. Interview evidence does, however, support that causal mechanism. My conversation with Robert, the director of an organization based in Amman but working in multiple countries, confirmed the importance of maintaining local access for his organization to survive and thrive. Robert explained that his organization had pursued somewhat more regime-compatible programs in Jordan than it had in nearby countries, where it runs programs but does not maintain an office. He conceded, "Here in Jordan, maybe we try to avoid issues that are very controversial. We are careful because we're practical: I don't want to get in trouble with Jordan."[41]

Yet later in the same interview, Robert noted that his organization could leave Amman if necessary and that he would like to (cautiously) fund local partners that did press for real political reform in Jordan. Yet Jordanian NGOs did not seem to be attracted to such programs. He explained, "Actually, I don't recall any controversial proposals coming to us in the first place … We thought we might get some proposals after the Arab Spring here in Jordan, but we still just got the same old anodyne programs about women. And women have already been done in Jordan."[42] We can infer from his comment that access problems are again more acute for Jordanian organizations than for non-Jordanian organizations working in Jordan, and that those access problems encourage local organizations to pursue regime-compatible programs such as women's political participation. Those reflections are consistent with my theoretical expectations.

The final point that it is important to recognize about access problems is that worries about organizational survival can become worries about

---

[41] Interview 145, with a director of an international organization, in person, Amman, May 27, 2012.
[42] Interview 145, with a director of an international organization, in person, Amman, May 27, 2012.

personal survival for Jordanian staff. I asked Ahmed, the director of an NGO based in Amman who used to work for an American democracy donor, how he chose what programs to pursue. He revealed that he and his family were living in Jordan as refugees. He explained, "I know that I don't want to talk about political rights here in Jordan because of my delicate personal situation, even though I'd like to. So all I can do is women's issues, rather than more political issues."[43]

Those worries, as expected, had implications for programming. Ahmed's NGO focused mainly on supporting women's groups and women's political participation in Jordan, two types of programs that are both measurable and regime-compatible. It did so not because Ahmed viewed such activities as particularly important for political reform in Jordan, nor because he thought they were particularly effective. Instead, it pursued programs related to women because Ahmed viewed such programs as relatively unlikely to jeopardize his family's living situation in Amman. His NGO's choice to work on supporting women's groups and women's political participation in Jordan to maintain access is consistent with broader trends in democracy support in the Middle East.

*Summary: organizational survival* Evidence from Jordan confirms that organizations working in the democracy establishment are driven by both their ideals and their incentives to survive, which involves pleasing both government donors and the Jordanian government. Activists want to create real political change in Jordan. But democracy cannot be promoted if organizations do not obtain funding. Data on the funding sources of organizations working on political reform in Jordan underscored the importance of winning foreign government grants for organizations' survival.

Moreover, concerns about organizational survival had important implications for the design and implementation of democracy aid in Jordan. Organizations, both local and international, pursued measurable programs to appeal to government donors in the absence of easy observation and control. Moreover, organizations (especially local ones) pursued regime-compatible programs that helped them maintain access to Jordan when they had some discretion from donors. Yet there is another salient aspect of the taming of democracy assistance: the field's professionalization, which has encouraged NGOs to increasingly focus on organizational survival. It is to that issue that I now turn.

[43] Interview 48, with a director of a Jordanian NGO, in person, Amman, October 26, 2009.

*Professionalization*

Chapters 5 and 6 focused extensively on the changes that have occurred in American democracy assistance as a consequence of the field's professionalization. My argument predicted that competition and professional norms in the democracy establishment should have increased over time and that both should have led organizations to pursue more measurable and regime-compatible programs. Case studies of organizations – including Freedom House, the Institute for Democracy in Eastern Europe, and the Open Society Foundations – as well as the systematic analysis of a new data set of US democracy-assistance projects confirmed that the argument yields a more complete understanding of the taming of democracy assistance than do existing approaches on their own.

My case study of democracy assistance in Jordan is not focused on those dynamics. Nevertheless, it does offer a chance to further explore the contours and consequences of the professionalization of democracy assistance. As such, I can evaluate the support in Jordan for some of the causal mechanisms associated with my theory. First, do people working in Jordan's democracy establishment share professional norms and identities, developed through their work over the past three decades both inside and outside of Jordan? Second, do professional norms and competitive pressures encourage them to pursue tamer forms of democracy assistance? Finally, do professionals feel tensions between their ideals of advancing democratic change and their pressures to help their organizations survive and thrive and resolve those tensions usually by promoting democracy in measurable and regime-compatible ways?

*The contours of professionalization* The field of democracy assistance in Jordan, like many domains of civil society there, is highly professional. A scan of the staff at democracy-related organizations in Jordan confirms that – with their backgrounds developed through work experience and educational training – they are largely professionals. Ellen, for example, was the director of the Civil Society Program of the Academy for Educational Development (AED) in Jordan. She entered the field in 1991 by working for George Soros in Prague, later worked for OSI in New York and Budapest, then directed Freedom House's office in Jordan, and finally worked for AED in Jordan. Osama, the founder of the Arab Foundation for Development and Citizenship, started his Amman-based NGO in 2007 after previously working for the National Endowment for Democracy and the Center for the Study of Islam and Democracy in Washington, DC. Johan, the director of the OSI Jordan office, previously worked for the Konrad Adenauer Stiftung in the

Middle East and also as a consultant for the European Union. As those careers suggest, circulation across organizations over the course of a career is typical.

The professionalization of democracy assistance in Jordan, as elsewhere, has had both endogenous and exogenous sources. Much of the literature focusing on NGO professionalization in the Arab world emphasizes how the process has been driven by funding competition. NGOs want to demonstrate credibility and obtain funding from foreign donors that may view them as insufficiently professional.[44] Moreover, they want to compete successfully for foreign funding against the relatively professional royal and quasi-governmental NGOs that dictators have set up to infiltrate civil society.[45] After all, they are operating in a context where, as one former American democracy donor ironically put it, "If you want the best civil society work in Jordan, you go to the Queen."[46] At the same time, professionalization was also linked to wider changes in activism in the Arab region, which feminist scholar Islah Jad has aptly referred to as the "NGO-ization of social movements."[47] Changes in activism relate to broader trends in higher education and the global political economy, which has created markets in philanthropy through neoliberalism and deregulation.[48]

*The consequences of professionalization: convergence* According to the findings in Chapters 5 and 6, one of the core consequences of the democracy establishment's professionalization has been its convergence on measurable and regime-compatible approaches to democracy assistance. Of course, there are some differences in approaches across international donors. Several European countries have supported gay and lesbian rights in Jordan, an issue the United States ignores; the Friedrich Ebert Stiftung, which is linked to the Social Democratic Party in Germany, worked with Jordanian unions, in contrast to the more economically conservative Konrad Adenauer Foundation, which is linked to a more right-wing party, the Christian Democratic Union.

On the whole, however, the recipients of democracy aid in Jordan perceived donors as remarkably similar. In my interviews, I asked every Jordanian NGO, "How are the international donors different

---

[44] Hawthorne (2005, 105).
[45] Clark and Michuki (2009, 329, 332); Hammami (2000).
[46] Interview 71, with a former officer at an international donor, in person, Amman, July 1, 2010.
[47] Jad (2004).
[48] Hopgood (2008, 103–11).

from each other?" The only differences they cited were logistical – specifically, application procedures – or, as discussed above, pertained to donors' monitoring abilities. Otherwise, interviewees perceived the donors' priorities as shifting in unison according to fads; over the period of my field research, the fads involved youth groups, women's groups, and social media.

The earlier chapters found that the field's convergence on particular programmatic strategies occurred through competitive learning as well as through professional norms. Reflecting some of those professional norms, my interviewees frequently used the terms "toolbox" and "best practices" to describe their approaches, in contrast to the previous era's "trial and error." Professionals translated, both literally and figuratively, programs they knew about and thought worked well from other countries. AED's Jordan civil society program was adapted from its general global program; the Solidarity Center's work in Jordan's qualified industrial zones (QIZs) was based on work that its director had pursued in QIZs in Indonesia and East Africa in the 1990s. Meanwhile, a Jordanian NGO received foreign funding to translate the materials of an American NGO, the Center for Civic Education, into Arabic for distribution in Saudi Arabia, Bahrain, Egypt, Tunisia, and the West Bank. As that NGO's director explained, "The books were all the same except the first two or three pages that talked about the country."[49] In some cases, interviewees stated that they had mimicked the previous programs they thought were effective; in other cases, they said that the models they were following were simply "how things are done."

As my argument would predict, government donors have played an important role in fostering local convergence. One mechanism of convergence involved donor officials suggesting particular approaches to Jordanian NGOs; another involved donor officials fostering networks among their grantees. As the director of an organization that relies on funding from the NED explained, "Many times they [the NED] have given us contacts in other countries – like in Lebanon especially – that we can learn from and benefit from the experience of."[50]

In addition, donor agencies and democracy NGOs share social and professional networks that encourage convergence. Donor officials attend some of the same events and hold regular information-sharing meetings in Amman, even if many think coordination could still improve. Outside of official functions, international staff live in the same upscale

---

[49] Interview 52, with a director of a Jordanian NGO, in person, Amman, November 19, 2009.
[50] Interview 77, with a director of a Jordanian NGO, in person, Amman, October 18, 2009.

neighborhoods and eat at the same restaurants, especially when locals are fasting. Previous researchers have used the concepts of "aidland" and "peaceland" to describe the overseas worlds inhabited by development practitioners and international peacebuilders, respectively.[51] Evidence from Jordan suggests that there is also a "democracy land" that fosters further convergence rather than differentiation.

Finally, donor officials fostered convergence with their choices of who and what to fund. As noted in Chapter 5, donors such as the NED are themselves subject to pressures to secure funding from elected officials and to adhere to professional norms. Because they, too, are agents, donors want to fund professional NGOs with established reputations and track records. As Rula, a grant-maker based in Jordan explained, "We don't mind at all duplicating other donors – many of them [our projects] are duplicates. You can't just give half a million dollars to a brand-new organization. ... [Also], it is good to link ourselves with other international donors to enhance our profile and raise awareness of our work in the region."[52] It is safer, given donor agencies' needs to report back to elected officials, to take the roads already trod by other donors rather than to differentiate via innovation. At the extreme, donor agencies in Jordan fund identical projects. Two Jordanian NGOs, for example, told me separately that they had written a joint grant proposal for a parliamentary monitoring project. They split up when they found it difficult to work together and each successfully won a grant from a different international donor to implement the original project, simultaneously.

Competition and norms have not only fostered convergence in general but also convergence specifically on tame programs. Interviewees described their shifts toward tame approaches in pragmatic terms. Peter, a longtime practitioner based in Jordan, described his transition from idealist to pragmatist (and sometimes pessimist) over more than two decades in the field. The experience of promoting democracy at the end of the Cold War was euphoric but ultimately singular: "When I first [started working in the field], I was sort of anti-Communist and I wanted to root out all the bad guys. We were a bit too idealistic and ideological in those days – we were on the right side of history for Eastern Europe. Now, we've become much more practical."[53] Peter identified the source of his evolution as his increasingly professional mindset, not changes in donor governments or in the contexts in which he worked.

[51] Autesserre (2014); Mosse (2011).
[52] Interview 9, with an officer at an international donor, in person, Amman, October 19, 2009.
[53] Interview 50, with a director of an INGO, in person, Amman, December 13, 2009.

184 Testing the argument

As one would expect, some of the field's pioneers chafed at the field's professionalization. Dima, the director of a Jordanian NGO, told me, for example, that she was so frustrated that she had considered closing her NGO. She said, "We started doing the legal aid as a voluntary thing ... Now working on human rights and democracy has become a business. So for me, it's a very big challenge to keep working on human rights even though many donors want to fund my organization."[54] Others are happier with the field's evolution. Such tensions are what we would expect when organizations gradually start to prioritize their survival.

### What about private donors?

Thus far, my analysis has focused on government-funded democracy assistance. But private donors, such as the Soros and Ford Foundations, also fund democracy assistance. In general, I expect privately funded democracy assistance to be less measurable than government-funded aid. In contrast to private foundations, which are typically governed by boards, government donors are held accountable via democratic elections. Because they are agents of the public, elected officials are more likely to value and thus fund measurable programs than other grant-makers. Although a foundation's leaders are also principals to be pleased, they have different incentives and are less likely to reward measurable programs.

In Jordan, I also expect privately funded democracy assistance to be less regime-compatible than government-funded aid. One of the general principles in this book is that the more donors prefer measurable or regime-compatible programs, the more organizations in the democracy establishment will pursue them. It pays to do what the funder wants. As discussed previously, many Western democracy donors have security partnerships with the Jordanian regime. As a general rule, they may be relatively favorable to regime-compatible programs. Since privately funded donors do not have countervailing foreign-policy priorities in Jordan, we would expect them to fund less regime-compatible programs.

To test those hypotheses, I coded all the democracy-assistance projects that took place in Jordan in 2009. When I did so, I found that around 25 percent of the programs that were funded by private donors in Jordan were measurable and around 25 percent were regime-compatible. Both proportions are markedly lower than the proportions of measurable and regime-compatible assistance funded by government donors in Jordan. Indeed, both bilateral and multilateral government donors selected

---

[54] Interview 5, with a director of a Jordanian NGO, in person, Amman, November 5, 2009.

programs that were measurable, regime-compatible, or both more than half of the time. Those comparisons suggest that, as expected, private foundations promoted democracy differently than government donors in Jordan because they have different preferences and delegation structures. Since all donors were operating in the same political context, those differences cannot be explained by the characteristics of the Jordanian regime.

Interviews with grant-makers from private foundations suggest that the reasons why they pursue less measurable and regime-compatible programs are the ones emphasized by my argument. When I asked a staff member at the Soros Foundation in Amman why he did not fund more measurable projects, he responded that it was because voters do not hold the Soros Foundation accountable. He explained, "We have been less systematic than other donors, for sure ... We are dealing with private funds, money that comes from the Soros Fund, so we are not dealing with so much pressure for quantitative results."[55] Likewise, he suggested that the Soros Foundation was able to fund fewer regime-compatible programs than government donors because it was less beholden to countervailing strategic pressures. He stated, "We are not putting pressure on governments, per se, for the sake of putting pressure ... But sometimes when you have a friendly relationship like between [the] USA and Jordan, it means they [government donors] don't put on any pressure."[56] In other words, the qualitative evidence supports my causal mechanisms about principal–agent dynamics in democracy aid.

## Conclusions

Despite being one of the largest recipients of democracy assistance in the Middle East, Jordan remains autocratic and remained stable amid the Arab uprisings in 2011. Although there is no guarantee that any democracy assistance would have democratized Jordan, some observers have nevertheless criticized programs there for being too anodyne to be successful.[57] Scholars have argued that democracy promotion has been shaped inexorably by the donors' relationships with the Jordanian government and that it therefore lacks bite and credibility.

---

[55] Interview 61, with an international donor representative, in person, Amman, July 1, 2010.
[56] Interview 61, with an international donor representative, in person, Amman, July 1, 2010.
[57] Carapico (2002); Heydemann (2007); Wittes (2008).

This chapter took a different tack, emphasizing the importance of transnational actors in democracy aid. Democracy assistance in Jordan takes place far away from the Western capitals studied in previous chapters, and thus the organizations that implement programs there have considerable discretion. Competition for donor funding drove democracy-assistance organizations to pursue measurable programs, while access problems drove them, especially local ones, to pursue regime-compatible programs. These patterns were accentuated when funders are not present in Jordan. Although my focus in this chapter has not been on change over time, its evidence suggests that competition and professionalization have played a role in fostering convergence on measurable and regime-compatible programs. The findings have important implications for how democracy assistance in the Middle East should be reformed, to which I return in the book's conclusion.

Despite the chapter's insights, case studies are best in pairs that generate comparisons. Moreover, a concern with the Jordanian case is that its strategic value to donor governments may influence outcomes on such a fundamental level that it is hard to observe. Thus, in the next chapter I examine democracy assistance in another country that was typical in the statistical analysis: Tunisia. Tunisia, like Jordan, is a relatively small, relatively developed state, but it does not have strong security ties to foreign donors. Moreover, during the period of analysis, Tunisia experienced a regime change, giving me the opportunity to examine the effects of domestic shocks on democracy assistance. If we observe similar causal effects in Tunisia to the ones observed in Jordan, then the argument will be strongly supported.

*May we dare dream? But then, doesn't every reality start as a dream?*
*"Should the people one day truly aspire to life, then fate must respond!"*[1]

Tunisia inspired mass uprisings throughout the Arab world after popular protests forced its long-standing dictator, Zine El Abidine Ben
Ali, to step down on January 14, 2011. Tunisians had long resisted
and contended with Ben Ali's tyranny. But like other revolutions,
their successful uprising – against one of the world's most repressive
dictators – took most observers by surprise. Its immediate catalyst
was the public suicide of a fruit vendor, Mohamed Bouazizi, who set
himself on fire on December 17, 2010, to protest the corrupt police
in his town; the police had allegedly harassed Bouazizi, flipping over
his fruit cart and confiscating his fruit-weighing scales. Bouazizi's self-
immolation served as a lodestar for a young population fed up with
the government's corruption, bad economic policies, and repression.
It prompted protests across the country that brushed aside Ben Ali –
Tunisia's president since 1987 – within less than a month. Ben Ali and
his wife managed to escape, flying to Saudi Arabia after France turned
them away.

The main goal of this chapter is to evaluate the extent to which
the theory presented in Chapter 2 explains democracy assistance after
Ben Ali. To complement the analysis presented in Chapter 7, I focus
primarily on the professionalization hypotheses, drawing on twenty-
five field-based interviews, organizations' documents, news articles, and
secondary research. The first step is to evaluate the values of the key
variables. The chapter thus explores variation over time in democracy
assistance in Tunisia, comparing the immediate post-revolution period
to dynamics eighteen months later. One of the advantages of this
longitudinal approach is that it holds constant potentially confounding
factors – such as the strategic importance and regime type of the target

---

[1] *Economist* (online).

Table 8.1 *Summary of variables in Tunisia.*

| Years | Competition | Professional norms | Strategic importance | Freedom House rating | Expected aid |
|---|---|---|---|---|---|
| Early 2011 | Low | Low | Low–medium | Partly free | Very untame |
| Mid 2012 | Low–medium | Low–medium | Low–medium | Partly free | Untame |

*Notes:* Details about coding the variables are in the text. Note that the expected aid should also vary by delegation relationship, although I am not studying those variations in this chapter.

country – and thus allows me to focus on my key variables of interest. Table 8.1 previews the findings.

The second step is to evaluate the evidence in support of the hypothesized causal mechanisms. First, when competition is higher, organizations should work harder to get funding via measurable programs and to gain access via regime-compatible programs (Hypothesis 4). Organizations should use those strategies to promote survival. Second, when organizations in the democracy establishment are more professional, they should pursue more measurable and regime-compatible programs (Hypothesis 5). The first reason is that professionals value organizational survival more than non-professionals. The second reason is that professionals are more likely to view such programs as appropriate. Finally, because organizations want to win funding and survive, I expect them to respond to donor officials' preferences (Hypothesis 6).

The chapter continues as follows. The first section provides domestic and international context. The second section observes how democracy aid went "back to the future" immediately after the revolution with relatively untame democracy assistance. Since competition for donor funding in Tunisia was less fierce than elsewhere and civil society was relatively unprofessional, NGOs did not often pursue measurable and regime-compatible programs. The third section discusses the rapid emergence of survival concerns and their effects. The fourth section concludes.

### Context for the case study

This chapter seeks to explain the design and implementation of democracy assistance in Tunisia after the Jasmine Revolution. A necessary first step, therefore, is to understand the domestic and international contexts in which aid took place. Two important dynamics are the political opening of 2011, followed by instability, and the rapid investment by foreign donors, followed by retrenchment.

*The domestic context*

Tunisia is often called the "most European" Arab country. A small state bordered by Libya and Algeria, Tunisia is separated from Italy by less than 100 miles of sea. The country gained independence from France in 1956 and was ruled for the next three decades by Habib Bourguiba. In 1975, Bourguiba was elected "president for life" by Tunisia's National Assembly, a legislature filled with his party supporters. In 1987, Prime Minister Zine El Abidine Ben Ali, a former army general and diplomat, contrived to replace Bourguiba. Ben Ali's ascendance was called a "medical coup d'état" since state doctors helped remove Bourguiba by declaring him senile. With Bourguiba in exile until his death in 2000, Ben Ali pulled down the trappings of his predecessor, both literally (such as a massive equestrian statue of him in Tunis) and figuratively.

Although observers hoped that Ben Ali would democratize Tunisia, Bourguiba's departure did not lead to many fundamental changes. Early on, Ben Ali made several moves toward pluralism: allowing opposition parties in parliament for the first time since independence, creating a constitutional council to oversee new legislation, and temporarily amending the constitution to limit the president's tenure to two consecutive re-elections. As Figure 8.1 shows, the level of freedom in Tunisia increased notably at that time. But as the figure also shows, freedom quickly reverted to the mean. Repeating a familiar pattern, Ben Ali's so-called reforms did not lead to democratization and arguably supported his regime's survival.[2] Indeed, Tunisia's parliament had little power over policy, the press was not free, and opponents of the government were harassed.[3]

Nevertheless, many scholars were optimistic about Tunisia's prospects for democratization.[4] First, the economic structure was conducive to democracy: Tunisia had achieved "upper middle income" status according to the World Bank without relying on natural resources. Second, Ben Ali's regime lacked two traits – strategic value to the West and a military heavily invested in its maintenance – that preserved authoritarianism in the Middle East.[5] Finally, in contrast to other Arab rulers, Bourguiba and Ben Ali were fiercely secular, advocating women's education and

---

[2] Sadiki (2002).
[3] Angrist (1999).
[4] Durac and Cavatorta (2011, 13).
[5] Bellin (2004, 2012, 134–5).

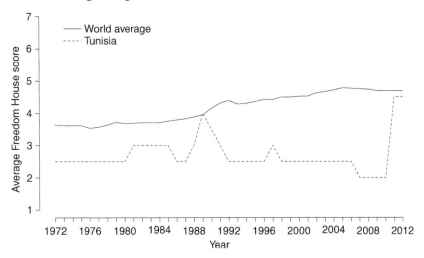

Figure 8.1 Freedom in the world and in Tunisia, 1972–2012.
*Note:* I averaged countries' political liberty and civil rights scores, which
were rescaled so that 1 represents the least democracy and 7 the most.
*Data source:* Freedom House (1973–2013).

full equality – significant factors since gender inequalities can impede
democracy.[6]

The Jasmine Revolution that overthrew President Ben Ali seemed
initially to justify such optimism. After Ben Ali's exit, the Islamist
Ennahda Party won a plurality of seats in the Constituent Assembly
election. The election brought the party's Hamadi Jebali to power as
prime minister in December 2011 as part of a governing coalition.
International election monitors hailed the election as free and fair,
with Freedom House deeming Tunisia "partly free" due to "increased
freedoms of speech, press, assembly, and religious expression; and
greater freedom for academics and nongovernmental organizations."[7]
During this initial opening, Tunisia's government generally welcomed
international aid to help with the transition. As a consequence, local and
international INGOs did not face many pressures to tame programs in
order to maintain access.

Yet neither the ouster of a long-running dictator nor the holding of
multi-party elections is sufficient for democratization to occur. Soon
after the election, several threats to Tunisia's transition emerged. First,

[6] Inglehart and Norris (2003).
[7] Freedom House (2012).

Tunisia's economy lapsed into crisis, stoking dissatisfaction and prompting protesters to return to the streets. Indeed, a survey sponsored by the International Republican Institute in the summer of 2012 found that 23 percent of adults were unemployed and actively looking for a job.[8] Second, the political atmosphere in Tunisia became violently polarized, as evidenced by attacks throughout 2012 on liquor stores, "un-Islamic" concerts, and the American Embassy. A key point of contention was the role of Islam in politics, with Salafis (Islamic "puritans") pushing to bring the country closer to sharia and the more moderate, but still Islamist, Ennahda Party positioning itself ambiguously, leaving many in doubt as to the party's true intentions.

### The international context

Despite some optimism about Tunisia's democratic prospects, Western donors invested little money there prior to 2011. Out of more than one billion dollars spent by the US government aiding democracy in the Middle East in the five years preceding the Arab uprisings, less than four million dollars went to Tunisia. Although European donors had a larger presence, their largest commitments (in 2002 and 2003) never totaled more than two million dollars. Moreover, even those EU dollars that were budgeted for Tunisia often went unspent.[9]

In terms of diplomatic pressure, representatives from the United States government occasionally criticized the Tunisian government (over, for example, lack of internet freedom) or had lunch with opposition parties. Such actions sought to give activists moral support and signal the United States' position on democracy. They were not, however, designed to encourage regime change, and nor did they end up fostering it. In fact, American officials later assessed the parties they met with as not having played a role in ousting Ben Ali.[10] European leaders did even less to jeopardize Tunisia's stability. Although the EU included Tunisia in the European Neighbourhood Policy and Euro-Mediterranean Partnership – initiatives that sought to encourage political reform – it did not invoke economic conditionality despite its considerable potential leverage.[11]

One explanation for the dearth of democracy promotion prior to the Jasmine Revolution was the repressive environment. During Ben Ali's rule, NGOs that accepted foreign funding could have had their

[8] Williams and Associates (2012).
[9] Bicchi (2009, 73).
[10] Interview 143, with an American diplomat, in person, Tunis, May 11, 2012.
[11] Powel (2009, 64–5).

staff arrested (or worse). Moreover, the regime lashed out against diplomats who were perceived as interfering. A second explanation was the geopolitical context. Although Tunisia (unlike Jordan) was not an American client state, the post-September 11 focus in the Middle East was still on fighting terrorism. All the same, two-thirds of the political activists that I spoke to in Tunis criticized international actors for not doing more to help them under Ben Ali, criticisms that some of them, such as Neila Charchour Hachicha, also made openly at the time.[12]

Unsurprisingly, given the context, some democracy assistance efforts in Tunisia were quite anodyne. Examples included a MEPI-funded seminar on good governance and government procurement and a university scholarship program.[13] A cable from the United States embassy in Tunis to Washington explained MEPI's timid approach thus: "Although projects directly and exclusively targeting political reform remain a rarity, we continue to look for openings where we find them and hope we can help Tunisian civil society to push the boundaries, however incrementally."[14]

Despite the circumstances, the international community also funded a number of politically-sensitive activities. Some INGOs maintained unofficial operations by flying under the radar of the government and collaborating closely with local activists, especially outside Tunis.[15] Other activities were managed from neighboring countries, such as Jordan and Morocco. Tunisian dissidents were commonly brought overseas – for example, to Morocco – for training. Kholoud, a Tunisian woman in her twenties, participated in such a program. Selected because of her volunteer work with a Tunisian NGO, Kholoud was terrified to attend – her legs shook at the airport en route to the training and she believed that the government monitored her emails afterwards. But she described the training session as a turning point, encouraging her to believe, "I have to fight and struggle for my freedom."[16] Later, after reading about activists' plans via Facebook, Kholoud joined the pro-democracy protests on Avenue Habib Bourguiba in Tunis in December 2010, often being forced to run away from security forces' tear gas and shots but never doubting that Ben Ali would step down.

Kholoud's story makes clear that relatively untame democracy assistance is possible – even in the twenty-first century, even in a country as repressive as Tunisia once was. If the book's argument is correct, the

---

[12] Hachicha (2005).
[13] Middle East Partnership Initiative (2009).
[14] United States Embassy in Tunis (2008).
[15] Interview 152, with an INGO director, in person, Tunis, May 17, 2012.
[16] Interview 128, with a Tunisian activist, in person, Tunis, May 16, 2012.

aftermath of the revolution, with its abundance of international funding and relative absence of competition and professional Tunisian NGOs, should be characterized by relatively large numbers of such programs, as was also the case in the 1980s and early 1990s, when NGOs were also less competitive and professional. Yet changes in democracy assistance should emerge as NGOs face new challenges in terms of survival, causing them to professionalize and converge on more measurable and regime-compatible programs.

## Democracy assistance immediately after Ben Ali

One of the core arguments in this book is that when organizations compete more for democracy assistance, they pursue tamer programs because competition focuses organizations on their survival. Another is that when organizations are more professional, they should pursue tamer programs because professionals value organizational survival more than non-professionals and they are more likely to take for granted tame programs as appropriate.

Although previous chapters showed that competition and professionalism are associated with tamer democracy assistance, on average, they did not show how democracy assistance would be designed today in the absence of those forces. Because there are many aspects of world politics that have changed since the 1980s, it is difficult to fully account for all the potential omitted variables. Perhaps, for example, broader changes in the culture of non-profit organizations fully explain the rise of tame programs.

One advantage of studying democracy assistance in Tunisia is that it enables me to, at least partially, answer the "what if?" question: what would democracy assistance look like today in an atmosphere of relatively abundant international funding and relatively unprofessional NGOs? In this section, I answer that question by making two claims. First, due to the political context, Tunisia has been relatively insulated from rising competition and professionalism in the democracy establishment. Second, the relative absence of competition and professionalism contributed to less tame democracy-assistance programs, such as activities supporting elections, political parties, and dissidents, in Tunisia in 2011 than in most other countries at that time.

*Back to the future? Less professionalism, less competition in Tunisia*

Appreciating Tunisia's pre-revolution political context helps us understand the atmosphere in the democracy-assistance community following the revolution. Autocratic Tunisia, with its repression, surveillance, and corruption, was, unsurprisingly, not the site of a vibrant civil society. When Ben Ali stepped down, many new NGOs were created.[17] Many of those new NGOs consisted of single individuals or small groups of people working out of their homes – hardly professionals with technical expertise and knowledge of field-specific norms.

Even older NGOs working toward political reform in Tunisia were less professional than their counterparts abroad. None of the Tunisian NGO staff that I interviewed, for example, had graduate degrees in related fields. That is a significant point since an alternative explanation for my findings about the taming of democracy assistance is that they reflect general changes in the non-profit sector. Although part of the cause of the lack of civil society development was Ben Ali's repression, NGOs in an autocracy can be quite professional, as the last chapter showed. That was generally not the case in Tunisia, where people entered the field, despite its uncertain financial benefits and potential risks, because they wanted to spread freedom. One NGO director illustrated his commitment in response to a question about how donors held his organization accountable: "I don't feel accountable to the donors – I feel accountable to the people I work with, who are more important than the donors. My first responsibility is a moral one to youth leaders. Every Saturday they take time out of their weekends to make this country better."[18] Hearing such a comment in Tunisia – an environment where NGO directors lack years of work experience in the field, relevant graduate degrees, and so on – is consistent with my argument.

Meanwhile, the international community's initial commitment to aiding the Tunisian transition discouraged NGO funding competition. Consider, for example, the United States government's pledges, which were striking not only because they were the largest in dollar terms but also because they represented the greatest reversal from the Ben Ali era. In the first six months after Ben Ali's ouster, the United States allocated just $40 million in bilateral aid since it was difficult to allocate funds to a country that had previously received little aid. But after opening a local USAID office (including an Office of Transition Initiatives), the United States allocated an additional $400 million to support democracy, human rights, and good governance, including $45 million in direct grants to democracy-assistance NGOs. In addition, the United States sent millions of dollars via the Middle East Response Fund, MEPI, and the NED, among other instruments, and selected Tunisia for an

[17] Chomiak (2011, 78).
[18] Interview 133, with an NGO director, in person, Tunis, May 11, 2012.

MCC Threshold Program that provided $20–30 million and potentially much more.[19]

As a consequence, local and international NGOs in Tunis did not sense any intense competition for funding in early 2011. As expected, the relative absence of competition afforded them freedom. Stephen, the director of a country office of an international NGO, said, for example, "I don't think about donors – I don't have to. That's an advantage. We have more funding flexibility than elsewhere and so we can be more effective."[20] Likewise, Hannah, the director of another INGO, put it this way: "The international community's desire to support the Tunisian transition was profound last year ... As an organization that had a track record in Tunisia and was here early, we've been able to get everything that we need. I hope that will continue. We've had some freedom and maximum flexibility to adapt quickly as needed."[21] As those comments indicate, the funding environment for democracy assistance in Tunisia was atypical and discouraged the competition that affects NGOs in many countries today. What were the consequences for democracy-assistance programs?

### Consequences for programming

Many factors affect how organizations design and implement democracy aid, including the political environments where they work and donor governments' preferences. But two important, and until now largely overlooked, factors that also play a crucial role are how professional the NGOs are and how fiercely they compete for donor-government funds. When one or both of those factors are high, I expect NGOs to converge on the tame programs that help them survive and thrive as organizations – even in the absence of clear evidence that such programs democratize target countries. When one or both of those factors are low, I expect NGOs not to pursue such tame strategies. Measurable programs help NGOs appeal to donor governments that otherwise have a hard time observing and controlling them. Regime-compatible programs help NGOs maintain access to target states that dislike foreign meddling. Unfortunately, as discussed in Chapter 3, neither type of program is clearly associated with democratization, and both have been associated with negative consequences in at least some cases.

[19] McInerney (2012, 26).
[20] Interview 129, with an INGO director, in person, Tunis, May 18, 2012.
[21] Interview 146, with an INGO director, in person, Tunis, May 9, 2012.

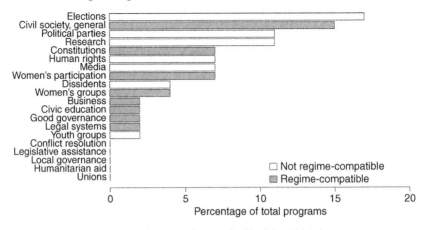

Figure 8.2 Democracy assistance in Tunisia, 2011, by category.
*Data source:* Author's coding based on interviews and organizations' materials.

Consistent with the argument, democracy assistance in Tunisia in 2011 was less measurable and regime-compatible than in other countries – both on average and in countries at the same level of democracy as Tunisia. Figure 8.2 summarizes the internationally funded projects, highlighting which projects were regime-compatible. In contrast to Jordan, most programs in Tunisia were *not* regime-compatible (58 percent). In other countries during 2011, only 41 percent of the aid was not regime-compatible; in other countries that, like Tunisia, were ranked "partly free" by Freedom House, the figure was even lower: 26 percent. The trends are similar for measurable programs. About 50 percent of the programs in Tunisia during 2011 and early 2012 were measurable, in contrast to 55 percent for all countries in the world and 82 percent for countries ranked "partly free."

Regime change may create openings for a few years of untame programming because of distinctive conditions or donor priorities. Yet Tunisia's aid was distinctively untame even among post-revolutionary states in a way that is consistent with my argument. As discussed above, Tunisia received little democracy assistance under Ben Ali. Since NGOs adopt professional practices in part to demonstrate credibility to donors and win funding,[22] Tunisian NGOs faced few isomorphic pressures until recently. In contrast, some other countries in the past decade – Serbia, Georgia, Kyrgyzstan – received considerable aid prior to their

[22] Boulding (2012).

revolutions. Thus, they should have had more professional NGO sectors, which is consistent with their relatively tame programs.

As Figure 8.2 shows, several categories of aid have been particularly common. Aid in several relatively confrontational categories – including political parties, research institutions, human rights, and the media – was plentiful. In contrast, aid to women's groups and governance – two tame types of democracy assistance that are globally and regionally prominent – was rarer.

Some of the trends can be explained by Tunisia's needs. Electoral aid is, for example, typical in a transitioning country. But it is hard to argue that Tunisia had no need for programs supporting women's groups and women's political participation. After the revolution, many people, both locally and internationally, worried that the rise of Islamist parties was causing a decline in women's rights.[23] Nevertheless, organizations working in Tunisia were drawn to the types of projects that were more prominent in the early days of democracy assistance during the Cold War, which they thought were likely to be effective.

My argument suggests that organizations' relative lack of concern with survival due to few challenges in terms of funding and access should have caused the relative prominence of tame aid programs. Interviewees' descriptions of their programming decisions confirmed that sincere beliefs about how to effect democratization drove their programming choices. Marcus, the director of an INGO based in Tunis, told me, for example, that he had a great deal of confidence in continued funding and worried little about donors' monitoring. He even shifted some of his NGO's efforts from technical assistance on constitutions (a measurable and regime-compatible category) to civic education (a regime-compatible but not measurable category). He said, "Politically, the EU [one of his major donors] isn't going to not fund us after 2013 because they're just very committed to the Tunisian transition. They understand that they can't always get quick results ... Initially our program did not have money for educational events, but I was able to reallocate the funds."[24]

Donor preferences also, as would be expected, significantly affected the design of democracy-assistance programs. USAID efforts to support democracy in Tunisia were, for example, often channeled through the Office of Transition Initiatives (OTI), a mechanism for aiding democracy that involves smaller grants being issued in a freer manner than is typical for USAID. At USAID, OTI's grants are relatively "flexible,

---

[23] Amara (2012).
[24] Interview 140, with an INGO director, in person, Tunis, May 17, 2012.

nimble, and fast," in the words of one OTI staff member. The OTI field office in Tunisia, which oversaw $100 million, therefore had less desire for measurable programs than a typical USAID field office. Moreover, OTI's field operations enhanced its monitoring capabilities relative to a typical USAID office, thus giving its NGO partners less incentive as well as less opportunity to implement tame programs. OTI's small-scale and less measurable civil society and civic education programs stand in sharp contrast to the large projects bankrolled by USAID elsewhere, such as the extensive legislative-assistance programs described in Chapter 7.

Evidence from post-revolutionary Tunisia therefore supports my theory, which emphasizes how organizations in the democracy establishment respond to incentives created by donor and target states. Both qualitative examples and quantitative data suggest that in the counterfactual case, when competition and professionalism are low, relatively untame democracy assistance can still result. But if my argument is correct, the passage of time should be linked to the rise of funding competition and professional norms. Was 2012 too soon for such forces to start emerging?

## The ongoing transformation of democracy aid

As the last section showed, democracy assistance in Tunisia was initially characterized by a heady idealism and experimentation that recalled earlier eras of democracy assistance. But one year later, the field started to change. The same forces – funding competition and professional norms – that caused the taming of democracy assistance elsewhere also started to emerge in Tunisia. Although the transformation was incomplete – professionalization does not happen overnight – it proceeded faster than in the 1990s, likely due to pressures created by the existence of the global field. The changes started to tangibly affect programs. Relatively regime-compatible programs related to good governance and civil society (residual), for example, both increased by 27 percent from 2011 to 2012.

What else could explain those nascent changes in democracy aid in Tunisia? One possibility is a shift in American or European relations with the Tunisian government. Positive relations between a democracy donor and an autocratic target state, for example, tend to be correlated with tamer democracy assistance, according to Chapter 5. But Tunisia is not a Western client, and donors have enjoyed largely cooperative relations with the Ennahda Party. Donors want Tunisia to set an example of Arab democracy.

Another possibility is a shift in Tunisian politics. The biggest development in that regard has been the rise of Islamism, starting with an unexpectedly successful showing by Islamists in the December 2011 election. Yet the key moments when the battle over Islam in Tunisia turned violent (such as the American embassy attack in September 2012) occurred after my period of field research, when the trends I discuss below had already begun. Moreover, none of my interviewees openly anticipated that violent turn or stated that they were redrafting their programs as a consequence. Thus, I conclude that organizational survival and emerging professional norms – in combination with other factors – do help explain the ongoing transformation of the democracy establishment in Tunisia.

### An emerging fight for organizational survival

Surviving and thriving as an organization in the democracy establishment requires both winning funding, usually from Western governments, and also gaining or maintaining access to undemocratic or democratizing target states. Both factors were relevant for democracy-promotion organizations in Tunisia starting in mid 2012, although, as would be expected for a country that seemed to largely be on a sincerely democratizing trajectory, funding was a more acute worry than access in Tunisia. I consider each aspect of organizational survival in turn.

Despite the survivalist focus among organizations that I document below, it is important to underscore that, like other transnational civil society actors, most people working for NGOs in Tunisia's democracy establishment are motivated by more than organizational survival. Kholoud, the former dissident who now helps run a Tunisian NGO, told me that she receives many emails from international donors inviting her to submit funding applications. Such donor invitations can create agency slack, giving her some latitude to choose programs that suited her organization's interests. But Kholoud does not want to have as much funding as possible. In her words, "We want to do one or two projects and do them really well. In a few years, there won't be so many grants in Tunisia and so we want to focus on our own vision."[25] But Kholoud's attitude is not shared by everyone in Tunisia or even in her organization. As another colleague at her NGO said, "In an ideal world, we would like to work with every ministry and every sector of the society."

[25] Interview 128, with a Tunisian activist, in person, Tunis, May 16, 2012.

*Funding pressures* Because the international community initially allocated a lot of democracy assistance in Tunisia, the NGO sector in the country quickly blossomed. Among the INGOs that were working in Tunisia by mid 2012 on democracy-assistance projects were the American Bar Association's Rule of Law Initiative, AMIDEAST, the Carter Center, Catholic Relief Services, Electoral Reform International Services (ERIS), Freedom House, Friedrich Ebert Stiftung, Friedrich Naumann Stiftung, IFES, IRI, Konrad Adenauer Stiftung, Mercy Corps, NDI, Search for Common Ground, and World Learning. With a few exceptions, those NGOs did not have programs in Tunisia prior to the revolution. With many new civil society organizations forming in 2011, the number of Tunisian NGOs seeking democracy funding also increased; indeed, working in international development offered a lucrative field for a young population facing high levels of unemployment.[26]

Because of the growth of Tunisia's civil society and the new presence of INGOs, the initial sensation of abundant democracy assistance faded during 2012. Many Tunisians expressed disappointment to me that, despite foreign powers' good will, Tunisia was not receiving a Marshall Plan. Others worried about Tunisia's funding being redirected to Egypt and Libya. Yet others complained that European donors were issuing no-cost extensions to democracy-assistance programs in order to concentrate instead on social and economic development, despite 2012 and 2013 being critical moments for democracy. Western diplomats received such complaints with incredulity, viewing their countries' commitments to Tunisia as unprecedented and generous. Nevertheless, practitioners' sense of funding scarcity was real and growing. Their frustrations were heightened because some of donors' biggest financial pledges, such as the Deauville Partnership from 2011, were missing.[27]

Salma, the president of a Tunisian NGO, vividly expressed her funding concerns to me with a recent example. The Arab Partnership Fund, a new British initiative supporting political reform, offered a workshop in 2012 in Tunis on submitting grant applications. When Salma showed up, she was stunned to see that about four-fifths of the approximately twenty-five attendees had come from INGOs with dedicated fundraising staff. She commented:

Now, we have a market for international funds in Tunisia ... Many international organizations are just using our country as a way to get funds, with limited knowledge of the country and few local partners. That scares me. They're bigger and have better relationships with the donors, but they can bid for the same funds

---

[26] Chomiak (2011, 78).
[27] Hamid and Mandaville (2013, 100).

that we are trying to bid for. I think it's a dictatorship of INGOs. Is Tunisia just another cake that international organizations are trying to share the pieces of?[28]

Since obtaining foreign funding is crucial to NGOs' survival, Salma's organization, which traditionally worked on youth programs, was pursuing partnerships with INGOs and programs in new areas, such as women's representation, to remain competitive. Notably, those new programs were tamer according to my definition, reflecting the general programming models pursued by INGOs globally.

Salma's frustrations were common among Tunisian NGOs, but not unique to them. Some INGOs also found themselves struggling to secure grants for their post-2013 programs. One American NGO director that I spoke to in Tunis, for example, was trying to pitch general civil society programs modeled on work her organization had done elsewhere in the region to funders with little success. She pointed out that the arrival of several highly professional organizations working in the same area – such as the Institute of International Education and Education for Employment – was making her life more difficult.[29] Another INGO director told me that his organization was just as corrupt in the search for donor funding as the non-Western NGOs he was trying to reform.[30]

An organizational strategy for coping with heightened competition is to pursue programs with measurable outputs and outcomes. As in Jordan and elsewhere, international donors in Tunisia faced considerable barriers to effective observation and control. Many of the old regime-affiliated NGOs from Ben Ali's time still existed, sometimes with different names. International donors that previously did not give out many (or any) civil society grants struggled to identify those NGOs and avoid funding them.[31] Even governments that did have a history of working with Tunisian civil society organizations, such as the United States with its local MEPI Regional Office, have found it difficult to monitor programs. As one US official explained, "One of the hardest challenges of these efforts is keeping track and reconciling all the different vehicles. There are lots of resources being directed at Tunisia right now, which is an absolute obsession in Washington."[32]

Aware of those challenges, savvy NGOs sought out measurable programs. NGO directors emphasized that they were not being forced to generate measurable programs, but that such programs represented

---

[28] Interview 134, with a Tunisian NGO director, in person, Tunis, May 14, 2012.
[29] Interview 130, with an INGO director, in person, Tunis, May 15, 2012.
[30] Interview 142, with an INGO director, in person, Tunis, May 9, 2012.
[31] Interview 128, with a Tunisian activist, in person, Tunis, May 16, 2012.
[32] Interview 143, with an American diplomat, in person, Tunis, May 11, 2012.

a savvy survival strategy. Their comments are consistent with donors' requests for applications, which called for measurement strategies, but not measurable programs, such as aid to support local governance instead of aid to support political parties, per se. For example, MEPI stated in 2011 that successful applicants should be "able to measure program success against proposed measurable achievements and completion dates."[33] Similarly, the EIDHR asked for Tunisian proposals that were "SMART: specific, measurable, achievable, relevant, and timely."[34]

Thus, donors' preferences influenced, but did not dictate, organizations' strategies. Adel, the director of the Tunis office of an INGO, put his strategy this way: "I know that they [donors] want to see results, even though they're not calling us every week or standing right behind us. We know that we have to generate tangible, real results quickly ... The way that we work today is to develop projects that are grounded in measurable projects and indicators."[35] Examples of the programs he chose to generate tangible results were activities supporting media freedom and media professionalization – programs that fall into this book's measurable category. Adel's comment is consistent with this book's argument that measurable programs help NGOs appeal to donor governments that want and need results but have a hard time monitoring their grantees.

*Access pressure* Since Tunisia's leaders appeared to be sincerely committed to democratization, one might assume that access was not a problem for organizations in the democracy establishment there. Organizations in a country such as Jordan certainly had a harder time operating than they did in Tunisia. Still, INGOs and local NGOs did face some access problems.

The main emerging source of access problems in Tunisia was popular and elite suspicion of foreigners. In the context of their study on anti-Americanism, political scientists Peter Katzenstein and Robert Keohane offered a definition of sovereign–nationalists, or people who focus on "the importance of not losing control over the terms by which polities are inserted in world politics and the inherent importance and value of collective national identities."[36] Sovereign–nationalist sentiments, especially

---

[33] United States Department of State (2011, 7). The State Department used similar language in the February 2012 request for applications for the Forum for the Future Civil Society Reform Initiative.

[34] European Instrument for Democracy and Human Rights (2012, 28).

[35] Interview 133, with an INGO director, in person, Tunis, May 11, 2012.

[36] Katzenstein and Keohane (2007, 32).

sovereign–nationalist anti-Americanism, were present in Tunisia after the revolution. Only 25 percent of the population in mid 2012 reported that it was good that American ideas and customs were spreading in their country.[37] More infamously, the American embassy in Tunis was one of the several US embassies in the Middle East that were attacked by protesters in September 2012, who broke windows and ignited fires inside the compound.

Sovereign–nationalist frustrations about democracy aid had existed for some time, with, according to one leaked American government cable, "MEPI" in Ben Ali's Tunisia being used as a "four-letter word."[38] Post-revolution, the backlash seemed to occur most often in the sensitive areas of elections and political-party aid. Articles in the Tunisian press targeted IFES, questioning its motives and comparing its staff members to CIA operatives, thus frightening many donors and international NGOs into thinking that highly political or well-publicized programs might create a problem.[39] As expected, media programs, another type of confrontational aid, also received local scrutiny.[40]

Some of the problems took place on a small scale, such as when individual Tunisian political activists rejected international programs and advice due to perceived slights. A particularly galling aspect of many international programs from the Tunisian perspective was that foreigners specializing in support to political parties, elections, and constitutions would draw on their experiences working in Iraq and Afghanistan – common ports of call for democracy practitioners, but countries that many Tunisians viewed as less advanced politically, economically, and socially than their own.[41] International experts were also occasionally piqued by their Tunisian interlocutors, such as when Tunisian officials would reject the advice and publicly disavow the participation of people with years of relevant technical experience.[42]

A few people working in the democracy establishment in Tunisia told me that they feared losing access not because of general sovereign–nationalist sentiment but because of the Ennahda Party's illiberalism. Debating the true intentions of Tunisia's ruling Islamists – whether they embraced a moderate form of Islam or were actually more extreme – was a common political pasttime in Tunisia after the party won a plurality in the Constituent Assembly. Constitutional debates over women's rights

[37] Pew Global Attitudes Project (2012a, 27).
[38] United States Embassy in Tunis (2008).
[39] Global Net (2011).
[40] Ghribi (2011).
[41] Interview 139, with a Tunisian politician, in person, Tunis, May 16, 2012.
[42] Interview 137, with an INGO director, in person, Tunis, May 14, 2012.

and the criminalization of blasphemy in 2012 generated particular controversy, and skeptics believed that Ennahda did not actually want democracy.

Some foreigners in the democracy establishment were happy to cooperate with Ennahda. Yet others – especially people who ascribed to the French concept of *laïcité* – were less sanguine. Peter, the director of an INGO, told me he believed that Ennahda members were monitoring his whereabouts and emails, and that he included their representatives in all his programs to avoid reprisals. The extent to which his fears were well founded remains uncertain, but they illustrate the perception of real access problems in mid 2012. And such beliefs tamed programming. Peter found programs supporting civic education, less politicized civil society groups, and the rule of law more appealing than political-party programs given the circumstances.[43]

*Summary: organizational survival* In summary, my research in Tunisia showed how organizations working in the democracy establishment are driven both by their desires to promote freedom and their needs to continue to win funding and maintain access. As activists, they sought to advance democracy in the most effective and efficient way possible. But winning funding for 2013 was more difficult than for 2012. Therefore, organizations focused more on the measurable programs that would help them maintain and expand their funding levels. They also pursued more regime-compatible programs when possible because of perceived hostility towards foreigners and illiberalism within Ennahda.

### Emerging professionalism

At the same time as worries about organizational survival started to affect organizations in Tunisia, so too did global norms about promoting democracy. Those norms encouraged people working in Tunisia to import techniques from other global contexts and, in so doing, to implement more measurable and regime-compatible programs. Moreover, the start of the professionalization of activism in Tunisia reinforced nascent tendencies among local NGOs to focus on the tamer types of programs that will help them survive as organizations. Although those trends were new to Tunisia, the hallmarks of professionalism that I observed in Jordan and elsewhere were already present, despite the relatively favorable funding environment and youth of many NGOs.

---

[43] Interview 142, with an INGO director, in person, Tunis, May 9, 2012.

*Some examples of professionalization* Foreign professionals working in the democracy establishment in Tunisia in 2012 had remarkable careers spanning many years and countries. The director of the International Republic Institute country office in Tunis began working for IRI in Serbia as a political activist and then worked in the field in Iraq, South Africa, Somaliland, Sudan, and Thailand, as well as in the organization's headquarters in Washington, DC. Afaf worked for an INGO (Search for Common Ground) by day and had a leadership position with a local Tunisian NGO (Voix de Femmes) by night. The country director for the ERIS office in Tunisia started out working for the UN in Jerusalem. Working on an election there ended up leading to a multiple-decade career that included work for the OSCE and other organizations in such diverse locations as the Democratic Republic of Congo and the Gambia. None of those people, and few in the broader field of which they are examples, were employed in the democracy establishment in Tunisia prior to mid 2011.

Recall that being an NGO professional involves relevant knowledge, experience, and education. What the aforementioned examples illustrate is that the democracy establishment in Tunisia, mostly thanks to people coming from abroad to work in Tunisia after the revolution, became more professional after the ouster of Ben Ali. The technical know-how and identities that democracy practitioners in Tunis possessed had been built over a period of many years and through work with a variety of organizations in a variety of political contexts. For some Tunisians working in the field that had an activist background, the influx of professionals was off-putting. One long-time activist, without professional credentials, complained to me about the "colonization of civil society by NGOs."[44]

The incipient professionalization of democracy assistance in Tunisia had several causes. First, the flood of donor funding for democracy assistance led to an influx of INGOs, which brought with them highly trained professionals from their global stables of short- and medium-term staff. Second, local NGOs – already worried about winning funding due to competition from the growing number of other local NGOs – had to demonstrate credibility to donors in order to compete successfully against those organizations. One strategy for doing so was to pursue partnerships with INGOs, which teach local organizations professional practices. Finally, there were general trends in Arab activism and humanitarianism at play that encouraged professionalization.[45] But

---

[44] Interview 134, with a Tunisian NGO director, in person, Tunis, May 14, 2012.
[45] Hopgood (2008); Jad (2004).

what difference, if any, did the emergence of professional norms make to democracy assistance in Tunisia?

*The consequences of professionalization* This book makes the case that professional norms foster convergence over time among organizations on tame democracy assistance. One reason is that professionalization causes organizations to value organizational survival more and thus to converge on the programs that help them achieve it. Another reason is that professionalization causes organizations to value certain tame programs in and of themselves as "appropriate" ways to promote democracy. A good example of this dual logic is the rise of aid to support women's political participation, a strategy that helps NGOs survive because it is both measurable and regime-compatible. Yet such aid also enjoys many principled supporters, who believe that women's representation is a core component of democracy and therefore that aiding it ought to be part of any democracy-promotion toolbox.

Given that professionalization was a new and ongoing process in the democracy establishment in Tunisia, it was too soon to see extensive changes in 2012. Many of the effects should be seen in the years to come. As I stated in the previous chapter, I have left extensive study of historical change to Chapters 4 and 5, which took a longer temporal view. Nevertheless, there was evidence in Tunisia that supports the causal mechanisms of my argument about professionalization.

First, recipients of democracy assistance in Tunisia perceived diverse government donors to prefer funding similar programs and NGOs to those in Jordan. Those similarities are not just confined to election aid, the most common form of aid in the country, but they are also present in work on civil society, women's representation, constitutions, and good governance. The director of a Tunisian NGO observed, for example, "The EU wants to work on the same thing as the United States and Canada and Eastern Europe. You get the feeling that they want to fund the same programs."[46] It would be wrong to say that donors did not differ at all in Tunisia. For example, the United States was often more comfortable with Islamist political parties than the European donors, who hail from countries influenced by the French tradition of *laïcité*. Nevertheless, none of my Tunisian interviewees identified *significant* differences among the international donors' approaches. One convergence mechanism was that donor and INGO staff lived, worked, and played in the same neighborhoods, such as the attractive suburbs La Marsa and Sidi Bou Said. Information and practices thus could be easily

---

[46] Interview 134, with a Tunisian NGO director, in person, Tunis, May 14, 2012.

shared across organizations, leading to complementary approaches, such as when NDI conducted focus groups to complement IRI's public opinion polls to help local political actors develop their platforms.

Second, anecdotes abound of the foreign models of democracy assistance brought into Tunisia after the Jasmine Revolution. Freedom House's office, for example, used the transitional justice and national reconciliation experiences of Nigeria to help guide a new rule-of-law program. Meanwhile, OTI rolled out "get out the vote" and civic education campaigns that were reminiscent of efforts that its director had overseen previously in Nepal. As one foreign professional working in Tunisia explained, "There are generic models that can be used everywhere and then you tweak them ... There are certain criteria that might change, even within the same region, but a lot of it [our programming] is generic."[47] The international models proffered by experts visibly affected local outcomes. The polling manual prepared by Tunisia's electoral commission (EC) for the Constituent Assembly elections, for example, used cartoons and drawings from a similar manual in Sudan and formatting from Lebanon.[48]

Those anecdotes are significant because imported projects tended to be tamer than those that local activists might develop on their own, including their initial programs in 2011. After all, as the previous section showed, the initial democracy-assistance programs implemented in Tunisia were notably less tame than the average programs in the world today. Thus, it is no coincidence that many of the imported programs, such as the civic education, election, and rule-of-law examples, fell into measurable and regime-compatible categories. Untame programs supporting dissidents, research, or unions were less commonly brought in from practitioners' previous experiences. All of those "copycat" programs are consistent with my argument's expectation that learning and emulation, although not necessarily learning about best practices for democratization, help diffuse practices in the democracy establishment.

Finally, as in Jordan, government donors and INGOs encouraged NGOs in Tunisia to converge on tame programs. One way that foreign funders and INGOs did so was by teaching local organizations professional practices. A Tunis-based INGO director, for example, explained how he would talk through basic tasks with his grantees, such as creating participant lists with signatures, not to mention more complicated ones, such as keeping track of expenses electronically. Many Tunisian NGOs

---

[47] Interview 131, with an INGO staff member, by telephone, May 7, 2012.
[48] Interview 137, with an INGO director, in person, Tunis, May 14, 2012.

were eager to learn such skills because doing so helped them appeal to more funders.

Another way that foreign donors and INGOs encouraged convergence was by fostering social and professional networks among grantees. They did that not only within Tunisia but also between Tunisia and other countries by fostering transnational connections between aid-recipient organizations. To take one example, Romania – a potential model for Tunisia given its similar history and size – sent its electoral commission to Tunisia to participate in an exchange sponsored by UNDP; NDI also used Romania as an example in its programs.

### Conclusions

Many people have compared the revolutionary wave of 2011 that began in Tunisia to the revolutions that swept through the Soviet Union in 1989. A less-appreciated fact is that democracy-assistance programs in Tunisia in 2012 resembled democracy-assistance programs that emerged in Central and Eastern Europe in the 1990s. One cause of those similarities is that the needs of post-revolutionary governments are similar. Another is that donor governments are often sincerely committed to democratization in such cases.

But this chapter has made the case that international democracy assistance in Tunisia today also resembles earlier eras of democracy assistance due to relatively unprofessional and non-competitive civil society organizations in both contexts. The previous absence and current abundance of democracy-assistance funding in Tunisia freed NGOs there to promote democracy in the ways they deemed best. The result is programs that are less tame than the programs in most other countries today, including those countries most similar to Tunisia.

Yet even without a major change in regime type or donor intentions in the two years post-revolution, democracy assistance in Tunisia changed. The blossoming of civil society in Tunisia and the arrival of INGOs fostered competition and professionalization. After all, local NGOs' lack of professionalism hampered them when competing for international grants in a marketplace growing crowded with INGOs with dedicated fundraising staff. Alongside those trends, I observed the importance of democracy-assistance programs by overseas professionals and an increasing attention to measurement. I expect those trends to accelerate in the coming years and lead to greater convergence on measurable and regime-compatible programs, as has been the case globally.

*Part III*

# Conclusions

# 9    Should democracy promoters be set free?

> *Progress towards human rights is neither linear nor guaranteed ... we're in a journey here.*[1]

The end of the Cold War transformed world politics in many ways. As the world moved from bipolar great power competition to American dominance, the ways that Western countries interacted with the developing world changed. For one thing, the foreign economic aid transferred from wealthy industrialized states to poorer states dropped significantly. When foreign aid increased again in the twenty-first century, it was notably different: Western countries and international institutions used aid less as a geostrategic tool and more as a way to genuinely support development and good governance in needy countries.[2]

Western countries and international institutions also reoriented their support for democracy in the developing world. Whereas American support for anti-communist tyrants during the Cold War was infamous, the United States increasingly – though not uniformly – prioritized democracy abroad after the collapse of the Soviet Union. Other advanced democracies and international institutions, such as the European Union and the United Nations, also prioritized democracy promotion. As the third wave of democratization swept through Africa, Asia, Europe, and Latin America, international actors did their best to support and advance democratic transitions in many countries around the world.

This book has aimed to improve our understanding of democracy assistance after the end of the Cold War. International democracy promotion represents the first and largest sustained attempt by many states and international organizations to transform the domestic political practices and institutions of other countries while generally still preserving those states' sovereignty. The goals of democracy promoters are urgent: according to Freedom House in 2014, 2.5 billion people, or 35 percent of the world's population, live in conditions that are

---

[1] Posner (2012).
[2] See Bermeo (2008) and also Wright and Winters (2010).

fundamentally "not free."[3] Highly repressive regimes, from North Korea to Equatorial Guinea, continue to intimidate and jail dissidents. Also troublingly, Freedom House has recorded a notable decline of freedom in democracies such as Mexico and Ukraine in the second decade of the twenty-first century. Indeed, although more democracies in the world existed at the dawn of the twenty-first century than ever before, there clearly remains a need for improvements in human rights, democracy, and freedom in many countries around the world.

Yet despite that need, the current outlook in the public discourse on international democracy promotion is pessimistic. Democracy promotion has been portrayed as ineffective as well as hypocritical, the latter because democracy-promoting states are not themselves perfect democracies and their support for democracy abroad is inconsistent. Skepticism of democracy promotion has multiple sources: a backlash against democracy-promotion NGOs in Egypt and elsewhere; a reaction against American foreign policy in Afghanistan and Iraq under President George W. Bush; concerns about the rise of anti-Western Islamist political parties in the Middle East, which could become empowered should the region democratize; a general disappointment in the failure of democracy promotion (especially in the former Soviet states) to generate long-term democratization; and the rise of China, which has been accompanied by renewed concerns that democracy does not support economic growth.

Although the topic had never been far from the headlines since 1989, the Arab Spring of 2011 reignited public interest in and debate surrounding democracy promotion. Much remains unknown about the long-term effects of popular mobilization in Tunisia, Egypt, and elsewhere. But it is alarmingly clear that the transformations that many Arab protesters and their allies abroad hoped would result in lasting democratization will be neither straightforward nor linear. That development is normatively troubling. Not only is democracy desired by most people in the world, but it is generally thought to bring with it a number of other benefits, including economic development, peaceful transfers of power, and peaceful relations with other democracies.[4]

What the foreign policies of the United States and other Western countries and international institutions should be toward Arab states in these changing times has emerged as a critical question for policymakers. Democracy assistance – foreign aid explicitly given with the goal of advancing democracy in another country – is the most common

[3] Freedom House (2014, 6).
[4] McFaul (2010, Ch. 2).

tool used to support transitions abroad, taking place in more than one hundred countries. Yet many previous academic studies – not to mention much of the skeptical popular discourse – argue that it is not successful. The time is therefore ripe for an in-depth examination of the factors that shape the design and implementation of democracy assistance.

The starting point for this study has been that, despite considerable popular debate about democracy promotion, we know remarkably little about how democracy aid operates on the ground and why. This micro-level study of democracy assistance reveals that many projects do not seek to directly confront dictators. Some of the most common types of democracy assistance in the twenty-first century support good governance and women's representation, in contrast to more forceful American aid programs supporting dissidents and political parties that were common in the 1980s. Worthy though the more recent programs may be, evidence does not suggest that they are particularly effective at spurring transitions from dictatorship to democracy. So what explains the shift?

Conventional wisdom suggests that the complete answer to that question lies in changes in target states' characteristics or donor countries' preferences. Although both sets of actors play an important role shaping the design and implementation of democracy assistance, they do not tell the entire story. Instead, the story of the taming of democracy assistance requires also telling the story of the people and organizations that make up what I call the democracy establishment. Those organizations are more likely to survive and thrive when they aid democracy in ways that are measurable using quantitative outcomes and maintain access to target countries. Growing competition and professionalism have fostered convergence among democracy practitioners on the approaches that help them survive and thrive.

That argument should not be misunderstood. Promoting democracy is hard, and I do not claim that it would always (or even usually) work if organizations did not have incentives to design programs in relatively tame ways. Moreover, in wanting to survive and thrive, I do not imply that organizations in the democracy establishment behave differently (or worse) than any of us would were we working in the same dangerous, frustrating situations. Finally, I do not argue that the ideas and incentives of organizations in the democracy establishment explain everything. Organizations respond to variations in the regime types of target countries, which determine the feasibility of different programs, as well as to changes in preferences of donor states. Autocracies that are strategically valuable to democracy donors, and especially the United States, for example, receive less confrontational forms of democracy aid. Moreover, the conflicting foreign-policy preferences of democracy donors create a situation where it is easy (or at least easier) for organizations in the democracy establishment to design their preferred programs. Nevertheless, diverse evidence shows that organizations' preferences and strategies consistently explain a consequential amount of the variations in the design and implementation of democracy assistance and therefore represent an important, if largely overlooked, component of any discussion about how to aid democracy today.

The remainder of this conclusion pursues three goals. First, it reviews some of the book's major findings. Second, it situates my findings within the scholarly literature, explaining how they build upon and contribute to literature on the anatomy of foreign influence, NGOs in world politics, and delegation. Finally, it explains how the findings contribute to ongoing debates about democracy promotion. Democracy-assistance programs increasingly prioritize quantitative outcomes and compatibility with target countries' regimes, which are potentially troubling trends. Making causal inferences on these matters is full of challenges. Yet a rigorous series of quantitative and qualitative tests supports the argument. Millions of people continue to live without political freedom. Although states give billions of dollars a year with the goal of trying to help them, their tools of foreign influence may not be ideally designed to do so because of the incentives created and reinforced by the government-funding structure. Reforms are needed to set the right kind of democracy assistance free.

### Transnational power and the taming of democracy assistance

This book has sought to understand how and why democracy assistance evolved after the end of the Cold War. It was motivated by the observation that many democracy-assistance efforts in the twenty-first century are not designed to confront dictators, in contrast to the confrontational aid that dominated the early era of democracy assistance. Why has democracy promotion been tamed over time? More broadly, the puzzle this book has addressed is: how and why do states and international institutions seek to influence a target state's domestic political institutions and practices, and under what conditions do they succeed?

#### *Why tame? The paradox of organizational survival*

States have multiple tools to promote democracy: economic sanctions and rewards; diplomacy; military intervention; and, as this book focuses on, democracy assistance. Within the broad tool of democracy assistance, however, states also have many different options – applying direct pressure in dictatorships by aiding dissident groups, helping free information reach more eyes and ears, and training lawyers to be more professional, among other things. Each year, in each of the more than one hundred countries that receive democracy assistance, democracy promoters must make the same decision: what type of program will we design and implement?

To answer that question requires an understanding of how democracy-assistance programs are funded and implemented. State governments set aside funding both bilaterally and multilaterally to support democracy. But governments and multilateral institutions do not implement and, in many cases, do not design democracy-assistance programs themselves. Instead, they delegate to non-governmental organizations. They do so because they have neither the expertise nor, given the sensitive and controversial nature of much democracy assistance, the inclination to implement programs themselves. Delegating democracy assistance is just one of the many ways that governments delegate and contract out foreign-policy programs today.

That act of delegation matters because "contractors" and "contractees" rarely share identical preferences. The organizations that implement democracy assistance sincerely want to advance democracy, which is what they are hired to do, but they also want to survive and thrive as organizations, which is not the goal of most democracy donors. To survive and thrive, democracy NGOs need to win government grants and maintain access to target countries. Maintaining access to target countries helps them win even more grants, not to mention avoid harassment, surveillance, and arrest. My approach treats the organizations in the democracy establishment are "normal" organizations and bureaucracies, despite the field's ideological origins. Practitioners have readily noted the "business" side of democracy promotion.[5] But their insights have not generally penetrated to scholarly and popular debates.

So what types of democracy assistance help democracy-promotion NGOs survive? I focused on two dimensions: measurability and regime-compatibility. Programs that are measurable using quantitative outcomes and are compatible with the regimes of the target countries help NGOs obtain funding and maintain target-country access. The more difficult it is for donors to observe and control organizations in the democracy establishment, the more likely those organizations are to pursue the tame programs that help them survive. A paradox arises because such

---

[5] Bjornlund (2001); Mitchell (2009).

programs succeed at winning government grants even though they do not clearly succeed at democratizing target countries and, in at least some cases, fail to do so.

There was also a temporal dimension to the story. Competition and professional norms have fostered convergence among democracy practitioners on programs that help their organizations survive. Over time, organizations in the democracy establishment learned about the best ways to gain funding and access. As they became more professional, practitioners also become less committed to an ideological, confrontational approach to democracy promotion and placed more value on organizational survival. Several characteristics of the government delegation structure, such as its reliance on short-term contracts, speeded up the natural processes of competition and professionalization. The normative and competitive pressures diffused practices such as promoting women's political participation so thoroughly that the democracy establishment has played an important role in the global spread of quotas for women in legislatures.[6]

Of course, since organizations in the democracy establishment care about their survival, they do not implement their preferred programs in a vacuum that is disconnected from states' preferences. Domestic political variations in donor governments as well as changes in the political relationships between donor and target states also influenced the design of democracy assistance. For the United States, Egypt and Togo are not equivalent target states. Despite that critical insight, however, states' preferences did not tell the whole story of the taming of democracy assistance.

### Evidence for the transnational approach

The typical approach to understanding democracy assistance emphasizes how donor governments use this aid to enhance their global power or to advance their interests, whether economic or political. Many scholars have observed continuities between American foreign-policy-making during and after the Cold War, noting that the United States has selectively promoted democracy in both eras according to its own selfish motives.[7] Without donor governments that are sincerely committed to democratic reform, democracy aid has little hope of bringing freedom and human rights to regions such as the Middle East and, in the worst cases, even prevents democracy there.

[6] Bush (2011).
[7] Brownlee (2012); Guilhot (2005); Lowenthal (1991); Robinson (1996).

Those dominant characterizations of democracy assistance generate valuable insights. Yet they assign almost all the causal weight to the state governments that fund democracy assistance, ignoring the NGOs that design and implement the projects on the ground overseas. I suggest that students of democracy assistance should partially shift their theoretical focus from states to transnational agents. Information problems prevent democracy donors from perfectly observing and controlling democracy assistance. As a consequence, organizations have some discretion to promote democracy in the tamer ways that help them survive but do not clearly help the cause of democracy. This book's transnational approach, which emphasizes the agency of organizations in the democracy establishment, may not surprise anthropologists, who have long focused on the middlemen (and women) of foreign assistance.[8] Political scientists, however, have not generally learned enough from their insights.

The book's transnational approach to explaining the taming of democracy assistance generates a number of empirical implications that should be true if it is persuasive. At its core, the book's logic rests on an assumption that there is a clash between organizations' desires to survive, which they pursue through tamer programs, and donors' desires – however ambivalent at times – to advance democracy. If the rewards that those organizations gain from pursuing tame democracy-assistance programs do not come, at least sometimes, at the cost of effective democracy assistance, then this argument would not hold water. Moreover, when donor governments are able to closely observe and control the NGOs they fund, those NGOs should be less likely to pursue tame programs. Finally, organizations should respond to variations in donors' preferences since they want to win funding.

The book also advanced a more sociological explanation of the taming of democracy assistance. I have argued that organizations in the democracy establishment have become more professional as a consequence of funding competition and normative change. Those changes should be observable and should concretely affect the nature of democracy assistance. The more competitive the funding environment, the harder organizations should work to please donors with measurable programs and to gain access to target states with regime-compatible programs. The more professional the organizations, the more they should value programs that enhance their survival.

From a researcher's perspective, the ideal way to test this argument would be in a laboratory where one variable at a time – the extent of information problems, how professional NGOs are, and so on – was

[8] Brown (2006); Coles (2007); Ferguson (1990); Jackson (2005).

randomly changed while holding all other variables constant. Of course, the real world is much more complicated. The approach of this book was to bring together a variety of forms of evidence to give the argument the hardest possible test. I have assembled new and existing data sets of democracy-assistance projects that covered multiple decades and donors and more than one hundred target countries. Those data allowed me to examine general correlations and make some counterfactual inferences. I then interviewed more than 150 democracy-assistance practitioners, with multiple trips to Jordan and Tunisia, and delved into organizational archives and a recent survey of practitioners. Those data helped me validate the argument's assumptions, test the argument in a more fine-grained manner, and show the causal mechanisms that are necessary to have more confidence in the statistical inferences.

A crucial step in the empirical tests was the development of a new typology of democracy-assistance projects in Chapter 3. I divided democracy-assistance programs into twenty categories. Drawing on interviews with practitioners as well as insights from the literatures on democratization and authoritarianism, I argued that certain programs are generally measurable or regime-compatible. I used the typology to classify thousands of democracy-assistance projects. Evidence suggested that measurable and regime-compatible projects can come at the expense of effective democracy assistance. Even on its own, this chapter represented an important contribution since most previous studies of democracy assistance have not disaggregated the overall concept, which is necessary to effectively study its causes and effects.

But the main point of the new typology was to use it to test the argument. In order to do so, the book moved through each step in the delegation chain, from donor governments to quasi-governmental donor organizations, to NGOs in donor states, to NGOs in target states. Chapter 4 explored delegation in democracy assistance across a wider swathe of donors. It showed that practitioners are more likely to pursue tame programs when donor governments have a harder time observing and controlling them. Donor governments, for example, have a harder time observing and controlling NGOs from target states than NGOs from their own countries. As a consequence, foreign NGOs were 16 percent more likely to pursue measurable projects and 8 percent more likely to pursue regime-compatible programs than donor-state NGOs. I established that relationship, and others, using data on recent democracy-assistance programs funded by all bilateral government democracy donors.

Chapter 5 analyzed an original data set of projects funded by the National Endowment for Democracy, a prominent American donor.

After explaining why the NED's projects provided a good test of the argument, I showed that rising competition and professionalism are associated with tamer democracy assistance, even after controlling for other relevant factors. Relatively tame programs increased from only around 20 percent of the NED's grants in 1986 to around 60 percent in 2009 – a striking trend. The trend over time seemed to hold among projects funded by another main American donor, USAID. Evidence from the NED's grants also suggested that when it is more difficult for the NED to observe and control its grantees, they pursue less tame democracy assistance.

Chapter 6's goal was to understand change and convergence in NGOs in the democracy establishment. It focused on the historical development of several American organizations involved in democracy assistance. On the one hand, Freedom House adapted to become a powerful agenda-setter for the overall field through its successful fundraising and global reach. On the other hand, the Institute for Democracy in Eastern Europe resisted professional norms and did not adapt so successfully. Thus, drawing on interviews and organizational records, I showed how competition and professionalization fostered convergence. Network analysis and evidence from a survey of more than 1,000 democracy-assistance practitioners also demonstrated that the transactions that take place between organizations in the network as well as between those organizations and donor states are both crucial for the field.

The subsequent two chapters complemented the analysis in the previous ones with case studies of contemporary democracy assistance in two Arab countries: Jordan and Tunisia. They aimed to show what tame programs looked like on the ground, how delegation operated in practice, and how democracy-assistance professionals made decisions. In so doing, they contributed to ongoing policy debates about how to support democracy after the Arab Spring.

Chapter 7 explored democracy support in the shadow of geopolitics in Jordan. It showed that – contrary to conventional wisdom – donor governments' strategic interests do not offer a complete explanation of the salient recent variations in democracy assistance in Jordan. Drawing on the previous chapters' transnational approach, I developed a more complete explanation, illustrating the importance of organizational survival, both in terms of funding and access, and of professional norms in terms of how democracy assistance operates in Jordan. The chapter also explored private foundations' democracy-assistance efforts.

Chapter 8 shifted focus to understand support for reform after the revolution in Tunisia. Little democracy assistance occurred in

Tunisia under dictator Zine El Abidine Ben Ali. In the post-revolution era, however, the funding environment for democracy assistance became quite plentiful. With less funding competition, organizations in Tunisia reverted to a less tame slate of activities reminiscent of international activities in the 1980s and early 1990s. Nevertheless, the forces of funding competition and professionalism had started to appear just one year after Ben Ali's ouster. It is likely that they will only grow stronger over time as the bountiful funding shrinks and NGOs become more professional, thus shaping programs.

In sum, the evidence strongly supported the book's transnational approach to understanding democracy assistance. That is not to say that this approach explains everything. Donor governments' preferences clearly still mattered, with, for example, the evidence in this book offering support for the idea that the United States funds democracy assistance with the intention of protecting its undemocratic allies. Moreover, target countries' political environments and important geo-political events, such as the end of the Cold War and September 11, 2001, generated the contexts in which democracy practitioners work. Finally, not every organization in the democracy establishment was intensely focused on its survival. The goal of this book, however, was not to reject those alternative explanations. Instead, it has sought to illustrate a general trend toward competition and professionalism in the democracy establishment and show how that general trend has led to a taming of democracy assistance on average. Evidence from inside organizations as well as from overseas vantage points helped support the argument.

## Scholarly contributions

In some ways, the simplest version of the argument presented in this book may seem straightforward: organizations in the democracy establishment have their own interests, which shape how they do their work. And yet the argument runs counter to much of the prevailing wisdom in international relations. In this section, I consider the book's implications for scholarly understandings of the anatomy of foreign influence, NGOs in world politics, and delegation.

### The anatomy of foreign influence

A burgeoning literature examines how international actors promote the spread of a variety of forms of political and economic liberalization around the world.[9] That literature represents the post-Cold War variety of what political scientist Peter Gourevitch called the "second image reversed."[10] The tools of foreign influence include shaming and socialization, economic sanctions and rewards, political conditionality, foreign aid, diplomatic measures, and military intervention. One of the underlying questions of this body of research is: under what conditions can states and international institutions successfully influence a target state's domestic political institutions and practices?

That question is typically answered by focusing either on the preferences of the states and international institutions attempting to influence other countries or on the preferences of the target states. With regards to the preferences of the states and international institutions that are "influencers," research has shown that strategic motives guide those actors. States and international institutions have been shown, for example, to disregard the characteristics of target states that tend to affect foreign-aid effectiveness in favor of giving foreign aid as a reward or a bribe for policy concessions from recipient governments.[11] As a consequence, we should expect many attempts at foreign influence to fail because they are not really meant to transform the target states at all.

States and international institutions do, however, sometimes attempt to influence target states' domestic political institutions and practices more sincerely. Yet when donors use tools of foreign influence sincerely, certain target states are more likely to be willing to transform themselves than others. Some states may, for example, use aid corruptly or for the purposes of strengthening their repressive rule. Countries may invite international election monitors but engage in "strategic manipulation" prior to the election to stay in power without alarming the monitors with obvious signs of fraud.[12] Thus, the effectiveness of foreign influence depends not only on donors' intentions, but on how likely the target states are to resist or accept the goals of the sending states.

My research suggests that the dominant perspectives do not tell the whole story about the anatomy of foreign influence. Sending states have a difficult time observing and controlling their overseas efforts, which take place in distant countries and may be funded through a long process of delegation with multiple actors. Furthermore, there is no direct feedback

---

[9] Hyde (2007); Kelley (2008); Levitsky and Way (2005); Pevehouse (2002); Simmons, Dobbin, and Garrett (2006).
[10] Gourevitch (1978).
[11] Alesina and Dollar (2000); Alesina and Weder (2002); Bueno de Mesquita and Smith (2009); Dreher, Sturm, and Vreeland (2009); Easterly (2006); Stone (2004, 2002, 2008).
[12] Beaulieu and Hyde (2009).

loop between people living in the target states – the people those efforts seek to help – and donors. For those reasons, among others, we should expect actors between and outside of states to also influence outcomes.

Recognizing the potential for principal–agent problems in foreign influence is not new.[13] Yet with a few important exceptions,[14] the micro-politics of the transnational actors in the transnational delegation chain have been left relatively unexplored. That omission is unfortunate since these normative and strategic transnational actors shape the imprint that international forces make on domestic politics. This study provides insight into one set of such actors, the democracy establishment, and explains why its members promote democracy in certain ways and not others. I show that their influence is felt not only on the design of democracy-assistance programs but also on the institutions and practices adopted by the developing countries in which the democracy establishment works. My theoretical approach can thus be used to study the actors in between sending and target states in a host of other areas of foreign influence.

### NGOs in world politics: a mixture of idealism and self-interest

Scholars of transnational NGOs have long characterized the organizations as involving a mixture of idealism and self-interest.[15] On the one hand, optimists tend to view the organizations in transnational networks as altruists and document their positive influence on world politics. On the other hand, cynics tend to view such actors as just as materially motivated as firms despite their high-minded rhetoric, and show how moral movements can have adverse consequences. This book's argument about the democracy establishment's blend of idealism and self-interest and how that the balance between the two motives changes over time gives yet another account that challenges any simple dichotomy. More importantly, it offers a general framework about the evolution of moral entrepreneurship that can be applied to other issue areas.

Margaret Keck and Kathryn Sikkink advanced a relatively opti-mistic take in their now classic book, *Activists Beyond Borders*. The authors showed how networked political entrepreneurs make moral claims that impact global public policy-making through case studies of

---

[13] Easterly (2006); Martens *et al.* (2002); Milner (2006); Milner and Tingley (2013); Schneider and Tobin (2013).

[14] Kelley (2009); Brown (2006).

[15] Bob (2005); Carpenter (2007); Keck and Sikkink (1998); Kennedy (2005); Lecy, Mitchell, and Schmitz (2010); Ron, Ramos, and Rodgers (2005); Sell and Prakash (2004).

transnational activism in the areas of human rights, the environment, and women's rights. Some research in this tradition takes international non-governmental organizations to some extent at face value, although it does generally recognize the strategic dimension of activism; nevertheless, the organizations say that they are motivated by various altruistic concerns, and scholars show that they mostly are. Among the research that confirms that point of view is a statistical study that shows how humanitarian motives shape the allocation decisions for foreign aid given by a number of prominent private organizations.[16]

Other research has taken a more cynical turn. Keck and Sikkink distinguished among transnational networks according to their motives: instrumental (as with networks of corporations); causal (as with epistemic networks); or principled (as with transnational advocacy networks).[17] But perhaps transnational networks are just as instrumental as transnational corporations. An exemplar of research in this more cynical tradition is an influential paper by political scientists Alexander Cooley and James Ron that examined the behaviors of transnational organizations working in the fields of humanitarian relief and development.[18] They found that competition over funding drives organizations to pursue ineffective and dysfunctional programs.

Drawing on seminal sociological theories of organizations, I joined the debate by examining in depth how an idea-driven network changes over time. In general, change in international organizations and non-state actors in world politics remains understudied when compared to issues such as when and why states establish such organizations.[19] I have shown the importance of ideas in the democracy establishment's origins but the increasing influence of survival as time passed. The balance between ideals and interests evolved. Building from important previous research by political scientist Michael Barnett,[20] I provided a general framework for predicting the likely blend between idealism and incentives at different points in a transnational movement's life-cycle.

Indeed, competition and professional norms will emerge in many domains of transnational activism. To understand the evolution of principled activism in world politics, we must pay attention to the structural conditions that affect moral entrepreneurs and that are often set by state governments. The survival incentives that arise in democracy

---

[16] Büthe, Major, and de Mello e Souza (2012).
[17] Keck and Sikkink (1998, 30).
[18] Cooley and Ron (2002). For other important contribution in this tradition, see Dicther (2003); Hancock (1989).
[19] Barnett and Coleman (2005, 593–4).
[20] Barnett (2009).

assistance for funding and access ought to matter elsewhere, such as with environmental and humanitarian aid or in the field of human rights. How and why activists across issue areas respond to structural incentives is likely to be a fertile area for future research. I hypothesize that domains of transnational action that require more NGO access for implementation will be especially prone to the dynamics illustrated in this book.

### A model of transnational delegation

One of the central arguments of this book – that the taming of democracy assistance is influenced by the structure through which Western governments delegate authority to promote democracy – draws on principal–agent arguments that have recently gained prominence in the study of world politics.[21] Previous studies have largely examined delegation between states and international organizations. I built from those studies' insights to examine transnational delegation, which involves transfers of authority across state boundaries as well as both supra- and sub-state actors.

The transnational setting of democracy assistance reveals new tensions that occur when agents must answer not only to their principals but also to the governments that host them. I show how state governments on both ends of democracy assistance's delegation chain – democratic donors on the sending side and pseudo-democracies on the target side – affect the strategies pursued by organizations in the democracy establishment. Democracy assistance is thus part of that ever-denser set of transnational relations – formal and informal ties across societies, states, and various types of non-state organizations – that Robert Keohane and Joseph Nye studied in their seminal work on complex interdependence.[22]

Some evidence suggests that the model of transnational delegation developed in this book is portable to other issue areas. Ethnographers of foreign-aid organizations, such as anthropologist James Ferguson, have shown that the survival advantages of technical, depoliticized measures and the need to negotiate compromises between funding and host states are common across many issue areas and target states.[23] By showing how the professional and competitive pressures that they identified operate

---

[21] Bradley and Kelley (2008); Gutner (2005a); Hawkins *et al.* (2006); Johnson (2010); Nielson and Tierney (2003); Pollack (1997).
[22] Keohane and Nye (1977).
[23] Ferguson (1990). See also Brown (2006); Jackson (2005).

within a broader framework involving the government-funding structure of democracy assistance, I have developed an approach to studying democracy assistance that should apply cross-nationally and over time. The approach should also apply to other issue areas, including human rights, development, and humanitarian action.

Consider, for example, the field of environmental assistance. Environmental assistance resembles democracy assistance in many ways. Encouraged by domestic support for environmental aid in some donor countries, bilateral environmental aid roughly quadrupled between 1980 and 1999 and multilateral environmental aid roughly doubled over the same time period.[24] As with democracy assistance, however, donor countries do not necessarily seek to export their own practices. Meanwhile, target states often do not desire environmental aid projects, creating resistance. At a minimum, target-state leaders prefer forms of assistance that will give them a direct political or economic benefit; at a maximum, they want to prevent or undermine programs supporting some of the donors' favored goals, such as conserving biodiversity, which can come at the expense of local economic development.

As with democracy assistance, the organizations that design and implement environmental assistance are likely to face pressures from donors and host countries and consequently confront incentives to design programs in ways that will keep their funding sources flowing and access open. That conflict of interests leaves the intermediary organizations stuck between their ideals and their interests and between their donors and the target states. Perhaps as expected, a study of environmental aid in Kazakhstan shows that local implementing organizations that received international aid did not carry out work on urgent local environmental concerns (for example, impure water) but instead pursued the favorite issue areas of foreign donors (for example, biodiversity).[25] A similar approach to the one developed in this study could thus be used to study environmental assistance and likely other domains of foreign influence too. Given the rising significance of contracts in domains from military affairs to diplomacy to development, the theoretical framework has broad relevance.[26] Extending it to other issue areas would not only provide a comparative perspective on democracy assistance, but also help illuminate broader debates about foreign influence and effectiveness.

---

[24] Roberts *et al.* (2009, 12).
[25] Weinthal and Luong (2002).
[26] Stanger (2009).

## Implications for democracy promotion

Finally, this book has sought to illuminate ongoing debates about democracy promotion among scholars and practitioners. As reviewed earlier in the book, previous findings about the impact of democracy assistance have been mixed. Two influential studies, for example, found that American democracy assistance has often, but not uniformly, encouraged democratization in competitive authoritarian regimes.[27] In some contexts – such as the revolutions that occurred in the post-communist states between 2000 and 2006 – democracy assistance successfully spread ideas and fostered transnational linkages among activists, while contemporaneous efforts nearby – as in Russia – largely failed.[28] One of the most comprehensive assessments of democracy assistance's impact found that $10 million of US democracy and governance aid was associated with a quarter of a point improvement in Freedom House's seven-point scale of democracy.[29]

Yet macro-level correlations between democracy assistance and democracy levels offer little guidance for practitioners about how democracy-assistance programs might be most effectively designed. The difficulty of translating research on democracy assistance's impact into practice is part of a broader scholar–practitioner divide on democracy assistance.[30] An important cause of that divide is that, outside of the democracy-assistance field, there is little knowledge of what democracy-assistance programs actually do where, and why.

To accurately evaluate democracy-assistance programs, we need to understand what they are trying to accomplish. As I have shown in this book, democracy-assistance programs deliberately vary a great deal in the extent to which they confront authoritarian regimes. One way of understanding many of the pessimistic or ambiguous results in terms of the effects of democracy assistance writ large is that not all democracy-assistance programs are designed to create short- or even medium-term changes in countries' scores on a democracy scale.

That observation may encourage deep skepticism about democracy-assistance programs. But if developed democracies abandoned democracy assistance, how else could they encourage those states to transition and consolidate? Replicating and extending many of the major quantitative findings about democratization, political scientist Jan Teorell found that the key triggers of democratization include economic

---

[27] Bunce and Wolchik (2011); Levitsky and Way (2010).
[28] Beissinger (2007); Bunce and Wolchik (2006b); Mendelson (2001).
[29] Finkel, Pérez-Liñán, and Seligson (2007).
[30] Mitchell (2010).

crisis, democratization in a neighboring country, participation in democratic regional organizations, peaceful demonstrations, and multi-party systems in autocracies. Meanwhile, factors such as Muslim populations and oil wealth impede democratization. Finally, socioeconomic modernization (specifically media proliferation) and economic freedom help sustain democracy; Muslim populations may reverse it.[31] Most of those factors do not change over time or, if they do, change slowly. Some of the other time-varying factors, such as economic crisis, would be unlikely events for the international community to want to encourage. One strategy suggested by those findings is to pressure autocracies to participate in democratic regional organizations. Otherwise, the most plausible points of influence would be for the international community to empower civil society actors that could peacefully demonstrate against authoritarian regimes, support multi-party elections, and promote media proliferation – activities that already fall under the rubric of democracy assistance.

Advanced democracies and international institutions could step away from democracy assistance and instead encourage countries to democratize through diplomatic leverage or other tools. That is what the democracy-assistance skeptics want. At best, they would point out, democracy assistance is fiendishly difficult to get right; and at worst, it is arrogant, counter-productive, and against donor states' national interests.

But democracy assistance is likely here to stay. Not only is there little historical evidence of foreign-assistance programs ending once started, but also democracy promotion has deep roots in the prevailing liberal international order.[32] Most American presidents have stated the United States' preference for democratization abroad. Furthermore, although the United Nations' Charter does not include the word "democracy," the 1948 Universal Declaration of Human Rights evinces a commitment to democracy, as does the 1948 Charter of the Organization of American States. Since then, democracy's place in international law has only grown.[33] Although budget battles over specific instruments of democracy assistance have taken place, no mainstream movement to eliminate democracy assistance exists. If Western states and international institutions are likely to continue to engage in democracy assistance, then the important question is: how best can they promote democracy in the developing world?

[31] Teorell (2010, 145–7).
[32] Ikenberry (2000).
[33] Franck (1992).

The research presented in this book suggests that the delegation structure of democracy assistance should be reformed. Although this book does not directly assess the causal impact of democracy-assistance programs, its central findings raise concerns. Specifically, the common tame programs do not directly threaten dictators by definition. Since many government officials want such actions to be part of democracy assistance in closed societies, it is necessary for them to think carefully about how they fund aid programs in the future.

### Lessons for democracy assistance reform

Many economists and political scientists have sought to understand how principals can better control agents. That subject is, in fact, the focus of an entire field: contract theory. I build from the basic insights of those scholars, as well as the book's empirical findings to suggest a number of simple but concrete ideas for reform. Other changes could also promote more effective democracy assistance, such as donor states that are more consistently committed to promoting democracy, regardless of their competing strategic interests. From the perspective of democracy promotion advocates, such changes are, alas, unlikely to occur soon.

The general principle that should guide reform to the funding structure of democracy assistance is simple: funders should gather more effective information about the projects they fund and more effectively control their agents. Democracy donors may have other foreign policy priorities even if they are often sincere. That means that mustering the appropriate energy and systems to observe and control agencies has often been, and may continue to be, difficult. Nevertheless, advocates of democracy promotion can help direct attention to the issue of foreign aid and press for reforms once they know which reforms might be effective. After all, as Chapter 4 suggested, when foreign aid is scrutinized more domestically, there are consequences for the way democracy is aided.

First, donor officials should *delegate to agents that are easier to observe and control*. The harder it is for donors to observe and control the organizations they fund, the more likely those organizations are to shift democracy-assistance programs away from donors' preferences. The lessons of this book suggest that several factors affect donor governments' abilities to observe and control their agents, including: how long the delegation chain is (shorter chains involve fewer information problems); the nationality of the NGO (certain donor-country NGOs are easier to observe and control); and the preference diversity of multilateral organizations (less diverse organizations are easier to observe and control). Donor officials may currently be prevented from delegating to more controllable agents by a lack of understanding of the problems described in this book. However, they may also be hamstrung by political rules that favor certain agents, and by cost. Such constraints are not easily overcome. Nevertheless, putting more emphasis on delegating to controllable organizations makes sense and should lead to less tame programs, especially in contexts where there are not competing geopolitical interests.

Second, donor officials should *use the private foundation model when possible.* In the United States, the NED, a quasi-private donor, promotes democracy in less tame ways than government agencies such as USAID. More generally, donors that are insulated from government bureaucracy and competing geopolitical objectives are more nimble and effective players in democracy assistance. They often also involve fewer steps of delegation and thus fewer information problems. Donor governments should more often delegate to such organizations. The creation of new funding mechanisms following the NED model, such as the European Endowment for Democracy in 2012, is promising.

Third, donor officials should *improve feedback loops between people on the ground in target countries and donor officials.* Monitoring currently occurs when donor governments go out and gather information about agents. An alternative method of monitoring would rely upon citizens and interest groups sounding alarms when democracy aid is going wrong. My field research suggests that locals have a great deal of information that they would like to share with donor governments. Rather than simply supporting ombudsman offices in other countries, donor governments could have foreign-aid ombudsmen. When possible, governments should send donor officials to target countries, where they can observe programs firsthand. In the United States, the Obama administration's participation in efforts such as the Open Government Partnership, a multilateral initiative to encourage civil society–government linkages, represents an important effort to foster feedback on foreign aid that will hopefully continue and expand.

Fourth, donor officials should *encourage the right kind of competition and discourage the wrong kind of competition.* The right kind of competition for funding rewards organizations that effectively promote democracy. Donors should encourage more applications for grants and contracts and specify more of their terms. Currently, democracy donors such as USAID work with a stable of favorite "primary implementing partners," but using such partners makes it more difficult for donors to ensure that their agents design and implement programs that are closer to donor preferences. Likewise, giving agents considerable discretion in the form of grants (as opposed to more rule-based contracts) makes it harder for donors to observe and control their agents. The wrong kind of competition for funding encourages NGOs to prioritize funding and access over effective democracy promotion. Making longer-term funding commitments (five years instead of one or two years) discourages the race for funding and encourages NGOs to seek out real change.

Fifth, donor officials should *conduct formal, institutionalized comparisons of programs with donors that fund similar programs.* One of the ways that principals can monitor their agents is by seeing multiple agents perform the same task and comparing their outcomes, the cost of their efforts, and so on. As shown in this book, most international donors promote democracy in remarkably similar ways, whether measured by the goals of their programs or the specific local NGOs that they ultimately fund overseas. Such donors therefore should undertake monitoring activities not just individually but collectively to improve their information.

Finally, donor officials should *use professional networks and institutions to foster new norms about democracy assistance.* As discussed throughout the book, professionalization has encouraged organizations to focus on their survival and fostered norms about the appropriateness of tame programs. Today, professional institutions foster convergence across organizations in the democracy establishment on relatively tame approaches to democracy assistance. Donors should work with those institutions – such as educational programs, conferences, think tanks, and other professional organizations and events – to help foster professional norms that are more conducive to effective democracy promotion.

As the last recommendation notes, my research on change in the democracy establishment over time found that strong professional norms and identities now exist in the field of international democracy assistance. As a consequence, even if donors enact some or all of the reforms suggested above, it is unlikely that the democracy establishment will change overnight. Norms are "sticky." Still, since actors in the democracy establishment do respond rationally in the long term to the incentives they face, reforms should eventually be effective. Furthermore, working with professional institutions may accelerate the change. What democracy assistance needs is engaged and informed donor governments and motivated yet idealistic aid recipients.

Donor officials should be receptive to making such changes. Some positive movements toward these recommendations are already underway, with the push for more rigorous and experimental impact assessments of democracy and governance at USAID.[34] International efforts to enhance transparency in the reporting of foreign-aid flows are

---

[34] Moehler (2010).

also underway. Now is the time to build on such efforts and take further steps to ensure that democracy aid promotes democracy effectively.

## Conclusions

Just thirty years ago, the term "democracy assistance" hardly existed. To the extent that anyone pursued democracy assistance, it was a small set of German political-party foundations. Although the United States – the world's largest democracy promoter today – vowed a commitment to democracy in the fight against global communism, empowering anti-communist allies was more often a guiding principle than promoting democracy. Today, democracy assistance represents a multi-billion dollar a year industry in which all the major Western countries and international institutions participate. The motivation for this book was to understand the nature of the shift from *realpolitik* to *idealpolitik*. In particular, it sought to understand how it is that a particular set of activities came to dominate the diverse global field of international democracy assistance. On a more basic level, the book also set out to document the rise of international democracy assistance and, in clear terms, define what it is and how we might classify its programs.

This book has argued that a profession called the democracy establishment has made a significant impact on the way that democracy is promoted abroad today. As time passed, organizations in the democracy establishment started working harder to pursue programs that would succeed at winning government grants and gaining access to the countries where they did their work, rather than just pursuing democratization. Motivated by incentives created by the government-funding structure of democracy assistance, those organizations pursued programs that were relatively tame. The end result has been democracy-assistance programs influenced not just by the preferences of the donor countries or the characteristics of the target states but also by the ideas and interests of organizations in the democracy establishment.

The democracy establishment's ideas and interests significantly affect the actual conduct of politics in many developing countries. As a result of the democracy establishment's direct and indirect influence, dozens of developing countries have adopted quotas for women's representation in national legislatures, and they have also pursued other practices such as inviting international election monitors and attempting to improve local governance. Since the democracy establishment has such a notable impact on world politics, it is all the more important that the political practices and institutions that it promotes in the developing world are the ones that are most likely to advance democracy – not ones that authoritarian leaders can easily co-opt in order to prolong their rule. My findings suggest that the funding structure for democracy assistance often rewards organizations that prioritize measurement over effectiveness and stability in target states over regime change. Aiding democracy abroad is a good thing, but democracy aid in its current form is not always. The funding structure of democracy assistance should be reformed to get the incentives right for organizations in the democracy establishment to succeed at their stated missions of advancing democracy around the world.

*Part IV*

Appendices and references

# Appendix A: Descriptions of categories of democracy assistance

This appendix provides fuller descriptions of the twenty categories of democracy assistance. I have used these categories throughout the book as a way of classifying and coding democracy-assistance programs.

- *Business*: These projects promote business, private enterprise, free market economies, and entrepreneurship. They include working with chambers of commerce, offering training and networking opportunities to would-be business leaders, disseminating information about free enterprise, and supporting research and education on related topics.
- *Civic education*: These projects inculcate democratic values and responsibilities among ordinary citizens. They include seminars that educate the public (and often, but not always, youth) about human rights, citizenship, and democratic values and programs that supply civic education materials to teachers and schools.
- *Civil society (general)*: These projects support the capacity and efforts of civil society organizations that are voluntary civic and social organizations. They include holding advocacy trainings for civil society leaders, publicizing civil society actors in the media, supporting events hosted by civil society organizations, and offering networking opportunities to civil society organizations. These projects refer to *general* civil society projects rather than efforts that primarily target business leaders, trade unions, women, or youth.
- *Conflict resolution*: These projects promote conflict resolution and peace under the umbrella of promoting democracy. They include holding training to reduce violent political actions, supporting peace agreements, and promoting reconciliation and co-existence across ethnic, religious, and racial lines.
- *Constitutions*: These projects support constitution-writing and constitutional reform. They include supporting constituent assemblies, disseminating draft constitutions, providing technical assistance (for example, on legal and historical issues related to constitutions), and

supporting civil society organizations' participation in the constitutional process.

- *Dissidents*: These projects foster the exchange of democratic ideas among dissidents and intellectuals. They include supporting literary publications, translating and disseminating key democratic texts or textbooks, and sponsoring conferences that promote the exchange of information about democracy. They support individuals that are activists (potentially abroad or underground) or democratic pioneers in the country, or both.
- *Elections*: These projects fund, train, and otherwise support election monitors and observers and also support free and fair elections in other ways. They include training political and civic leaders about the proper conduct of elections, offering voter education programs, conducting "get out the vote" campaigns, and supporting reforms or improvements to electoral processes by the government.
- *Good governance*: These projects promote the quality of the government's provision of basic services by working with elected officials and civil servants. Good governance is defined by the United Nations as: consensus-oriented; participatory; committed to the rule of law; effective and efficient; accountable; transparent; responsive; and equitable and inclusive. These projects support technical assistance and training on such topics as budgeting, office management, government anti-corruption, and communication with the public.
- *Humanitarian assistance*: These projects provide humanitarian assistance, which is foreign aid that is given to the needy in order to save lives and alleviate suffering, under the umbrella of democracy assistance. They typically target people who are poor, ill, refugees or forced migrants, or political prisoners.
- *Human rights*: These projects promote human rights. They include supporting human rights education, providing resources for citizens to monitor and report human rights abuses, aiding civil society organizations that work on human rights, publicizing human rights violations in the media, promoting basic freedoms (for example, of expression), and encouraging countries' participation in international human rights laws and institutions.
- *Legislative assistance*: These projects seek to improve the quality of a country's national legislature (i.e., its parliament or congress) and the legislation it produces. They include training parliamentarians and their staff on writing laws or running an office, supporting parliamentarians' constituent outreach, helping civil society actors monitor and lobby the legislature, financing a media office for the legislature, and encouraging parliamentary reform and modernization.

- *Local governance*: These projects seek to improve the effectiveness and democratic character of local or municipal governments. They are good governance projects that take place locally.
- *Media*: These projects seek to foster a free, independent, and professional media (including new media). They include giving direct grants or equipment to presses or newspapers, supporting press freedom, and training media professionals and students in good journalistic practice.
- *Political parties*: These projects seek to strengthen and professionalize political parties. They include training for political-party leaders and members in campaigning, communication strategies, and developing party platforms.
- *Research*: These projects support research on democracy and related issues (for example, human rights). They include study trips, supporting universities and think tanks in new research endeavors about democracy, such as conferences, workshops, public opinion surveys, or publications.
- *Rule of law*: These projects support the rule of law. They include supporting transitional justice institutions, educating citizens about their legal rights and duties, providing technical assistance for legal reform projects (for example, to a project to reform the criminal code), monitoring the legal system, pro bono legal assistance to civil society activists, and training for lawyers, paralegals, judges, and other legal professionals.
- *Unions*: These projects support trade unions and cooperatives. They include holding training for union leaders in advocacy, offering special civic and voter education opportunities for union members, supporting unions' advocacy campaigns, conducting research related to trade unions, and supporting international union exchange trips.
- *Women's groups*: These projects support women's civil society groups and women's standing in society. They include supporting women's legal rights, offering technical assistance and other forms of support to women's civil society groups, and promoting civic education among women.
- *Women's representation*: These projects promote women's participation in politics. They include supporting female candidate training, building the capacity of female elected officials and civil servants, and encouraging women to vote.
- *Youth*: These projects promote youth (or student) civil society organizations. They include supporting school parliaments, offering technical assistance and support to youth civil society groups, and promoting democratic values among youth through education and discussion.

# Appendix B:   List of interviewee affiliations

I conducted 152 interviews for this book between 2008 and 2012. Many interviews were conducted using "unattributable" or "off-the-record" terms. Accordingly, I either do not refer to those interviewees at all or do so without linking statements to interviewees. I assigned each interview a random number and refer to it using that number in the text so as to protect my interviewees' confidentiality.

To provide some sense of the scope of the interviews, I provide below a list of the affiliations of my interviewees. The affiliations listed are those that were held at the time of the interview. In the case of interviewees that were no longer working in the democracy-promotion field at the time of the interview, the affiliations listed are those that were last held. Many people had worked at several organizations and so the listed affiliations understate the breadth of organizations about which interviewees shared perspective. At many organizations, I interviewed multiple staff members and I occasionally interviewed the same person multiple times over the years. Each interview lasted for between 30 and 120 minutes and followed a semi-structured format.

## Interviews conducted in Jordan

Academy for Educational Development; Adaleh Center for Human Rights Studies; Al Hayat Center for Civil Society Development; Al Quds Center for Political Studies; Al Urdun Al Jadid Research Center; AMIDEAST; American Bar Association's Rule of Law Initiative; Amman Center for Human Rights Studies; AmmanNet; Arab Foundation for Development and Citizenship; Arab Network for Human Rights and Citizenship Education; Arab Women Leaders Training Institute; Arab Women Organization of Jordan; Associates in Rural Development, Inc., Jordan Local Governance Development Program; Canadian International Development Agency; Center for Defending Freedom of Journalists; Equitas International Centre for Human Rights Education;

European Commission, Delegation to Jordan; Foundation for the Future; Freedom House; Friedrich Ebert Stiftung; Good Life Studies Center; International Foundation for Electoral Systems (IFES); International Republican Institute; International Research and Exchanges Board (IREX); Islamic Action Front; Jordan Center for Social Research; Jordan Education Initiative; Jordanian Center for Civic Education Studies; Jordanian National Commission for Women; Jordanian Parliament; Karama; Konrad Adenauer Stiftung; Land and Human to Advocate Progress; Middle East Partnership Initiative; Millennium Challenge Corporation; MIZAN Law Group for Human Rights; Mosaweh Center for Democratic Research and Studies; National Centre for Human Rights; National Democratic Institute; Open Society Institute; Partners–Jordan; People in Need; Queen Zein Al Sharaf Institute for Development (ZENID); Sisterhood Is Global Institute; Solidarity Center; State University of New York, Center for International Development, Jordan Legislative Strengthening Program; United Nations; United Nations Development Programme; United States Agency for International Development; United States embassy; Women's Democracy Network; various political activists and local scholars.

### Interviews conducted in Tunisia

AMIDEAST; Arab Partnership Fund; Democracy Reporting International; Electoral Assistance Team of the European Union in Tunisia; Freedom House; Institute of International Education; International Foundation for Electoral Systems (IFES); International Republican Institute; Konrad Adenauer Stiftung; National Democratic Institute; Office of the Prime Minister; Search for Common Ground; Social Science Forum; Tunisian Association for Management and Social Stability; United Kingdom embassy; United Nations Development Programme; United States Agency for International Development; United States embassy; Voix des Femmes; various political activists and local scholars.

### Interviews conducted in the United States

Center for Democracy and Elections Management, American University; Carnegie Endowment for International Peace; Chemonics; Democracy International; DGMetrics, Inc.; Eurasia Foundation; European Union; Freedom House; German Marshall Fund of the United States; International Center for Non-Profit Law; International Foundation for Electoral Systems (IFES); International Republican Institute; Institute for Democracy in Eastern Europe; MacArthur Foundation;

MercyCorps; Middle East Partnership Initiative; National Democratic Institute; National Endowment for Democracy; Open Society Institute; Organization of American States; United Nations; US Agency for International Development; US Institute of Peace; US State Department; World Learning; various scholars and consultants for the UN and state governments.

# Appendix C:  Major organizations in the democracy establishment

This appendix lists 150 major institutions in democracy assistance. It includes multilateral organizations, government agencies, quasi-governmental organizations, and non-governmental organizations. The list was culled from scholarly resources on democracy promotion as well as the data set of grants funded by the National Endowment for Democracy that was created for this book.[1] Any list of "major" organizations inevitably involves some subjectivity. In the hopes of creating a valuable resource for future researchers, I cast a fairly wide net in creating this list. Of course, I still leave out many important actors promoting freedom in the world. I included NGOs only if they had received grants to work in at least three countries.

### Governmental and intergovernmental organizations

Canadian International Development Agency; Commonwealth Secretariat; Council of Europe; Danish International Development Agency; Department for International Development; European Initiative for Democracy and Human Rights; European Union; Friedrich Ebert Stiftung; Friedrich Naumann Stiftung; Hans Seidel Stiftung; Henrich Böll Stiftung; International Broadcasting Bureau; International Centre for Human Rights and Democratic Development; Konrad Adenauer Stiftung; Millennium Challenge Corporation; Norwegian Agency for Development; Organization for Economic Cooperation and Development; Organization for Security and Cooperation in Europe; Organization of African Unity; Organization of American States; Swedish International Development Authority; US Agency for International Development; US Department of State (DRL Bureau; MEPI; USIA); UN Democracy Fund; UN Electoral Assistance Unit; Westminster Foundation for Democracy; World Bank.

[1] See Diamond (1997); Carothers (1999); and the Program on Evaluating International Influences on Democratic Development at Stanford University (2010).

241

## Non-governmental and quasi-governmental organizations

Academy for Educational Development; African-American Institute; Africare; America–Mideast Educational and Training Services; American Bar Association's Rule of Law Initiative; American Committee for Aid to Poland; American Federation of Teachers; American University; America's Development Foundation; Arab Institute for Human Rights; Associates in Rural Development, Inc.; Asia Foundation; Asian Forum for Human Rights and Development; Association d'Appui au Développement des Initiatives Communautaires; Balkan Investigative Reporting Network; Capacitas International; Carnegie Corporation; Carter Center; Casal and Associates, Inc.; Center for Democracy and Human Rights; Center for Democracy and Reconciliation in Southeast Europe; Center for Foreign Journalists; Center for Global Communication Studies; Center for Human Rights Advocacy; Center for International Private Enterprise; Center for Justice and International Law; Center for the Study of Human Rights at Columbia University; Center of International Media Assistance; Checchi and Company Consulting, Inc.; Chemonics International; Civic Education; Club de Madrid; Committee to Protect Journalists; Congressional Human Rights Foundation; Creative Associates International; Delphi International; Democracy International; Development Alternatives; Digital Freedom Network; DPK Consulting; Esquel Group Foundation; Ethiopian Human Rights Council; Eurasia Foundation; Ford Foundation; Foreign Policy Research Institute; Foundation for a Civil Society; Foundation for Education for Democracy; Foundation for the Future; Freedom House; Fund for Peace; German Marshall Fund of the United States; Global Rights; Helsinki Citizens Assembly; Helsinki Committee for Human Rights in Republika Srpska; Human Rights Information and Documentation Center; Human Rights Protection; Institute for Democracy in Eastern Europe; Institute for North–South Issues; International Center for Global Communications Foundation; International Development Law Organization; International Federation of Journalists; International Foundation for Election Systems (IFES); International Human Rights Law Group; International Institute for Democracy and Electoral Assistance; International Press Institute; International Republic Institute; International Rescue Committee; James F. Byrnes International Center; Jan Bus Educational Foundation; Joint Baltic American National Committee; Joint Center for Political and Economic Studies; League of Women Voters; Legacy International; MacArthur Foundation; Management Sciences for Development; Mershon Center of Ohio State University; Milan Simecka Foundation; Millennium, IP3; Mott Foundation; National Center for State Courts; National Democratic Institute; National Endowment for Democracy; National Forum for Human Rights; National Forum Foundation; National Institute for Citizen Education in the Law; National Peace Foundation; Nonviolence International; Open Society Institute; Outreach International; PADCO; Pan American Development Foundation; Partners for Democratic Change; Partners of the Americas; People in Need; People in Peril Association; People's Action for Free and Fair Elections; Polish Czech–Slovak Solidarity Foundation; Private Agencies Collaborating Together; Pro Democracy Association; Puebla Institute; Research Triangle Institute; Resources for Action, Inc.; Robert F. Kennedy Memorial Center for Human Rights; Search for Common Ground; Smoloskyp; Solidarity Center; Soros Foundations; STINA News Agency; SUNY Center for International Development; International Center for Not-for-Profit Law; International City/County Management Association; Transparency International; US Institute of Peace; Union of Councils; United Nations Association of Georgia; US Overseas Cooperative Development Committee; Vital Voices Global Partnership; Washington Office for Democracy in Zambia; Women's Campaign International; Women's Learning Partnership; World Learning; World Press Freedom Committee; YMCA of the USA, International Division.

# Appendix D:  Data appendix

This appendix provides information about the nature and sources of the quantitative data that I used throughout the book. Although some issues of measurement and operationalization are discussed extensively earlier in the text (specifically with regard to the dependent variables in the analysis), in some cases I omitted a thorough discussion of the independent and control variables to aid the book's exposition. Below, I discuss those variables in the order that they appear in the text.

## Chapter 3

In this chapter, I examined whether changes in executive and legislative power were correlated with regime-compatible democracy assistance. The data on changes in countries' executive leaders came from the Archigos data set.[1] I relied upon the variable "Exit" to identify leaders who exited from office for reasons other than natural causes. The data on whether incumbents and incumbent parties won national elections came from the National Elections Across Democracy and Autocracy (NELDA) database.[2] Specifically, I used variable NELDA24 ("Did the incumbent's party lose?").

Later in the chapter, I calculated the proportions of elections that seemed unlikely beforehand to be free and fair and that monitors refused to observe. For those calculations, I again used NELDA; the specific variables used were NELDA11 ("Before elections, are there significant concerns that elections will not be free and fair?") and NELDA49 ("Did any monitors refuse to go to an election because they believed that it would not be free and fair?").

---

[1] Goemans, Gleditsch, and Chiozza (2009).
[2] Hyde and Marinov (2012).

## Chapter 4

In this chapter, I examined how delegation relationships shape the design and implementation of democracy assistance. Chapter 4 contains information about the nature and sources of the data for the dependent variables.

I used three different indicators of delegation relations in democracy assistance. The first indicator was *Donor-country NGOs* and applied to aid being channeled via NGOs. This dichotomous variable was coded 1 if a project was implemented by a donor-country NGO and 0 otherwise. The coding was based on donors' self-reported channel of delivery information to the Organisation for Economic Co-operation and Development.[3] The second indicator was *EU projects* and applied to aid being channeled via multilateral institutions. This dichotomous variable was coded 1 if a project was implemented by the European Union and 0 otherwise. The coding was also based on donors' self-reported channel of delivery information to the Organisation for Economic Co-operation and Development.[4] The third indicator was *Aid volatility* and applied to aid being channeled via government agencies. I calculated *Aid volatility* by taking the standard deviation of each donor country's total foreign-aid commitments between 2001 and 2010, as reported by the country to the OECD.[5] Recall that the standard deviation is a measure of the variance in a set of numbers.

I included a number of control variables in the analysis in this chapter. The first control variable was *Affinity*. The affinity score is calculated based on countries' similarity in voting records in the United Nations General Assembly (UNGA). This variable is made available from Erik Gartzke's data set, "The Affinity of Nations: Similarity of State Voting Positions at the UNGA."[6] The variable takes on values of between −1 and 1 and is based on a three-category coding of UN votes (yes, no, and abstain). The specific variable is called Sscore3i. The second control variable was *Democracy*. The primary measure for democracy in this chapter came from Freedom House, which measures countries' political rights and civil liberties on a scale of one to seven. I averaged and transformed those scores so that 1 represents the least democratic countries.[7] These scores are based on country experts' responses to questionnaires about various dimensions of freedom. Since Freedom

---

[3] Organisation for Economic Co-operation and Development (2010).
[4] Organisation for Economic Co-operation and Development (2010).
[5] Organisation for Economic Co-operation and Development (2010).
[6] Gartzke (1998).
[7] Freedom House (2012).

House's measures have sometimes been criticized, I also ensure that my results are robust to the Polity IV measure of democracy, which is a twenty-point scale on which −10 represents highly autocratic countries and 10 represents highly democratic countries.[8] The third control variable was the *Democracy*[2] variable. That variable was simply the square of the combined Freedom House score variable.

I also included regional fixed effects in some of the analyses in Chapter 4. The World Bank classifies countries into a number of regions: East Asia and Pacific; Europe and Central Asia; Latin America and the Caribbean; the Middle East and North Africa; South Asia; and Sub-Saharan Africa.[9] I used those categories to create indicator variables. Finally, I also conducted robustness checks using information on donor governments' gross national incomes. This variable was measured in constant US dollars and based on data from the World Bank.[10]

## Chapter 5

In this chapter, I examined how competition and professional norms shape the design and implementation of American democracy assistance. Chapter 5 contains information about the nature and sources of the data for the dependent variables and key independent variables.

The primary control variables in the analysis are: *Cold War*; *Military aid*; *Democracy*; *Democracy*[2]; and *Post-1994*. I discuss each variable in turn here. First, *Cold War* was a dichotomous variable that took the value of 1 for years before the end of the Cold War in 1990 (1992 in robustness checks) and 0 otherwise.

Second, *Military aid* was a continuous variable that captured the amount of US military aid that the target country received in the previous year. The data came from the USAID Greenbook. I added 1 before taking the natural log to eliminate zeroes.[11] In cases of missing data, I assumed the country received no aid. This variable sought to measure the concept of a country's strategic importance to the United States. In robustness checks, I instead used the target country's US economic aid and its political affinity with the United States in terms of UN votes as alternative indicators of strategic importance. The former data were also taken from the USAID Greenbook; the latter data were described above.

---

[8] Marshall, Gurr, and Jaggers (2009).
[9] World Bank (2012b).
[10] World Bank (2012a).
[11] United States Agency for International Development (2012).

Third, the *Democracy* and *Democracy²* were continuous measures of target countries' regime types. Both variables were described above. In robustness checks, I explored the significance of an additional indicator of regime type. Political scientist Barbara Geddes has classified authoritarian regimes into three categories: military, single-party, and personalist.[12] I used data from an extension of Geddes's categories that also includes the category of monarchies.[13]

Finally, *Post-1994* was a dichotomous variable that takes the value of 1 for years after 1994 and 0 otherwise.

[12] Geddes (1999).
[13] Wright (2008a).

# Bibliography

Abu-Lughod, Lila. 2002. "Do Muslim Women Really Need Saving? Anthropological Reflections on Cultural Relativism and its Others." *American Anthropologist* 104(3): 783–90.

Alesina, Alberto and David Dollar. 2000. "Who Gives Foreign Aid to Whom and Why?" *Journal of Economic Growth* 5(1): 33–63.

Alesina, Alberto and Beatrice Weder. 2002. "Do Corrupt Governments Receive Less Foreign Aid?" *American Economic Review* 92(4): 1126–37.

Amara, Tarek. 2012. "Thousands Rally in Tunisia for Women's Rights." *Reuters*, August 13.

Angrist, Michele Penner. 1999. "Parties, Parliament, and Political Dissent in Tunisia." *British Journal of Middle Eastern Studies* 4(4): 89–104.

Arvin, B. Mak. 2002. *New Perspectives on Foreign Aid and Economic Development.* Westport, CT: Praeger.

Autesserre, Sèverine. 2014. *Peaceland: Conflict Resolution and the Everyday Politics of International Intervention.* Problems of International Politics Series. New York: Cambridge University Press.

Azpuru, Dinorah, Steven E. Finkel, Aníbal Pérez-Liñán and Mitchell A. Seligson. 2008. "Trends in Democracy Assistance: What has the United States Been Doing?" *Journal of Democracy* 19(2): 150–9.

Barabasi, Albert-Laszlo. 2003. *Linked: How Everything is Connected to Everything Else and What it Means for Business, Science, and Everyday Life.* New York: Plume.

Barkan, Joel D. 2012. "Democracy Assistance: What Recipients Think." *Journal of Democracy* 23(1): 129–37.

Barkan, Joel D. and Fred Matiangi. 2009. "Legislative Power in Emerging African Democracies." In: *Kenya's Torturous Path to Successful Legislative Development*, ed. Joel D. Barkan. Boulder, CO: Lynne Rienner Publishers, pp. 33–72.

Barnett, Michael N. 2009. "Evolution Without Progress? Humanitarianism in a World of Hurt?" *International Organization* 63(4): 621–63.

Barnett, Michael and Liv Coleman. 2005. "Designing Police: Interpol and the Study of Change in International Organizations." *International Studies Quarterly* 49(4): 593–619.

Baylouny, Anne Marie. 2005. "Jordan's New 'Political Development' Strategy." *Middle East Report* 35(3): 40–3.

Beaulieu, Emily and Susan D. Hyde. 2009. "In the Shadow of Democracy Promotion: Strategic Manipulation, International Observers and Election Boycotts." *Comparative Political Studies* 42(3): 392–415.

Beissinger, Mark R. 2007. "Structure and Example in Modular Political Phenomena: The Diffusion of Bulldozer/Rose/Orange/Tulip Revolutions." *Perspectives on Politics* 5(2): 259–76.

Bellin, Eva. 2004. "The Robustness of Authoritarianism in the Middle East: Exceptionalism in Comparative Theory." *Comparative Politics* 36(2): 139–57.

2012. "Reconsidering the Robustness of Authoritarianism in the Middle East: Lessons from the Arab Spring." *Comparative Politics* 44(2): 127–49.

Bermeo, Sarah Blodgett. 2008. "Foreign Aid, Foreign Policy and Strategic Development." PhD dissertation. Princeton University, Princeton, NJ.

Bicchi, Federica. 2009. "Democracy Assistance in the Mediterranean: An Overview." *Mediterranean Politics* 14(1): 61–78.

Birch, Sarah. 2012. *Electoral Malpractice*. Comparative Politics Series. Oxford University Press.

Bjornlund, Eric. 2000. "Civil Society Transformed: International Aid to New Political Parties in the Czech Republic and Slovakia." *Voluntas: International Journal of Voluntary and Nonprofit Organizations* 11(2): 161–79.

2001. "Democracy, Inc." *The Wilson Quarterly* 25(3): 18–24.

2004. *Beyond Free and Fair: Monitoring Elections and Building Democracy*. Baltimore, MD: Johns Hopkins University Press.

Blackwell, Matthew, Stefano Iacus, and Gary King. 2009. "cem: Coarsened Exact Matching in Stata." *The Stata Journal* 9(4): 524–46.

Bloodgood, Elizabeth A. 2011. "The Interest Group Analogy: International Non-Governmental Advocacy Organisations in International Politics." *Review of International Studies* 37(1): 93–120.

Bob, Clifford. 2005. *The Marketing of Rebellion: Insurgents, Media, and International Activism*. New York: Cambridge University Press.

Bogdanich, Walt and Jenny Nordberg. 2006. "Mixed U.S. Signals Helped Tilt Haiti Toward Chaos." *New York Times*, January 29.

Bollen, Kenneth, Pamela Paxton, and Rumi Morishima. 2005. "Assessing International Evaluations: An Example From USAID's Democracy and Governance Program." *American Journal of Evaluation* 26(2): 189–203.

Boulding, Carew. 2012. "Dilemmas of Information and Accountability: Foreign Aid Donors and Local Development NGOs." In: *The Credibility of Transnational NGOs: When Virtue is Not Enough*, ed. Peter A. Gourevitch, David A. Lake, and Janice Gross Stein. New York: Cambridge University Press, pp. 115–36.

Bradley, Curtis A. and Judith G. Kelley. 2008. "The Concept of International Delegation." *Law & Contemporary Problems* 71(1): 1–36.

Brady, Henry E. and David Collier, eds. 2004. *Rethinking Social Inquiry: Diverse Tools, Shared Standards*. Lanham, MD: Rowman & Littlefield.

Brancati, Dawn. 2014. "The Determinants of U.S. Public Opinion Towards Democracy Promotion." *Political Behavior* forthcoming.

Brancati, Dawn and Jack L. Snyder. 2011. "Rushing to the Polls: The Causes of Premature Post-Conflict Elections." *Journal of Conflict Resolution* 55(3): 469–92.

Britton, Hannah Evelyn. 2005. *Women in the South African Parliament: From Resistance to Governance*. Urbana: University of Illinois Press.

Brown, Keith. 2006. "The New Ugly Americans? Making Sense of Democracy Promotion in the Former Yugoslavia." In: *Transacting Transition: The Micropolitics of Democracy Assistance in the Former Yugoslavia*, ed. Keith Brown. Bloomfield, CT: Kumarian Press, pp. 1–22.

Brown, Stephen. 2001. "Authoritarian Leaders and Multiparty Elections in Africa: How Foreign Donors Help to Keep Kenya's Daniel arap Moi in Power." *Third World Quarterly* 22(5): 725–39.

  2004. "Theorising Kenya's Protracted Transition to Democracy." *Journal of Contemporary African Studies* 22(2): 325–42.

  2011. "'Well, What Can You Expect?': Donor Officials' Apologetics for Hybrid Regimes in Africa." *Democratization* 18(2): 512–34.

Brownlee, Jason. 2007. *Authoritarianism in an Age of Democratization*. New York: Cambridge University Press.

  2012. *Democracy Prevention: The Politics of the U.S.–Egyptian Alliance*. Cambridge University Press.

Bueno de Mesquita, Bruce and Alastair Smith. 2009. "A Political Economy of Aid." *International Organization* 63(2): 309–40.

Bunce, Valerie J. and Sharon L. Wolchik. 2006a. "International Diffusion and Postcommunist Electoral Revolutions." *Communist and Post-Communist Studies* 39(3): 283–304.

  2006b. "Transnational Networks, Diffusion Dynamics and Electoral Revolutions in the Postcommunist World." *Physica A: Statistical Mechanics and its Applications* 378(1): 92–9.

  2011. *Defeating Authoritarian Leaders in Postcommunist Countries*. New York: Cambridge University Press.

Burnell, Peter J., ed. 2000. *Democracy Assistance: International Co-operation for Democratization*. London: Routledge.

Burnside, Craig and David Dollar. 2000. "Aid, Policies, and Growth." *American Economic Review* 90(4): 847–68.

  2004. "Aid, Policies, and Growth: Revisiting the Evidence." Policy Research Working Paper Series 3251. Washington, DC: World Bank.

Bush, Sarah Sunn. 2011. "International Politics and the Spread of Quotas for Women in Legislatures." *International Organization* 65(1): 103–37.

  2013. "'Made-in-America' Democracy? Explaining Allocation Patterns in American Democracy Support." Paper presented at the 2013 Annual Meeting of the Midwest Political Science Association, Chicago, April 12.

Bush, Sarah Sunn and Amaney Jamal. 2015. "Anti-Americanism, Authoritarian Regimes, and Women's Political Representation: Evidence from a Survey Experiment in Jordan." *International Studies Quarterly* forthcoming.

Büthe, Tim, Solomon Major, and André de Mello e Souza. 2012. "The Politics of Private Foreign Aid: Humanitarian Principles, Economic Development Objectives, and Organizational Interests in NGO Private Aid Allocation." *International Organization* 66(4): 571–607.

Campbell, Donald T. 1976. "Assessing the Impact of Planned Social Change." Paper No. 8, Occasional Paper Series, The Public Affairs Center, Hanover, NH: Dartmouth College.

Carapico, Sheila. 2002. "Foreign Aid for Promoting Democracy in the Arab World." *Middle East Journal* 56(3): 379–95.

Carothers, Thomas. 1996. "Aiding Post-Communist Societies: A Better Way?" *Problems of Post-Communism* 43(5): 15–24.

 1999. *Aiding Democracy Abroad: The Learning Curve*. Washington, DC: Carnegie Endowment for International Peace.

 2005. "Choosing a Strategy." In: *Uncharted Journey: Promoting Democracy in the Middle East*, ed. Thomas Carothers and Marina Ottaway. Washington, DC: Carnegie Endowment for International Peace, pp. 193–208.

 2006a. "The Backlash Against Democracy Promotion." *Foreign Affairs* 85(2): 55–68.

 2006b. *Confronting the Weakest Link: Aiding Political Parties in New Democracies*. Washington, DC: Carnegie Endowment for International Peace.

 2009a. "Democracy Assistance: Political vs. Developmental?" *Journal of Democracy* 20(1): 5–19.

 2009b. "Democracy Assistance Without a Plan." LSE UNDP Development and Transition. Available at: www.carnegieendowment.org/2009/04/01/democracy-assistance-without-plan.

 2009c. "Revitalizing Democracy Assistance: The Challenge of USAID." Washington, DC: Carnegie Endowment for International Peace.

Carpenter, R. Charli. 2007. "Studying Issue (Non-)Adoption in Transnational Advocacy Networks." *International Organization* 61(3): 643–67.

 2011. "Vetting the Advocacy Agenda: Network Centrality and the Paradox of Weapons Norms." *International Organization* 65(1): 69–102.

Carpenter, R. Charli and Betcy Jose. 2012. "Transnational Issue Networks in Real and Virtual Space: The Case of Women, Peace and Security." *Global Networks* 12(4): 525–43.

Chicago Council on Foreign Relations and the German Marshall Fund of the United States. 2002. "Worldviews 2002." U.S. Leaders Topline Report. Available at: www.thechicagocouncil.org/files/Studies_Publications/POS/POS2002/Public_Opinion_Survey__Worldviews_2002.aspx.

Chikhladze, Giga and Irakli Chikhladze. 2005. "The Rose Revolution: A Chronicle." In: *Enough!: The Rose Revolution in the Republic of Georgia, 2003*, ed. Zurab Karumidze and James Wertsch. New York: Nova Science Publishers, pp. 1–20.

Chomiak, Laryssa. 2011. "The Making of a Revolution in Tunisia." *Middle East Law and Governance* 3(1): 68–83.

Christensen, Darin and Jeremy Weinstein. 2013. "Defunding Dissent: Restrictions on Aid to NGOs." *Journal of Democracy* 24(2): 77–91.

Clark, Ann Marie, Elisabeth J. Friedman, and Kathryn Hochstetler. 1998. "The Sovereign Limits of Global Civil Society: A Comparison of NGO Participation in UN World Conferences on the Environment, Human Rights, and Women." *World Politics* 51(1): 1–35.

Clark, Janine A. and Wacheke M. Michuki. 2009. "Women and NGO Professionalisation: A Case Study of Jordan." *Development in Practice* 19(3): 329–39.

Clinton, Hillary Rodham. 2009. "Address to the U.S. Agency for International Development Employees." Washington, D.C., January 23. Available at: http://iipdigital.usembassy.gov/st/english/texttrans/2009/01/2009012317060eaifas0.1295893.html.

Coles, Kimberley A. 2004. "Election Day: The Construction of Democracy through Technique." *Cultural Anthropology* 19(4): 551–80.

2007. *Democratic Designs: International Intervention and Electoral Practices in Post-War Bosnia-Herzegovina.* Ann Arbor: University of Michigan Press.

Collier, David and Steven Levitsky. 1997. "Democracy with Adjectives: Conceptual Innovation in Comparative Research." *World Politics* 49(3): 430–51.

Collier, David, Jody LaPorte, and Jason Seawright. 2012. "Putting Typologies to Work: Concept-Formation, Measurement, and Analytic Rigor." *Political Research Quarterly* 65(2): 217–32.

Cooley, Alexander and James Ron. 2002. "The NGO Scramble: Organizational Insecurity and the Political Economy of Transnational Action." *International Security* 27(1): 5–39.

Copelovitch, Mark S. 2010. "Master or Servant? Common Agency and the Political Economy of IMF Lending." *International Studies Quarterly* 54(1): 49–77.

Corn, David. 1993. "Beltway Bandits: Better Dead than NED." *The Nation*, July 12, pp. 56–7.

Corstange, Daniel and Nikolay Marinov. 2012. "Taking Sides in Other People's Elections: The Polarizing Effect of Foreign Intervention." *American Journal of Political Science* 56(3): 655–70.

Cox, Michael, G. John Ikenberry, and Takashi Inoguchi, eds. 2000. *American Democracy Promotion: Impulses, Strategies and Impacts.* Oxford University Press.

Crawford, Gordon. 2001. *Foreign Aid and Political Reform: A Comparative Analysis of Democracy Assistance and Political Conditionality.* New York: Palgrave.

Davenport, Christian. 2007. "State Repression and Political Order." *Annual Review of Political Science* 10: 1–23.

David, Assaf and Stefanie Nanes. 2011. "The Women's Quota in Jordan's Municipal Councils: International and Domestic Dimensions." *Journal of Women, Politics & Policy* 32(4): 275–304.

Democracy International, Inc. 2011. "Parliamentary Program of Azerbaijan Evaluation: Final Report." Bethesda, MD: Democracy International, Inc.

Diamond, Larry. 1997. *Promoting Democracy in the 1990s: Actors and Instruments, Issues and Imperatives.* New York: Carnegie Corporation of New York.

Dicther, Thomas W. 2003. *Despite Good Intentions: Why Development Assistance to the Third World Has Failed.* Amherst, MA: University of Massachusetts Press.

Dietrich, Simone. 2013. "Bypass or Engage? Explaining Donor Delivery Tactics in Foreign Aid Allocation." *International Studies Quarterly* 57(4): 698–712.

DiMaggio, Paul J. 1991. "Constructing an Organizational Field as a Professional Project: U.S. Art Museums, 1920–1940." In: *The New Institutionalism in Organizational Analysis*, ed. Walter W. Powell and Paul J. DiMaggio. University of Chicago Press, pp. 267–92.

DiMaggio, Paul J. and Walter W. Powell. 1983. "The Iron Cage Revisited: Institutional Isomorphisms and Collective Rationality in Organizational Fields." *American Sociological Review* 48(2): 147–60.

Donno, Daniela. 2010. "Who Is Punished? Regional Intergovernmental Organizations and the Enforcement of Democratic Norms." *International Organization* 64(4): 593–625.

2013. *Defending Democratic Norms: International Actors and the Politics of Electoral Misconduct.* Oxford University Press.

Dreher, Axel, Jan-Egbert Sturm, and James Raymond Vreeland. 2009. "Development Aid and International Politics: Does Membership on the UN Security Council Influence World Bank Decisions?" *Journal of Development Economics* 88(1): 1–18.

Drezner, Daniel W. 2008. "The Realist Tradition in American Public Opinion." *Perspectives on Politics* 6(1): 51–70.

Durac, Vincent and Francesco Cavatorta. 2011. "Strengthening Authoritarian Rule through Democracy Promotion? Examining the Paradox of the US and EU Security Strategies: The Case of Bin Ali's Tunisia." *Journal of North African Studies* 36(1): 3–19.

Easterly, William. 2002. "The Cartel of Good Intentions." *Foreign Policy* 131(July–August): 40–9.

2006. *The White Man's Burden: Why the West's Efforts to Aid the Rest Have Done So Much Ill and So Little Good.* New York: Penguin.

*Economist* (online). 2011. "Tunisia's Revolution in the Arab Press: What the Arab Papers Say." Available at: www.economist.com/blogs/newsbook/2011/01/tunisias_revolution_arab_press.

Elkins, Zachary. 2009. "Constitutional Networks." In: *Networked Politics: Agency, Power, and Governance,* ed. Miles Kahler. Ithaca, NY: Cornell University Press, pp. 43–63.

Embassy Cairo. 2007. "Egypt: Updated Democracy Strategy." Available at: www.aftenposten.no/spesial/wikileaksdokumenter/article4008796.ece.

Embassy Manama. 2010. "Guarding NDI's Flank." Available at: www.telegraph.co.uk/news/wikileaks-files/bahrain-wikileaks-cables/83344643/GUARDING-NDIS-

Epstein, Susan B., Nina M. Serafino, and Francis T. Miko. 2007. *Democracy Promotion: Cornerstone of U.S. Foreign Policy?* Washington, DC: Congressional Research Service.

European Instrument for Democracy and Human Rights. 2012. "EIDHR: Call for Proposals." Memorandum. Available at: www.eidhr.eu/files/dmfile/MicrosoftPowerPoint-EIDHR_FORUM2012_CfPObj1_publ.pdf.

European Parliament, Office for Promotion of Parliamentary Democracy. 2010. *Getting Acquainted: Setting the Stage for Democracy Assistance.* Brussels: European Parliament.

European Union. 2007. "The Council of the European Union." Treaty of Nice: A Comprehensive Guide. Available at: http://europa.eu/legislation_summaries/institutional_affairs/treaties/nice_treaty/nice_treaty_council_en.htm.

Fahim, Kareem. 2012. "As Hopes for Reform Fade in Bahrain, Protesters Turn Anger on United States." *New York Times,* June 23, p. A6.

Fahmy, Mohamed Fadel. 2012. "Captains Stay with their Crew." *Foreign Policy (online)*. Available at: www.foreignpolicy.com/articles/2012/05/02/captains_stay_with_their_crew.

Faust, Jörg and Melody Garcia. 2013. "With or Without Force: European Public Opinion on Democracy Promotion." Discussion Paper. Bonn: German Development Institute.

Fearon, James D. and David D. Laitin. 2000. "Ordinary Language and External Validity: Specifying Concepts in the Study of Ethnicity." Paper presented at the 96th Annual Meeting of the American Political Science Association, August/September, Washington, DC.

Ferguson, James. 1990. *The Anti-Politics Machine: "Development," Depoliticization, and Bureaucratic Power in Lesotho*. New York: Cambridge University Press.

Finkel, Steven E., Aníbal Pérez-Liñán, and Mitchell A. Seligson. 2007. "The Effects of U.S. Foreign Assistance on Democracy Building, 1990–2003." *World Politics* 59(3): 404–39.

Finnemore, Martha and Kathryn Sikkink. 1998. "International Norm Dynamics and Political Change." *International Organization* 52(4): 887–917.

Flores, Thomas Edward and Irfan Nooruddin. 2012. "The Effect of Elections on Postconflict Peace and Reconstruction." *Journal of Politics* 74(2): 558–70.

Fowler, Alan. 1996. "Demonstrating NGO Performance: Problems and Possibilities." *Development in Practice* 6(1): 58–65.

Franck, Thomas M. 1992. "The Emerging Right to Democratic Governance." *American Journal of International Law* 86(1): 46–91.

Freedom House. 1985–2014. *Freedom in the World* (annual reports). Washington, DC: Freedom House.

  2003. "Freedom House Statement on Iraq War." Available at: www.freedomhouse.org/article/freedom-house-statement-iraq-war.

  2012. "About Us." Available at: www.freedomhouse.org/template.cfm?page=2.

Freyburg, Tina. 2011. "Transgovernmental Networks as Catalysts for Democratic Change? EU Functional Cooperation with Arab Authoritarian Regimes and Socialization of Involved State Officials into Democratic Governance." *Democratization* 18(4): 1001–25.

Gandhi, Jennifer and Ellen Lust-Okar. 2009. "Elections Under Authoritarianism." *Annual Review of Political Science* 12: 403–22.

Gandhi, Jennifer and Adam Przeworski. 2007. "Authoritarian Institutions and the Survival of Autocrats." *Comparative Political Studies* 40(11): 1279–301.

Gartzke, Erik. 1998. "Kant We All Just Get Along? Opportunity, Willingness, and the Origins of the Democratic Peace." *American Journal of Political Science* 42(1): 1–27.

Geddes, Barbara. 1999. "What Do We Know About Democratization after Twenty Years?" *Annual Review of Political Science* 2: 115–44.

Gershman, Carl and Michael Allen. 2006. "New Threats to Freedom: The Assault on Democracy Assistance." *Journal of Democracy* 17(2): 36–51.

Ghribi, Asma. 2011. "State Department Program's Funding of Tunisian Media Comes under Scrutiny." *Tunisia Live*. Available at: http://goo.gl/NHcDCe.

Giannone, Diego. 2010. "Political and Ideological Aspects in the Measurement of Democracy: The Freedom House Case." *Democratization* 17(1): 68–97.

Girod, Desha M., Stephen D. Krasner, and Kathryn Stoner-Weiss. 2009. "Governance and Foreign Assistance: The Imperfect Translation of Ideas into Outcomes." In: *Promoting Democracy and the Rule of Law: American and European Strategies*, ed. Amichai Magen, Thomas Risse, and Michael A. McFaul. London: Palgrave Macmillan, pp. 61–92.

Global Net. 2011. "Abdelwahab El Hani: 'Les extrêmes sont un danger pour la Tunisie'." Global Net. Available at: http://goo.gl/2uTsgY.

Goemans, Henk E., Kristian Skrede Gleditsch, and Giacomo Chiozza. 2009. "Introducing Archigos: A Dataset of Political Leaders." *Journal of Peace Research* 46(2): 269–83.

Goldstein, Judith and Robert O. Keohane. 1993. "Ideas and Foreign Policy: An Analytical Framework." In: *Ideas and Foreign Policy: Beliefs, Institutions and Political Change*, ed. Judith Goldstein and Robert O. Keohane. Ithaca, NY: Cornell University Press, pp. 3–30.

Gourevitch, Peter A. 1978. "The Second Image Reversed." *International Organization* 32(4): 881–912.

Gourevitch, Peter A. and David A. Lake. 2012. "Beyond Virtue: Evaluating and Enhancing the Credibility of Non-Governmental Organizations." In: *The Credibility of Transnational NGOs: When Virtue is Not Enough*, ed. Peter A. Gourevitch, David A. Lake, and Janice Gross Stein. Cambridge University Press, pp. 3–34.

Green, Andrew T. and Richard D. Kohl. 2007. "Challenges of Evaluating Democracy Assistance: Perspectives from the Donor Side." *Democratization* 14(2): 151–65.

Green, Donald P., Soo Yeon H. Kim, and David Yoon. 2001. "Dirty Pool." *International Organization* 5(2): 441–68.

Guilhot, Nicolas. 2005. *The Democracy Makers: Human Rights and International Order*. New York: Columbia University Press.

  2007. "Reforming the World: George Soros, Global Capitalism, and the Philanthropic Management of the Social Sciences." *Critical Sociology* 33(3): 447–77.

Gutner, Tamar. 2005a. "Explaining the Gaps between Mandate and Performance: Agency Theory and World Bank Environmental Reform." *Global Environmental Politics* 5(2): 10–37.

  2005b. "World Bank Environmental Reform: Revisiting Lessons from Agency Theory." *International Organization* 59(3): 773–83.

Hachicha, Neila Charchour. 2005. "Tunisia's Election Was Undemocratic at All Levels." *Middle East Quarterly* 12(3): 77–81.

Hadenius, Axel and Jan Teorell. 2007. "Pathways from Authoritarianism." *Journal of Democracy* 18(1): 143–57.

Hafner-Burton, Emilie M., Miles Kahler, and Alexander H. Montgomery. 2009. "Network Analysis for International Relations." *International Organization* 63(3): 559–92.

Hamid, Shadi and Peter Mandaville. 2013. "Bringing the United States Back into the Middle East." *Washington Quarterly* 36(4): 95–105.

Hammami, Rema. 2000. "Palestinian NGOs since Oslo: From NGO Politics to Social Movements?" *Middle East Report* 214(Spring): 16–19, 27, 48.

Hancock, Graham. 1989. *The Lords of Poverty: The Power, Prestige, and Corruption of the International Aid Business.* London: Macmillan.

Haring, Melinda A. 2013. "Reforming the Democracy Bureaucracy." Philadelphia, PA: Foreign Policy Research Institute.

Hawkins, Darren G., David A. Lake, Daniel L. Nielson, and Michael J. Tierney. 2006. "Delegation Under Anarchy: States, International Organizations and Principal–Agent Theory." In: *Delegation and Agency in International Organizations,* ed. Darren G. Hawkins, David A. Lake, Daniel L. Nielson, and Michael J. Tierney. New York: Cambridge University Press, pp. 3–38.

Hawthorne, Amy. 2005. "Is Civil Society the Answer?" In: *Uncharted Journey: Promoting Democracy in the Middle East,* ed. Thomas Carothers and Marina Ottaway. Washington, DC: Carnegie Endowment for International Peace, pp. 81–114.

Hazaimeh, Hani. 2010. "Jordan Makes Tangible Progress in Reforms – EU." *Jordan Times,* May 13.

Henderson, Sarah L. 2000. "Importing Civil Society: Foreign Aid and the Women's Movement in Russia." *Demokratizatsiya: Journal of Post-Soviet Democratization* 8(1): 65–82.

   2002. "Selling Civil Society: Western Aid and the Nongovernmental Organization Sector in Russia." *Comparative Political Studies* 35(2): 139–67.

   2003. *Building Democracy in Contemporary Russia: Western Support for Grassroots Organizations.* Ithaca, NY: Cornell University Press.

Heydemann, Steven. 2007. "Upgrading Authoritarianism in the Arab World." Analysis Paper No. 13. Washington, DC: The Saban Center for Middle East Policy at the Brookings Institution.

Ho, Daniel E., Kosuke Imai, Gary King, and Elizabeth A. Stuart. 2007. "Matching as Nonparametric Preprocessing for Reducing Model Dependence in Parametric Causal Inference." *Political Analysis* 15(3): 199–236.

Hobson, Christopher and Milja Kurki. 2012. "Introduction." In: *The Conceptual Politics of Democracy Promotion,* ed. Christopher Hobson and Milja Kurki. London: Routledge, pp. 1–15.

Holsti, Ole R. 2000. "Promotion of Democracy as Popular Demand." In: *American Democracy Promotion: Impulses, Strategies and Impacts,* ed. Michael Cox, G. John Ikenberry, and Takashi Inoguchi. Oxford University Press, pp. 151–81.

Hood, Christopher. 1998. *The Art of the State: Culture, Rhetoric and Public Management.* Oxford University Press.

Hopgood, Stephen. 2008. "Saying 'No' to Wal-Mart? Money and Morality in Professional Humanitarianism." In: *Humanitarianism in Question: Politics, Power, Ethics,* ed. Michael Barnett and Thomas G. Weiss. Ithaca, NY: Cornell University Press, pp. 98–123.

House of Commons, International Development Committee. 2010. "Draft International Development (Official Development Assistance Target) Bill." Seventh Report of Session 2009–10. London: The Stationery Office.

Huntington, Samuel P. 1991. *The Third Wave: Democratization in the Late Twentieth Century.* Norman: University of Oklahoma Press.

Hyde, Susan D. 2007. "The Observer Effect in International Politics: Evidence from a Natural Experiment." *World Politics* 60(1): 37–63.

2010. "Experimenting in Democracy Promotion: International Observers and the 2004 Presidential Elections in Indonesia." *Perspectives on Politics* 8(2): 511–27.

2011. *The Pseudo-Democrat's Dilemma: Why Election Observation Became an International Norm*. Ithaca, NY: Cornell University Press.

2012. "Why Believe International Election Monitors?" In: *The Credibility of Transnational NGOs: When Virtue Is Not Enough*, ed. Peter A. Gourevitch, David A. Lake, and Janice Gross Stein. Cambridge University Press, pp. 37–61.

Hyde, Susan D. and Nikolay Marinov. 2012. "Which Elections Can Be Lost?" *Political Analysis* 20(2): 191–210.

Iacus, Stefano M., Gary King, and Giuseppe Porro. 2012. "Causal Inference Without Balance Checking: Coarsened Exact Matching." *Political Analysis* 20(1): 1–24.

Ibn Al Hussein, Abdullah, II. 2011. "Speech of His Majesty King Abdullah II on the Occasion of Arab Revolt, Army Day and Coronation Day." Amman, Jordan, June. Available at: http://kingabdullah.jo/index.php/en_US/speeches/view/id/478/videoDisplay/10.html.

Ichino, Nahomi and Matthias Schuendein. 2012. "Deterring or Displacing Electoral Irregularities? Spillover Effects of Observers in a Randomized Field Experiment in Ghana." *Journal of Politics* 74(1): 292–307.

Ikenberry, G. John. 1993. "Creating Yesterday's New World Order: Keynesian 'New Thinking' and the Anglo-American Postwar Settlement." In: *Ideas and Foreign Policy: Beliefs, Institutions and Political Change*, ed. Judith Goldstein and Robert O. Keohane. Ithaca, NY: Cornell University Press, pp. 57–86.

2000. "America's Liberal Grand Strategy: Democracy and National Security in the Post-war Era." In: *American Democracy Promotion: Impulses, Strategies and Impacts*, ed. Michael Cox, G. John Ikenberry, and Takashi Inoguchi. Oxford University Press, pp. 103–26.

Inglehart, Ronald and Pippa Norris. 2003. *Rising Tide: Gender Equality and Cultural Change*. New York: Cambridge University Press.

Institute for Democracy in Eastern Europe. 2001. "2000–2001 Activities." Available at: www.idee.org/ideeactivities2000-2001.html.

2012. "IDEE Program and Activities: 2010–2012." Available at: www.idee.org/ideeactivities2010-12.html.

International Center for Not-for-Profit Law. 2012. "NGO Law Monitor: Jordan." Washington, DC: International Center for Not-for-Profit Law.

Ishkanian, Armine. 2008. *Democracy Building and Civil Society in Post-Soviet Armenia*. New York: Routledge.

Jackson, Jeffrey T. 2005. *The Globalizers: Development Workers in Action*. Baltimore, MD: Johns Hopkins University Press.

Jad, Islah. 2004. "The NGO-isation of Arab Women's Movements." *IDS Bulletin* 35(4): 34–42.

Jamal, Amaney A. 2007. *Barriers to Democracy: The Other Side of Social Capital in Palestine*. Princeton University Press.

2012. *Of Empires and Citizens: Pro-American Democracy or No Democracy at All?* Princeton University Press.

Johnson, Tana. 2010. "Rethinking Non-State Actors: The Role and Impact of International Bureaucrats in Institutional Design." PhD dissertation. University of Chicago.

Jordan, Michael J. 1996. "Iliescu's Foes Say US Envoy Meddling in Romania Vote." *Christian Science Monitor*, October 11, p. 1.

*Jordan Times.* 2010. "Jordan Obtains 'Advanced Status' with EU." *Jordan Times*, October 27.

Kahler, Miles. 2009. "Networked Politics: Agency, Power, and Governance." In: *Networked Politics: Agency, Power, and Governance*, ed. Miles Kahler. Ithaca, NY: Cornell University Press, pp. 1–20.

Katz, Ethan. 2001. "Bias in Conditional and Unconditional Fixed Effects Logit Estimation." *Political Analysis* 9(4): 379–84.

Katzenstein, Peter J. and Robert O. Keohane. 2007. "Varieties of Anti-Americanism: A Framework for Analysis." In: *Anti-Americanisms in World Politics*, ed. Peter J. Katzenstein and Robert O. Keohane. Ithaca, NY: Cornell University Press, pp. 9–38.

Keck, Margaret E. and Kathryn Sikkink. 1998. *Activists Beyond Borders: Advocacy Networks in International Politics*. Ithaca, NY: Cornell University Press.

Kelley, Judith G. 2004. *Ethnic Politics in Europe: The Power of Norms and Incentives*. Princeton University Press.

2008. "Assessing the Complex Evolution of Norms: The Rise of International Election Monitoring." *International Organization* 62(2): 221–55.

2009. "D-Minus Elections: The Politics and Norms of International Election Observation." *International Organization* 63(4): 765–87.

2012. *Monitoring Democracy: When International Election Observation Works and Why it Often Fails*. Princeton University Press.

Kennedy, David. 2005. *The Dark Sides of Virtue: Reassessing International Humanitarianism*. Princeton University Press.

Keohane, Robert O. and Joseph S. Nye. 1977. *Power and Interdependence*. Boston: Little, Brown.

Khalaf, Roula. 2012. "Kings Trump Aid for Arab Spring Nations." *Financial Times*, July 16, p. 13.

King, Gary and Langche Zeng. 2006. "The Dangers of Extreme Counterfactuals." *Political Analysis* 14(2): 131–59.

Kirkpatrick, David K. 2012. "Egypt Defies U.S. by Setting Trial for 19 Americans on Criminal Charges." *New York Times*, February 5, p. A1.

Kopstein, Jeffrey. 2006. "The Transatlantic Divide over Democracy Promotion." *Washington Quarterly* 29(2): 85–98.

Korey, William. 1998. *NGOs and the Universal Declaration of Human Rights: "A Curious Grapevine"*. New York: St. Martin's Press.

Krisch, Henry. 2009. "George Soros." In: *Encyclopedia of Human Rights*, ed. David P. Forsythe. Oxford University Press.

Lake, David A. and Wendy H. Wong. 2009. "The Politics of Networks: Interests, Power, and Human Rights Norms." In: *Networked Politics: Agency, Power, and Governance*, ed. Miles Kahler. Ithaca, NY: Cornell University Press, pp. 127–50.

Lasota, Irena. 1999. "Sometimes Less Is More." *Journal of Democracy* 10(4): 125–8.

Lecy, Jesse D., George E. Mitchell and Hans Peter Schmitz. 2010. "Advocacy Organizations, Networks, and the Firm Analogy." In: *Advocacy Organizations and Collective Action*, ed. Aseem Prakash and Mary Kay Gugerty. Cambridge University Press, pp. 229–51.

Levitsky, Steven and Lucan A. Way. 2005. "International Linkage and Democratization." *Journal of Democracy* 16(3): 20–34.

  2010. *Competitive Authoritarianism: The Origins and Evolution of Hybrid Regimes in the Post-Cold War Era*. Problems of International Politics Series. New York: Cambridge University Press.

Lieberman, Evan S. 2005. "Nested Analysis as a Mixed-Method Strategy for Comparative Research." *American Political Science Review* 99(3): 435–52.

Lindberg, Staffan. 2006. *Democracy and Elections in Africa*. Baltimore, MD: Johns Hopkins University Press.

Lowenthal, Abraham F., ed. 1991. *Exporting Democracy: The United States and Latin America*. Baltimore, MD: Johns Hopkins University Press.

Ludwig, Robin. 2004. "The UN's Electoral Assistance: Challenges, Accomplishments, Prospects." In: *The UN Role in Promoting Democracy: Between Ideals and Reality*, ed. Edward Newman and Roland Rich. Tokyo: United Nations University Press, pp. 169–87.

Lumsdaine, David Halloran. 1993. *Moral Vision in International Politics: The Foreign Aid Regime, 1949–1989*. Princeton University Press.

Lust-Okar, Ellen. 2009. "Reinforcing Informal Institutions through Authoritarian Elections: Insights from Jordan." *Middle East Law and Governance* 1: 3–37.

Lust-Okar, Ellen and Amaney Ahmad Jamal. 2002. "Rulers and Rules: Reassessing the Influence of Regime Type on Electoral Law Formation." *Comparative Political Studies* 35(3): 337–66.

March, James G. and Johan P. Olsen. 1998. "The Institutional Dynamics of International Political Orders." *International Organization* 52(4): 943–69.

Marinov, Nikolay and Hein Goemans. 2014. "Coups and Democracy." *British Journal of Political Science* 44(4): 799–825.

Marshall, Monty G., Ted Robert Gurr, and Keith Jaggers. 2009. "Polity IV Project: Political Regime Characteristics and Transitions, 1800–2009." Dataset Users' Manual, Center for Systemic Peace, Vienna, VA. Available at: www.systemicpeace.org/inscr/inscr.htm.

Martens, Bertin, Uwe Mummert, Peter Murrell, and Paul Seabright. 2002. *The Institutional Economics of Foreign Aid*. New York: Cambridge University Press.

McCarthy, John D. and Mayer N. Zald. 2011. "Resource Mobilization and Social Movements: A Partial Theory." *American Journal of Sociology* 82(6): 1212–41.

McFaul, Michael. 2004–5. "Democracy Promotion as a World Value." *Washington Quarterly* 28(1): 147–63.

  2010. *Advancing Democracy Abroad: Why We Should and How We Can*. Lanham, MD: Rowman & Littlefield.

McInerney, Stephen. 2012. *The Federal Budget and Appropriations for Fiscal Year 2013: Democracy Governance, and Human Rights in the Middle East and North Africa*. Washington, DC: Project on Middle East Democracy.

McKinlay, R. D. and R. Little. 1977. "A Foreign Policy Model of U.S. Bilateral Aid Allocation." *World Politics* 30(1): 58–86.

McKoy, Michael K. and Michael K. Miller. 2012. "The Patron's Dilemma: The Dynamics of Foreign-Supported Democratization." *Journal of Conflict Resolution* 56(5): 904–32.

Melia, Thomas O. 2005. "The Democracy Bureaucracy: The Infrastructure of American Democracy Promotion." Discussion Paper. Princeton Project on National Security, Princeton University. Available at: www.princeton.edu/~ppns/papers/democracy_bureaucracy.pdf.

2006. "The Democracy Bureaucracy." *American Interest* 1(4): 122–30.

Mendelson, Sarah E. 2001. "Democracy Assistance and Political Transition in Russia between Success and Failure." *International Security* 25(4): 68–106.

Mendelson, Sarah E. and John K. Glenn, eds. 2002. *The Power and Limits of NGOs: A Critical Look at Building Democracy in Eastern Europe and Eurasia*. New York: Columbia University Press.

Merry, Sally Engle. 2011. "Measuring the World: Indicators, Human Rights, and Global Governance." *Cultural Anthropology*. 52(53): 583–595.

Middle East Partnership Initiative. 2009. "2009 MEPI Impact Stories." Available at: www.medregion.mepi.state.gov/mepi-impact-stories-archive.html/.

Milner, Helen V. 2006. "Why Multilateralism? Foreign Aid and Domestic Principal–Agent Problems." In: *Delegation and Agency in International Organizations*, ed. Darren G. Hawkins, David A. Lake, Daniel L. Nielson, and Michael J. Tierney. New York: Cambridge University Press, pp. 107–39.

Milner, Helen V. and Dustin H. Tingley. 2010. "The Political Economy of U.S. Foreign Aid: American Legislators and the Domestic Politics of Aid." *Economics and Politics* 22(2): 200–32.

2011. "Who Supports Global Economic Engagement? The Sources of Preferences in American Foreign Economic Policy." *International Organization* 65(1): 37–68.

2013. "The Choice for Multilateralism: Foreign Aid and American Foreign Policy." *Review of International Organizations* 8(3): 313–41.

Mitchell, Lincoln A. 2009. *Uncertain Democracy: U.S. Foreign Policy and Georgia's Rose Revolution*. Philadelphia: University of Pennsylvania Press.

2010. "The Democracy Promotion Disconnect." Paper presented at the 51st Annual Convention of the International Studies Association, February, New Orleans.

2011. "The New World of Democracy Promotion." *Current History* 110(739): 311–16.

Moehler, Devra C. 2010. "Democracy, Governance, and Randomized Development Assistance." *Annals of the American Academy of Political and Social Science* 628(1): 30–46.

Monten, Jonathan. 2005. "The Roots of the Bush Doctrine: Power, Nationalism, and Democracy Promotion in U.S. Strategy." *International Security* 29(4): 112–56.

Morrison, Kevin M. 2009. "Oil, Nontax Revenue, and the Redistribu-
tional Foundations of Regime Stability." *International Organization* 63(1):
107–8.

Mosse, David, ed. 2011. *Adventures in Aidland: The Anthropology of Professionals
in International Development*. Studies in Public and Applied Anthropology.
Oxford: Berghahn Books.

National Democratic Institute. 2010. "NDI: A Quarter Century of Working for Democracy and Making Democracy Work." Washington,
DC: National Democratic Institute. Available at: www.ndi.org/25th_
anniversary_publication/index.html.

National Endowment for Democracy. 1985–2012. *NED Annual Reports for 1985–
2012*. Washington, DC: National Endowment for Democracy.

2012a. "About NED." Available at: www.ned.org/about.

2012b. "Proposal Preparation Guidelines." Available at: www.ned.org/sites/
default/files/Proposal-Budget-Guidelines.pdf.

National Research Council, Committee on Evaluation of USAID Democ-
racy Assistance Programs. 2008. *Improving Democracy Assistance: Building
Knowledge Through Evaluations and Research*. Washington, DC: National
Academies Press.

Newman, Edward. 2004. "UN Democracy Promotion: Comparative Advan-
tages and Constraints." In: *The UN Role in Promoting Democracy: Between
Ideals and Reality*, ed. Edward Newman and Roland Rich. Tokyo: United
Nations University Press, pp. 188–207.

Nielson, Daniel L. and Michael J. Tierney. 2003. "Delegation to International
Organizations: Agency Theory and World Bank Environmental Reform."
*International Organization* 57(2): 241–76.

2005. "Theory, Data, and Hypothesis Testing: World Bank Environmental
Reform Redux." *International Organization* 59(3): 785–800.

Nixon, Ron. 2011. "U.S. Groups Helped Nurture Arab Uprisings." *New York
Times*, April 14, p. A1.

Norris, Pippa. 2008. *Driving Democracy: Do Power-Sharing Institutions Work?*
New York: Cambridge University Press.

Nuti, Paul J. 2006. "Toward Reflective Practice: Understanding and Negotiating
Democracy in Macedonia." In: *Transacting Transition: The Micropolitics of
Democracy Assistance in the Former Yugoslavia*, ed. Keith Brown. Bloomfield,
CT: Kumarian Press, pp. 69–94.

Obama, Barack Hussein. 2009. "Remarks by the President on a New Beginning." Cairo University, Egypt, June. Available at: www.whitehouse.gov/the_
press_office/Remarks-by-the-President-at-Cairo-University-6-04-09.

Open Society Foundations. 2012a. "About the Open Society Foundations."
Available at: www.soros.org/about.

2012b. "Expenditures." Available at: www.opensocietyfoundations.org/about/
expenditures.

Organisation for Economic Co-operation and Development. 2010. "Query
Wizard for International Development Statistics (QWIDS)." Development
Assistance Committee. Paris: OECD.

Ottaway, Marina. 2005a. "The Limits of Women's Rights." In: *Uncharted
Journey: Promoting Democracy in the Middle East*, ed. Thomas Carothers and

Marina Ottaway. Washington, DC: Carnegie Endowment for International Peace, pp. 115–30.

2005b. "The Problem of Credibility." In: *Uncharted Journey: Promoting Democracy in the Middle East*, ed. Thomas Carothers and Marina Ottaway. Washington, DC: Carnegie Endowment for International Peace, pp. 173–92.

Ottaway, Marina and Amr Hamzawy. 2011. "Protest Movements and Political Change in the Arab World." Washington, DC: Carnegie Endowment for International Peace.

Papke, Leslie E. and Jeffrey M. Wooldridge. 1996. "Econometric Methods for Fractional Response Variables with an Application to 401(K) Plan Participation Rates." *Journal of Applied Econometrics* 11(6): 619–32.

2008. "Panel Data Methods for Fractional Response Variables with an Application to Test Pass Rates." *Journal of Econometrics* 145(1–2): 121–33.

Paris, Roland. 2004. *At War's End: Building Peace after Civil Conflict*. New York: Cambridge University Press.

Peceny, Mark. 1999. *Democracy at the Point of Bayonets*. University Park: Pennsylvania State University Press.

Peters, Anne Mariel and Pete W. Moore. 2009. "Beyond Boom and Bust: External Rents, Durable Authoritarianism, and Institutional Adaptation in the Hashemite Kingdom of Jordan." *Studies in Comparative International Development* 44(3): 256–85.

Petrova, Tsveta. 2014. *From Solidarity to Geopolitics: Support for Democracy among Postcommunist States*. Cambridge University Press.

Pevehouse, Jon C. 2002. "Democracy from the Outside-In? International Organizations and Democratization." *International Organization* 56(3): 515–49.

Pew Global Attitudes Project. 2012a. *Global Opinion of Obama Slips, International Policies Faulted: Drone Strikes Widely Opposed*. Washington, DC: Pew Research Center.

2012b. "Opinion of the United States." Washington, DC: Pew Research Center.

Pollack, Mark A. 1997. "Delegation, Agency, and Agenda Setting in the European Community." *International Organization* 51(1): 99–134.

Posner, Michael H. 2012. "Briefing on the Release of the 2011 Human Rights Reports." Washington, DC, May 24. Available at: www.state.gov/j/drl/rls/rm/2012/190837.htm.

Powel, Brieg Tomos. 2009. "The Stability Syndrome: US and EU Democracy Promotion in Tunisia." *Journal of North African Studies* 14(1): 57–73.

Prakash, Aseem and Mary Kay Gugerty, eds. 2010. *Advocacy Organizations and Collective Action*. Cambridge University Press.

Pridham, Geoffrey. 1999. "Complying with the European Union's Democratic Conditionality: Transnational Party Linkages and Regime Change in Slovakia, 1993–1998." *Europe–Asia Studies* 51(7): 1221–44.

Program on Evaluating International Influences on Democratic Development at Stanford University. 2010. "Democracy Promotion Organizations in the United States." Freedom Spogli Institute, Stanford

University. Available at: http://fsi.stanford.edu/research/program_on_evaluating_international_influences_on_democr

Przeworski, Adam, Michael E. Alvarez, José Antonio Cheibub, and Fernando Limongi. 2000. *Democracy and Development: Political Institutions and Well-Being in the World, 1950–1990.* Cambridge University Press.

Reagan, Ronald. 1982. "Address to Members of the British Parliament." London, June 8. Available at: www.reagan.utexas.edu/archives/speeches/1982/60882a.htm.

1983. "Remarks at a White House Ceremony Inaugurating the National Endowment for Democracy." Washington, DC, December 16. Available at: www.presidency.ucsb.edu/ws/?pid=40874.

Richter, James. 2002. "Evaluating Western Assistance to Russian Women's Organizations." In: *The Power and Limits of NGOs*, ed. Sarah E. Mendelson and John K. Glenn. New York: Columbia University Press, pp. 54–90.

Roberts, J. Timmons, Bradley Parks, Michael Tierney, and Robert Hicks. 2009. "Has Foreign Aid Been Greened?" *Environment* 51(1): 8–19.

Robinson, Glenn E. 1998. "Defensive Democratization in Jordan." *International Journal of Middle East Studies* 30(3): 387–410.

Robinson, William I. 1996. *Promoting Polyarchy: Globalization, US Intervention, and Hegemony.* Cambridge Studies in International Relations. Cambridge University Press.

Rodin, Ivan. 2012. "Let's See the Colour of Your Grant Money: Signatures Are Being Collected on the Internet for a Law on the Control of Foreign Financing of the Country's Non-Commercial Organizations." *Nezavisimaya Gazeta* (BBC Monitoring), April 5.

Roessler, Philip G. 2005. "Donor-Induced Democratization and the Privatization of State Violence in Kenya and Rwanda." *Comparative Politics* 37(2): 207–27.

Ron, James, Howard Ramos, and Kathleen Rodgers. 2005. "Transnational Information Politics: NGO Human Rights Reporting, 1986–2000." *International Studies Quarterly* 49(3): 557–87.

Rubin, Barnett R. 2004. "Crafting a Constitution for Afghanistan." *Journal of Democracy* 15(3): 5–19.

Ryan, Curtis R. 1998. "Peace, Bread and Riots: Jordan and the International Monetary Fund." *Middle East Policy* 6(2): 54–66.

Sadiki, Larbi. 2002. "Bin Ali's Tunisia: Democracy by Non-Democratic Means." *British Journal of Middle Eastern Studies* 29(1): 57–78.

Savun, Burcu and Daniel C. Tirone. 2011. "Foreign Aid, Democratization, and Civil Conflict: How Does Democracy Aid Affect Civil Conflict?" *American Journal of Political Science* 55(2): 233–46.

Schedler, Andreas. 2006. "The Logic of Electoral Authoritarianism." In: *Electoral Authoritarianism: The Dynamics of Unfree Competition*, ed. Andreas Schedler. Boulder, CO: Lynne Rienner Publishers, pp. 1–26.

Schmitz, Hans Peter. 2004. "Domestic and Transnational Perspectives on Democratization." *International Studies Review* 6(3): 403–26.

Schneider, Christina J. and Jennifer L. Tobin. 2013. "Interest Coalitions and Multilateral Aid Allocation in the European Union." *International Studies Quarterly* 57(1): 103–15.

Schraeder, Peter J., Steven W. Hook, and Bruce Taylor. 1998. "Clarifying the Foreign Aid Puzzle: A Comparison of American, Japanese, French, and Swedish Aid Flows." *World Politics* 50(2): 294–323.

Schumpeter, Joseph A. 1942. *Capitalism, Socialism, and Democracy.* New York: Harper & Brothers.

Schwedler, Jillian. 2003. "More than a Mob: The Dynamics of Political Demonstrations in Jordan." *Middle East Report* 226(Spring): 18–23.

Schwirtz, Michael. 2010. "A Battle of Worldviews Is Playing Out in Postelection Belarus." *New York Times*, December 21, p. A6.

Scott, James M. and Carie A. Steele. 2005. "Assisting Democrats or Resisting Dictators: The Nature and Impact of Democracy Support by the National Endowment for Democracy, 1990–1999." *Democratization* 12(4): 439–60.

    2011. "Sponsoring Democracy: The United States and Democracy Aid to the Developing World, 1988–2001." *International Studies Quarterly* 55(1): 47–69.

Seawright, Jason and John Gerring. 2008. "Case Selection Techniques in Case Study Research." *Political Research Quarterly* 61(2): 294–308.

Sell, Susan K. and Aseem Prakash. 2004. "Using Ideas Strategically: The Contest between Business and NGO Networks in Intellectual Property Rights." *International Studies Quarterly* 48(1): 143–75.

Sharp, Jeremy M. 2012. *Egypt: Background and U.S. Relations.* Washington, DC: Congressional Research Service.

Shayne, Julie D. 2004. *The Revolution Question: Feminisms in El Salvador, Chile, and Cuba.* New Brunswick, NJ: Rutgers University Press.

Simmons, Beth A. 2009. *Mobilizing for Human Rights: International Law in Domestic Politics.* New York: Cambridge University Press.

Simmons, Beth A., Frank Dobbin, and Geoffrey Garrett. 2006. "Introduction: The International Diffusion of Liberalism." *International Organization* 60(4): 781–810.

Simpser, Alberto and Daniela Donno. 2012. "Can International Election Monitoring Harm Governance?" *Journal of Politics* 74(2): 501–13.

Sjoberg, Fredrik M. 2012. "Making Voters Count: Evidence from Field Experiments about the Efficacy of Domestic Election Observation." Columbia University Harriman Institute Working Paper 1. Available at: http://papers.ssrn.com/sol3/papers.cfm?abstract_id=2133592.

Soros, George. 1995. *Soros on Soros: Staying Ahead of the Curve.* New York: John Wiley.

Staggenborg, Suzanne. 1988. "The Consequences of Professionalization and Formalization in the Pro-Choice Movement." *American Sociological Review* 53(4): 585–605.

Stanger, Allison. 2009. *One Nation under Contract: The Outsourcing of American Power and the Future of Foreign Policy.* New Haven, CT: Yale University Press.

State University of New York's Center for International Development. 2010. "Legislative-Strengthening Program in Jordan 2005–2010." Albany, NY: SUNY.

Stein, Janice Gross. 2009. "The Politics and Power of Networks: The Accountability of Humanitarian Organizations." In: *Networked Politics: Agency,*

*Power, and Governance*, ed. Miles Kahler. Ithaca, NY: Cornell University Press, pp. 151–70.

Stone, Diane. 2010. "Private Philanthropy or Policy Transfer? The Transnational Norms of the Open Society Institute." *Policy & Politics* 38(2): 269–87.

Stone, Randall W. 2002. *Lending Credibility: The International Monetary Fund and the Post-Communist Transition*. Princeton University Press.

2004. "The Political Economy of IMF Lending in Africa." *American Political Science Review* 98(4): 577–91.

2008. "The Scope of IMF Conditionality." *International Organization* 62(4): 589–620.

Stroup, Sarah S. 2012. *Borders among Activists: International NGOs in the United States, Britain, and France*. Ithaca, NY: Cornell University Press.

Sundstrom, Lisa McIntosh. 2005. "Foreign Assistance, International Norms, and NGO Development: Lessons from the Russian Campaign." *International Organization* 59(2): 419–49.

Sussman, Leonard R. 2009. "Freedom House." In: *Encyclopedia of Human Rights*, ed. David P. Forsythe. Oxford University Press.

Teorell, Jan. 2010. *Determinants of Democratization: Explaining Regime Change in the World, 1972–2006*. Cambridge University Press.

Thiel, Rainer. 2010. *Nested Games of External Democracy Promotion: The United States and the Polish Liberalization of 1980–1989*. Heidelberg: VS Verlag für Sozialwissenschaften.

Tierney, Michael J., Daniel L. Nielson, Darren G. Hawkins, *et al.* 2011 "More Dollars than Sense: Refining our Knowledge of Development Finance using AidData." World Development 39(11): 1891–1906.

Tingley, Dustin H. 2010. "Donors and Domestic Politics: Political Influences on Foreign Aid Effort." *Quarterly Review of Economics and Finance* 50(1): 40–9.

Traub, James. 2008. *The Freedom Agenda: Why America Must Spread Democracy (Just Not the Way George Bush Did)*. New York: Farrar, Straus, and Giroux.

UN Millennium Project. 2009. "The 0.7% Target: An In-depth Look." Press release. Available at: www.unmillenniumproject.org/press/07.htm.

United Nations. 2005. "Declaration of Principles for International Election Observation and Code of Conduct for International Election Observation." New York: United Nations.

United Nations Democracy Fund. 2014. "About UNDEF." Available at: www.un.org/democracyfund/about-undef.

United States Agency for International Development. 2009. "USAID Fiscal Year 2009: Agency Financial Report." Washington, DC.

2012. "U.S. Overseas Loans and Grants: Obligations and Loan Authorizations, July 1, 1945–September 30, 2012." Washington, DC.

United States Agency for International Development, Center for Democracy and Governance. 1998. "Handbook of Democracy and Governance Program Indicators." Technical Publication Series. Washington, DC.

2010. "User's Guide to DG Programming." PN-ADR-500. Washington, DC.

United States Agency for International Development, Office of the Inspector General. 2008. "Audit of USAID/Jordan's Democracy and Governance Activities." Audit Report No. 6-278-09-001-P. Washington, DC.

United States Congress, House of Representatives Committee on Foreign Affairs. 2010. "Testimony of Jennifer L. Windsor, Executive Director of Freedom House." Press Release. Available at: http://democrats.foreignaffairs.house.gov/111/win061010.pdf.

United States Department of State. 2011. "Middle East Partnership Initiative: Local Grants Program." Program Statement. Washington, DC.

United States Department of State and United States Agency for International Development. 2008. "Master List of Standard Indicators." Washington, DC.

United States Department of State, Middle East Partnership Initiative. 2007. "U.S.–Middle East Partnership for Breast Cancer Awareness and Research." Press release. Available at: http://2002-2009-mepi.state.gov/infoshts/88273.htm.

United States Embassy in Tunis. 2008. "MEPI Update for Tunisia." Cable. Available at: http://wikileaks.org/cable/2008/04/08TUNIS373.html/.

United States General Accounting Office. 1991. *Promoting Democracy: National Endowment for Democracy's Management of Grants Needs Improvement.* Publication Number GAO/NSIAD-91-162. Washington, DC.

United States Government Accountability Office. 2006. *Foreign Assistance: U.S. Democracy Assistance for Cuba Needs Better Management and Oversight.* Publication Number GAO-07-147, Washington, DC.

2008. *Foreign Assistance: Continued Efforts Needed to Strengthen USAID's Oversight of U.S. Democracy Assistance for Cuba.* Publication Number GAO-09-165. Washington, DC.

2009. *Democracy Assistance: U.S. Agencies Take Steps to Coordinate International Programs but Lack Information on Some U.S.-Funded Activities.* Publication Number GAO-09-993, Washington, DC.

2013. *Cuba Democracy Assistance: USAID's Program Is Improved, but State Could Better Monitor its Implementing Partners.* Publication Number GAO-13-285, Washington, DC.

Usatin, Rebekah. 2013. "Evaluation of Democracy Assistance Grantmaking." University of Pennsylvania, Philadelphia, May 1.

Vachudova, Milada Anna. 2005. *Europe Undivided: Democracy, Leverage and Integration after Communism.* Oxford University Press.

Valiyev, Anar M. 2006. "Parliamentary Elections in Azerbaijan: A Failed Revolution." *Problems of Post-Communism* 53(3): 17–35.

Vitalis, Robert. 1994. "The Democratization Industry and the Limits of the New Interventionism." *Middle East Report* 187/8: 46–50.

Weaver, Catherine. 2008. *Hypocrisy Trap: The World Bank and the Poverty of Reform.* Princeton University Press.

Weber, Max. 1978 [1922]. *Economy and Society.* Berkeley: University of California Press.

Wedel, Janine R. 2001. *Collision and Collusion: The Strange Case of Western Aid to Eastern Europe.* New York: Palgrave for St. Martin's Griffin.

Weinthal, Erika and Pauline Jones Luong. 2002. "Environmental NGOs in Kazakhstan: Democratic Goals and Nondemocratic Outcomes." In: *The Power and Limits of NGOs: A Critical Look at Building Democracy in Eastern*

*Europe and Eurasia*, ed. Sarah E. Mendelson and John K. Glenn. New York: Columbia University Press, pp. 152–76.

Wilensky, Harold L. 1964. "The Professionalization of Everyone?" *American Journal of Sociology* 70(2): 137–58.

Williams and Associates. 2012. "Survey of Tunisian Public Opinion." Salem, MA. Available at: www.iri.org/sites/default/files/2012%20October%203%20Survey%20of%20Tunisian%20Public%20Opinion%2C%20July%2026-August%208%2C%202012.pdf/.

Winters, Matthew S. 2010. "Choosing to Target: What Types of Countries Get Different Types of World Bank Projects?" *World Politics* 62(3): 422–58.

Wittes, Tamara Cofman. 2008. *Freedom's Unsteady March: America's Role in Building Arab Democracy*. Washington, DC: Brookings Institution.

World Bank. 2012a. "Country and Lending Groups." World Bank Data. Available at: http://data.worldbank.org/about/country-classifications/country-and-lending-groups.

2012b. "World Development Indicators." World Bank Data. Available at: http://data.worldbank.org/products/wdi.

Wright, Joseph. 2008a. "Do Authoritarian Institutions Constrain? How Legislatures Affect Economic Growth and Investment." *American Journal of Political Science* 52(2): 322–43.

2008b. "To Invest or Insure? How Authoritarian Time Horizons Impact Foreign Aid Effectiveness." *Comparative Political Studies* 41(7): 971–1000.

Wright, Joseph and Matthew Winters. 2010. "The Politics of Effective Foreign Aid." *Annual Review of Political Science* 13: 61–80.

Yom, Sean M. 2009. "Jordan: Ten More Years of Autocracy." *Journal of Democracy* 20(4): 151–66.

Youngs, Richard. 2003. "European Approaches to Democracy Assistance: Learning the Right Lessons?" *Third World Quarterly* 23(1): 127–38.

2004. *International Democracy and the West: The Role of Governments, Civil Society and Multinational Business*. Oxford University Press.

Youngs, Richard and Tamara Cofman Wittes. 2009. "Europe, the United States, and Middle Eastern Democracy." In: *Promoting Democracy and the Rule of Law: American and European Strategies*, ed. Amichai Magen, Thomas Risse, and Michael A. McFaul. London: Palgrave Macmillan, pp. 93–117.

# Index

CPSIA information can be obtained
at www.ICGtesting.com
Printed in the USA
LVOW13s1922190117
521545LV00015B/229/P